Bigger Bombs for
a Brighter Tomorrow

Bigger Bombs for a Brighter Tomorrow

*The Strategic Air Command
and American War Plans
at the Dawn of the Atomic Age, 1945–1950*

JOHN M. CURATOLA

McFarland & Company, Inc., Publishers
Jefferson, North Carolina

LIBRARY OF CONGRESS CATALOGUING-IN-PUBLICATION DATA

Names: Curatola, John M., 1965– author.
Title: Bigger bombs for a brighter tomorrow : the Strategic Air Command and American war plans at the dawn of the atomic age, 1945/1950 / John M. Curatola.
Other titles: Strategic Air Command and American war plans at the dawn of the atomic age, 1945–1950
Description: Jefferson, North Carolina : McFarland & Company, Inc., Publishers, 2016 | Includes bibliographical references and index.
Identifiers: LCCN 2015043156 | ISBN 9780786494194 (softcover : acid free paper) ∞
Subjects: LCSH: Nuclear weapons—Government policy—United States—History—20th century. | Nuclear warfare—Government policy—United States—History—20th century. | United States. Air Force. Strategic Air Command—History. | Strategic forces—United States—History—20th century. | Military planning—United States—History—20th century. | United States—Military policy—History—20th century. | Cold War.
Classification: LCC U264.3 .C87 2016 | DDC 358.4/2097309045—dc23
LC record available at http://lccn.loc.gov/2015043156

BRITISH LIBRARY CATALOGUING DATA ARE AVAILABLE

ISBN (print) 978-0-7864-9419-4
ISBN (ebook) 978-1-4766-2137-1

© 2016 John M. Curatola. All rights reserved

No part of this book may be reproduced or transmitted in any form or by any means, electronic or mechanical, including photocopying or recording, or by any information storage and retrieval system, without permission in writing from the publisher.

On the cover: Mushroom cloud from the *Able* test of Operation Crossroads in the Bikini Atoll on July 1, 1946 (Joint Army/Navy Task Force One)

Printed in the United States of America

McFarland & Company, Inc., Publishers
 Box 611, Jefferson, North Carolina 28640
  www.mcfarlandpub.com

For my two greatest joys:
Jenny and Katie

Table of Contents

Preface   1

Introduction   7

Part I. The Bomb

1. Mr. X and the Fiscal Year (FY) 50 Debate   23
2. The Atomic Energy Commission and the Fight Over Custody   37
3. Inter-Service Squabbles   65

Part II. American War Planning

4. The Postwar World and the USSBS   77
5. National Security Objectives?   88
6. War Plans   96
7. Assessments   124

Part III. Strategic Air Command

8. Men   135
9. Machines   154

Conclusion: Turning the Corner   175

Chapter Notes   195

Bibliography   215

Index   223

Preface

For almost fifty years, the Strategic Air Command (SAC) was on the front line of the Cold War. Sitting atop the most potent and powerful weapons ever devised, the men and women of SAC stood as the bulwark against potential Communist expansion. With "Peace is our Profession" as their motto, SAC aircrews and personnel stood in a combat-ready status for most of the command's existence and dutifully served as defenders of the free world. A diversified force with both manned bomber aircraft and intercontinental ballistic missiles, SAC was capable of delivering megatons' worth of destruction upon the Soviet Union and her Warsaw Pact allies. Keepers of much of the nation's atomic weaponry, SAC provided considerable deterrent power for the U.S. military and offset the Red Army's numerical superiority. In addition to the destructive force inherent in its weapons, SAC also employed some of the most sophisticated intelligence-gathering platforms ever devised by man in order to try to gain a full appreciation of Soviet military posture and dispositions. From the 1950s up to the command's deactivation in 1992, SAC evolved into one of the most potent and professional military organizations ever constructed.

However, this incredible destructive power and professional acumen were not created overnight, nor were SAC's capabilities developed with a set procedural template. Military innovation is not a straightforward process and does not necessarily follow a given set of rules or procedures. Rather, developing new military capabilities and applications is often a messy process full of miscalculation, blunder, and confusion. The growth of SAC was no different. While the command eventually developed a global reach with enormous firepower, it started inauspiciously after the Second World War and had to mature over a number of years. Developing a global atomic strike force required assistance from other segments of the federal government and national agencies. SAC was subject to political winds, the vagaries of the budget, and changes in national sentiment. Its history is also replete with compromises, setbacks, and in some cases abject failures.

During the first few years of the command's existence, SAC was hardly a competent, capable military force. It was initially plagued by faulty leadership, poor resources, substandard training, and legacy equipment. After the war, SAC suffered the exodus of thousands of seasoned veterans. In addition to its internal problems, SAC also suffered from a lack of a coherent national strategy for the use of atomic weapons. Furthermore, SAC lacked guidance regarding U.S. goals and objectives vis-à-vis the Soviet Union. War plans in the late 1940s were infeasible, based upon capabilities that SAC did not possess, and the few capabilities SAC did have were not aimed at any particular political objective. Even if SAC did have the assets and training to execute the established war plans, what was a strategic bombing offensive supposed to accomplish if it had to go to war in the late 1940s? This question remained largely unanswered.

Furthermore, as the nation's only atomic delivery force at the time, SAC had very little control over or access to the weapons it was supposed to deliver. After the war, the Atomic Energy Commission (AEC) assumed control of all the materials left over from the Manhattan Project. As the custodians of America's atomic monopoly, the AEC jealously guarded fissionable materials and sought to limit military access to the few atomic components the nation had on hand. The AEC had its own organizational issues that precluded production of fissionable materials. While SAC had its internal problems, the nascent AEC and the inherited atomic infrastructure from the war were also in poor shape.

The confluence of these factors made SAC (and America's atomic monopoly during the late 1940s) a paper tiger with very little ability to prosecute war and leverage the nuclear advantage. While the Truman administration placed many of its military eggs into the atomic basket, there was very little capability actually resident in the nation's strategic bombing armada, with fissionable material also in short supply. Trying to offset the Red Army's numerical superiority, SAC and the atomic bomb served as the nation's primary foil against Communist expansion. Had the nation chosen to press its atomic prerogative, SAC would have been hard-pressed to execute the kinds of missions envisioned in any of the established war plans. Plain and simple, the nation was bluffing with regard to its atomic arsenal and capability, and most Americans were ignorant of the situation.

A number of published works discuss this particular topic. Harry Borowski's "A Hollow Threat" was one of the first books that highlighted the poor state of the postwar air force and its inability to conduct atomic warfare. His work, along with Walton Moody's detailed analysis in *Building a Strategic Air Force* and William Borgiasz's *The Strategic Air Command*, provided an excellent account regarding the internal functioning of SAC and its lack of capability during this period. These works have also been augmented recently by Phillip Meilinger's 2012 work *Bomber: The Formation and Early Years of Strategic Air Command*. All of these works have been useful in the development of this treatise. However, in 1990 Stephen Ross and David Allen Rosenberg provided the Cold War historian a great service by doing yeoman's work of making available, and publishing in their original form, the approved war plans developed during the immediate postwar period. These primary source documents are invaluable to the historian trying to gain an appreciation of American military thinking on war with the Soviets. Furthermore, in this series Ross and Rosenberg also published the Weapon System Evaluation Group Report of February 1950 that shed considerable light on the efficacy of the planned aerial offensive. Moreover, in 2006, a declassified SAC commander's briefing from April 1950 became available. This briefing provides unique insight regarding the state of the command late in 1949 and its ability to support the OFFTACKLE war plan. Included with the brief are parts of the commander's narrative comments and transcripts that elaborate further on the challenges facing both the nation and the Air Force. From these last two sources, this book draws heavily.

This book critically reviews the most prominent war plans during the postwar era and compares them with the actual capability resident in both SAC and other national organizations, specifically the AEC. What is found paints an even drearier picture of American atomic warfare capabilities than what previous books have articulated. This work looks at all three levels of war regarding the atomic aerial offensives in the various plans from 1945 to 1950. Review of the strategic, operational, and tactical levels of war shows that neither the AEC nor SAC were in position to execute or sustain either a conventional or atomic offensive against the USSR. While previous works discuss the larger strategic and operational issues facing SAC, this book seeks to provide greater depth, not only regarding the operational-level issues, but at the tactical level of the aerial offensive. It is at this tactical level that SAC's limitations are clearly illustrated and plainly evident.

This work, unlike others, will first analyze the problems inherent in the AEC regarding leadership, attitude, and infrastructure and address the relevant implications to the military. As the inheritors of the wartime Manhattan Engineering District, the AEC was faced with unique challenges after the war regarding the new technology and its supporting infrastructure. The AEC was hard-pressed to produce atomic weapons after the war and then maintain an adequate stockpile of munitions to support military operations. Furthermore, the commissioners of the AEC were less than impressed with American military leadership. Suspicion and distrust at the federal level between the AEC and the National Military Establishment (NME) precluded effective support from the civilian agency.

This distrust at the federal level also included the services themselves as the Air Force and Navy continuously fought over roles, missions, and, more importantly, their military budgets. Each service was trying to prove its relevancy in the postwar atomic world at the expense of the others. Naval aviation saw the new independent U.S. Air Force (USAF) as a threat to its existence and feared the marginalization of carrier aviation. The USAF in turn believed naval aircraft inconsequential in a future atomic conflict. Considerable tension existed not only between the civilian masters of nuclear technology, but also among the military services regarding responsibilities for atomic warfare. This book attempts to draw all of these factors together.

Secondly, this book will dissect the established war plans from 1945 to 1950 and not only compare them with the state of the AEC, but more importantly will review SAC's ability to execute them. This work will provide a critical review of the PINCHER, BROILER, HALFMOON, and OFFTACKLE war plans and address the feasibility of these designs given the state of SAC, the air force, and the AEC at the time. Each of these war plans had its own unique nuances, but the one common thread in all of them was SAC's inability to execute them. Significant logistical shortfalls combined with operational limitations precluded the successful execution of these plans if they were put into action, regardless of which ordnance—conventional or atomic—was called for. Furthermore, and more importantly, all of these plans outlined military operations that had little or no connection to a politically envisioned end state. Conspicuously absent were the larger American political objectives given a war with the Soviet Union.

Lastly, this book will provide a detailed look at the state of SAC itself following the war and up to the beginning of 1950. For much of the postwar period, SAC, like the rest of the U.S. military establishment, was poorly trained, manned, and equipped. Outside of airshows, flyovers, and public-relations stunts, the Air Force was a shell of its wartime size and capability. Furthermore, it was hardly the atomic combat ready force Truman or the American public thought it was. While the Truman administration put much of its military strategy in the atomic realm, SAC was unprepared for its assigned responsibilities. Both in terms of manpower and in equipment, SAC suffered badly from poor leadership, policies, and equipment. Airframes resident in the fleet were either legacy systems that were showing their age or new airframes that had not yet worked out the bugs associated with new aircraft design. For most, if not all, of this period, SAC was a broken organization, and it took the leadership skills and abilities of General Curtis LeMay to shake the command out of its doldrums. However, taking over in late 1948, LeMay could only do so much and needed not only time, but money and resources to fix the command's problems. As a result, until the Korean War, SAC would remain an organization with significant problems.

Preface

As the U.S. became the protector of the free world following the war, the nation placed its trust in the bomb and the Air Force's ability to prosecute atomic war. America's atomic monopoly was viewed as the shield to counter the Red Army's numerical superiority and the perceived threat of global monolithic communism. As America put its trust in atomic weaponry, a tongue-in-cheek comment at the USAF Weapons Laboratory was that they were building "bigger bombs for a brighter tomorrow." However, America's atomic capabilities were clearly not up to the task, and its ability to prosecute atomic warfare was largely an illusion. In all, this book looks to provide further insight into postwar U.S. military strategies as they relate to the aerial offensives envisioned. It also seeks to help explain the tenuous nature of the civilian military relationship at the time and how that affected capability. It is hoped that this book illustrates the perils of postwar planning and the dangers of assumptions in national security.

Introduction

Shortly after August 6, 1945, following the dropping of the first atomic bomb on Hiroshima, the United States attempted to warn the Japanese people about the power of the newly developed bomb. In an effort to encourage the Japanese to sue for peace, Americans dropped leaflets over the home islands. Written on leaflets prior to the Nagasaki detonation was an ominous warning:

To the Japanese People:
America asks that you take immediate heed of what we say on this leaflet. We are in possession of the most destructive explosive ever devised by man. A single one of our newly developed atomic bombs is actually the equivalent in explosive power to what 2000 of our giant B-29s can carry on a single mission. This awful fact is one for you to ponder and we solemnly assure you it is grimly accurate.
We have just begun to use this weapon against your homeland. If you still have any doubt, make inquiry as to what happened to Hiroshima when just one atomic bomb fell on that city.... You should take steps now to cease military resistance. Otherwise, we shall resolutely employ this bomb and all our other superior weapons to promptly and forcefully end the war.
EVACUATE YOUR CITIES.[1]

Because of Japanese inaction regarding surrender proceedings, early on the morning of August 9, a specially configured B-29 Superfortress piloted by Major Charles Sweeney took off from Tinian Island, traveling northwest. The plane's mission was to drop a second atomic bomb. Major Sweeney's primary target was the military arsenal located in the center of the city of Kokura on the northern end of the island of Kyushu.[2] Prior to dropping the bomb, the flight plan called for Sweeney to rendezvous with two aircraft over the island of Yakoshima off the southern coast of Kyushu. During the preflight inspection, Sweeney discovered that the solenoid in the pump for a 600-gallon auxiliary fuel cell was inoperative. The fuel cell was installed in the rear bomb bay, and it was installed merely to offset the B-29's center of gravity due to the weight of the "Fat Man" bomb's 10,000 pounds. Fixing the pump might take hours.[3] After considering his option of scrubbing the mission, Sweeney finally replied, "The hell with it.... I want to go, we're going."[4] He took off at 0245, a little behind schedule. After five hours of flying he reached Yakoshima. However, one of the two planned rendezvous aircraft failed to join up with the bomb-laden plane. Sweeney orbited the island in hopes of eventually joining with the aircraft carrying high speed photographic equipment.[5] Though instructed to make only one short orbit over the rendezvous point, Sweeney orbited for 45 minutes.[6] At 30,000 feet altitude, the B-29 consumes some 500 gallons of fuel per hour. Having delayed his attack and with no success in finding the other plane, Sweeney departed for his primary target.

Misfortune continued. Directed to drop his ordnance using only visual bombing methods, upon arriving over Kokura, bombardier Captain Raymond "Kermit" Beahan failed to locate his aiming point due to smoke drifting over from the nearby city of Yawata. The smoke was the result from a conventional fire-bombing raid conducted earlier by 20th Air Force B-29s.[7] In an effort to find the aim point visually, the B-29 made three passes over the town. In each pass, the aim point failed to reveal itself. The three passes over the town caused another delay in bombing and cost Sweeney's aircraft another 55 minutes' worth of precious fuel.[8]

Because of the smoke and inability to locate the target, Sweeney then turned the B-29 toward the designated alternate target—the city of Nagasaki on the southern end of Kyushu. Nagasaki was a military-industrial center for many years.[9] Located in the center of the Urakami Valley, Nagasaki was home to the Mitsubishi shipbuilding yard and steel factory, and it possessed a robust rail system connected to a large, capable seaport.

Falling critically short on fuel because of the earlier decision to orbit for the escort aircraft and the three unsuccessful passes over Kokura, the bomber continued to Nagasaki, only to find the view of the city also obscured, this time by clouds.[10] Fuel calculations estimated that the bomber had only enough gas to make one bomb run over the city. Despite instructions to drop the bomb using visual bombing techniques, rather than abort the mission and drop the atomic device into the sea, Major Sweeney ordered Beahan to release the weapon using radar bombing methods.[11] However, with the aircraft just 25 seconds from the release point, an opening in the clouds appeared and Beahan yelled: "I've got it! I've got it!"[12] Acknowledging Beahan's claim, Sweeney replied, "You own it!" At 11:01 the bombardier dropped his ordnance, which ironically detonated near the largest Catholic Church in the Far East.[13]

After discharging the weapon, Major Sweeney conducted a steep left turn to avoid the blast effect of the bomb. The bomb exploded at an altitude of approximately 1,500 feet with a blast estimated to be three times as powerful as the previous Hiroshima explosion.[14] Upon detonation, a large white flash ensued with a tremendous roar, accompanied by a crushing blast wave and intense heat.[15] Analysis conducted after the war by the U.S. Strategic Bombing Survey (USSBS) estimated:

> Within a radius of 1 km from ground zero men and animals died almost instantaneously from the blast and pressure and heat; houses and other structures were smashed, crushed, and scattered; and fires broke out. The strong complex steel members of the structures of the Mitsubishi Steel Works were bent and twisted like jelly and the roofs of reinforced concrete [at the] National Schools were crumpled and collapsed, indicating a force beyond imagination.[16]

Heat from the explosion melted the granite off the façades of surrounding buildings, and some estimates report the temperature from the ensuing explosion ranged from three thousand to nine thousand degrees centigrade.[17]

After observing the detonation, and now critically short on fuel, Sweeney and his crew headed for Okinawa and landed their plane with engines sputtering and propellers "windmilling" because of fuel starvation.[18] After the landing, ground crews had to tow the plane to the parking ramp because its fuel tanks were completely dry. Sweeney had risked both the mission and the aircrew because of poor fuel management. Upon Sweeney's return to Tinian, General Curtis LeMay, commander of the XXI Bomber Command, chided Sweeney: "You fucked up, didn't you, Chuck?"[19] To this query, Sweeney had no reply and only stood in silence. According to the pilot's group commander, Colonel Paul Tibbets, Sweeney's silence "spoke volumes."[20]

After the B-29 departed the target area, smoke and dust engulfed the Urakami Valley, and survivors claim that darkness descended upon the city.[21] Those not killed in the immediate blast suffered from extreme heat and radiation burns. Victims were burnt so badly that their skin was peeling and hung from their extremities like loose clothing, and those facing the explosion appeared as though the skin from their faces had melted.[22] Blackened, burnt bodies were everywhere, and thousands had their skin turned as "red as cooked lobsters."[23] Many victims jumped into the Urakami River or nearby ponds of water to escape the intense heat, and many of these bodies were found hanging onto shorelines, with some left half-floating or completely immersed.[24] An estimated one-third of the casualties in Nagasaki died from flash burns and expired in a few minutes or a few hours.[25] In the conflagration that ensued, between fifty thousand and one hundred thousand people were estimated to have been injured, and the number of dead was placed at over thirty-five thousand.[26]

However, the lingering effects of radiation caused up to 20 percent of the deaths, many unaware of their affliction for weeks.[27] Radiation exposure was largely based upon one's proximity to the blast itself and usually caused the victim to have bloody diarrhea and/or vomiting, lethargy, lesions, a complete loss of white blood cells, deterioration of bone marrow, loss of feeling in the legs, hair loss, and acute inflammation of the mucus membranes of the throat, lungs, and stomach.[28] These same victims also suffered from fevers that went as high as 106 degrees for extended periods and endured swelling of the gums, mouth, and pharynx.[29]

Unfortunately for the survivors, 80 percent of Nagasaki's hospital beds were located within a few thousand feet of the detonation and were obliterated.[30] Because of the damage from the initial blast and the subsequent fire, the city lacked adequate medical supplies and facilities to treat the thousands of victims. Even if adequate medical services had been available, scientists estimated that the radiation casualty rate would have dropped only 5 to 8 percent.[31]

Because of the bombing, subsequent flights of aircraft over the city sent survivors scurrying for shelter.[32] Fear of additional atomic bombings led to a constant sense of uneasiness and nervousness among the remaining population.[33] The state of shock the inhabitants of Nagasaki experienced hampered recovery efforts, as residents displayed either aimlessness or hysteria, or decided to leave the city altogether for areas containing shelter and food.[34]

Weeks later in the United States, 85 percent of Americans polled approved of the use of the atomic bomb on Japanese cities, with only 10 percent dissenting and another 5 percent having no opinion.[35] In September, 69 percent of polled Americans thought that it was a "good thing" that the bomb was developed, with only 17 percent dissenting.[36] Even four months after the attacks and well after the war had ended, 22.7 percent of Americans polled wished that the U.S. had had the opportunity to drop many more atomic bombs before the Japanese had surrendered.[37]

While popular sentiment supported the bombing, a duality of sentiment existed within the national leadership. A message sent to Truman from Senator Richard Russell lauded the bombing and advocated more atomic missions. In an August 7 telegram, the senator told the president that we "should continue to strike the Japanese until they are brought groveling to their knees. We should cease our appeals to Japan to sue for peace. The next plea for peace should come from an utterly destroyed Tokyo."[38] However, in response to this message, the president demurred and stated that he did not believe in "wiping out a whole population" and that he had "humane feelings for the women and children of Japan."[39] Similarly, when head of the Manhattan Engineering District (MED) Major General Leslie Groves and U.S. Army Air Force (USAAF) Chief General Henry H. Arnold met with Army Chief of Staff General George C. Marshall after the Hiroshima bombing, Marshall cautioned against being too elated by the attack because it had caused so much death and destruction.[40] After Marshall's comment, Groves responded that he was not too concerned about the Japanese deaths considering the suffering of Americans at the hands of the Japanese.[41] Once outside of Marshall's office, Arnold reportedly turned to Groves and stated, "I am glad you said that; it's just the way I feel."[42]

Based upon the poll data and other evidence, most Americans at the time would have agreed with the president in a response he sent to Sam Cavert, General Secretary of the Federal Council of the Churches of Christ in America, regarding the attack on Hiroshima. The president wrote on August 11, 1945, "The only language they [Japanese] seem to understand is the one we have been using to bombard them. When you have to deal with a beast, you have to treat him as a beast. It is most regrettable but nevertheless true."[43] Later evidence of Truman's duality regarding the bombing is also evident in a memo sent to Secretary of State Dean Acheson on May 7, 1946. In the memo, Truman tells Acheson about a visit by Oppenheimer to the White House that occurred months earlier. Truman begins by calling Oppenheimer a "cry baby" and writes, "He came into my office some five or six months ago and spent most of his time wringing his hands and telling me they had blood on them because of the discovery of atomic energy."[44] While accounts of Truman's response to Oppenheimer may be apocryphal, he supposedly offered the scientist his handkerchief from his pocket and replied, "Well here, would you like to wipe your hands?"[45]

* * *

At the Massachusetts Institute of Technology Mid-Century Convocation in March 1949, former British Prime Minister Winston Churchill presented a speech entitled "Social Implications of Scientific Progress." During the address Churchill spoke on the role of technology in future military conflict. With the advent of human flight and the introduction of atomic weaponry, Churchill proffered, "Humanity was informed that it could make machines that would fly through the air.... The conquest of the air and the perfection of the art of flying fulfilled the dream which for thousands of years had glittered in human imagination. Certainly it was a marvelous and romantic event.... For good or ill air mastery is today the supreme expression of military power, and fleets and armies, however necessary, must accept a subordinate rank."[46]

Churchill's comments rang true to many, especially to Lieutenant General Curtis LeMay, Commander of the USAF's Strategic Air Command (SAC).[47] LeMay was so enamored of this quotation that he had the words printed, framed, and hung in his office at Offutt Air Force Base, Nebraska.[48] While other military services may have bristled at such a statement and taken umbrage with the idea of atomic strategic bombardment, many within the U.S. government and the defense establishment agreed with Churchill's observations. America's experiences in the recent global conflict and its infatuation with new technology, both atomic and aeronautical, certainly drew many to the conclusion that future wars were to be largely aviation-centric endeavors. In a 1946 speech given to the Economic Club of Detroit, future Air Force Secretary Stuart Symington proffered, "Whether to keep the peace, or win a war, our strength in the air will decide the destiny of America."[49]

With an atomic monopoly following the war, America found itself the preeminent power in the world, both economically and militarily. With the defeat of the Axis, most of Europe in ruins from six years of war, parts of Asia devastated, England teetering on financial chaos, and the Soviet Union facing a huge rebuilding and recovery effort, the U.S. was the sole economic and industrial power in the world. America still had its entire infrastructure intact, possessed easy access to an abundance of natural resources, and could expect an adequate labor pool to operate the nation's industries. America's service as the "arsenal of democracy" for the Allied powers stimulated the American economy as U.S. exports by 1944 exceeded $14 billion.[50]

Furthermore, the U.S. arguably possessed the most potent war machine on earth. In addition to having cracked the code on nuclear fission and developed atomic weapons, as the war ended in September 1945 the U.S. military had 95 army and marine ground divisions, approximately 230 Army Air Force groups, more than 85,000 aircraft, 1,166 Navy com-

General Curtis LeMay, second commander of SAC. He corrected many of the problems he inherited from his predecessor and established a climate that made the command one of the most professional and powerful military organizations ever built. His no-nonsense attitude and faith in constant training made him a feared but also a revered leader. He eventually went on to become the Air Force Chief of Staff (U.S. Air Force photograph).

bat ships, and over 12 million men and women in uniform.[51] By every measure of national power in 1945, the United States stood as the most dominant state on the globe.

However, with the end of the war, most of those in uniform looked forward to returning to civilian life and, hopefully, a job in the postwar economy. America returned to its tradition of maintaining only a small peacetime military as loud cries of "bring the boys home" forced the military services to demobilize as fast as possible. Symptomatic of this sentiment, Secretary of the Interior Harold Ickes warned that unless the military began discharging men, civilian populations would be short of fuel and coal for the upcoming winter.[52] Also reflective of the demobilization sentiment, Congressman Edwin Johnson called the Army's measured demobilization plan "blind, stupid, and criminal," and charged that the Army was unnecessarily holding men.[53] In an October 1945 presidential cabinet meeting, newly appointed Secretary of War Robert Patterson and his counterpart from the Navy, future Secretary of Defense James Forrestal, decried the hasty demobilization. The two men argued that a quick demobilization threatened the American position given the postwar security environment.[54] President Truman agreed with the secretaries' observations but countered, "The press and congress ... drown us out ... the American people had chosen to scuttle their military might."[55]

While debate ensued regarding the speed of the demobilization process, the armed services began releasing men from active duty. In a four-month period from September to December 1945, an average of 1 million men left the Army each month for civilian life.[56] The Army alone had approximately 8 million men in uniform at the end of August 1945, while a year later that number had dwindled to 2 million.[57] The U.S. Army Air Force (USAAF) had its strength overseas cut by more than half during the same period and dropped from 1 million men to only 385,000.[58]

While some complained of lethargy in the demobilization process, others agreed with the secretaries' and the president's assessments. According to one Air Force leader, "Demobilization was not demobilization; it was a rout. We just walked away and left everything."[59] Supporting this observation, by September 1946, the air force consisted of only 55 groups, down from the previous 230, with only two groups listed as operationally effective.[60] Less than two years after the war, by April 1947, the Army (including the Army Air Force) was but a shell of its former self with approximately 1 million men left in uniform.[61]

Despite the military drawdown, a sense of security pervaded America, flush from victory over the Axis and possessing an atomic monopoly. An Air Force officer in the service's academic periodical, *Air University Quarterly Review* (AUQR), wrote that if peace was to permeate on the globe, it would be a "Pax Americana."[62] He argued that "just as the instrument of Pax Britannica a century ago was sea power ... in the event of another war our first and perhaps only major offensive effort will be strategic air attacks."[63] Possessing a strategic air fleet armed with atomic weapons, Americans felt themselves relatively safe in the new "American Pax Atomica."[64] With the Pax Atomica, not only would America be secure, but the free nations of the world could depend upon the American atomic shield to keep them safe from communist encroachment.

With this secure feeling, most Americans focused their concerns domestically. A poll taken in October 1945 asked Americans the question, "What do you think is the most important problem facing the country during the next year?" The answers of jobs, strikes, and reconversion were by far the three prevailing responses.[65] A little over a year later in 1946, polls again queried Americans after the November midterm elections and asked the question, "What is the first problem you would like to see the new Congress take up?" The four most frequent responses were: control of strikes, prices and the high cost of living, tax reform, and the housing shortage.[66] Americans were happy to move from a wartime economy, focus their efforts domestically, and place a majority of the nation's national defense burden on atomic weaponry.

Reflecting the nation's economic and military dominance, in December 1947, Secretary Forrestal acknowledged the primacy of atomic weapons in American strategy in testimony to the Senate Armed Services Committee. Forrestal argued that there were only "four outstanding facts in the world at this time":

(1) Predominance of Russian land power in Europe and Asia.
(2) Predominance of American sea power.
(3) Our exclusive possession of the atomic bomb.
(4) American productive capability.

He asserted further, "As long as we can out-produce the world, control the sea, and strike inland with the atomic bomb, we can assume risks otherwise unacceptable in an effort to restore world trade, to restore the balance of power—military power—and to eliminate some of the conditions that breed war."[67] While most understood that the atomic monopoly would not last forever, in the postwar era, President Truman put stock in American atomic might and was seemingly open to its use. In 1949, while speaking to newly elected Democratic members of Congress, Truman discussed the decision to pull the atomic trigger by stating, "If it has to be made for the welfare of the United States, and the democracies of the world are at stake, I wouldn't hesitate to make it again."[68] As a result, it appeared that America had both the means and the will to conduct an atomic offensive. War plans in the immediate postwar period called for dozens of powerful atomic weapons that targeted Soviet infrastructure and production capacities. Reminiscent of

World War II bombing strategies, postwar planners envisioned using atomic ordnance on many of the same kinds of targets hit during the Combined Bombing Offensive (CBO) in Europe.

However, the reality was quite different. Despite its military might in 1945, America's atomic capability was "a hollow threat."[69] While Americans placed much of their national security in the atomic realm, this newfound capability was missing a coherent doctrine, strategy, and application. A lack of consensus existed at the national level regarding the use of atomic weapons. When it came to atomic bombs, there were more questions than answers. How many of these weapons were to be built? Who was to maintain the stockpile? How were they to be employed, and who would deliver them? If war came, where and when should these bombs be dropped? Lastly, and more importantly, what ends did we hope to achieve by utilizing these weapons? These were all questions that had no real answers. While some planners had ideas about certain aspects of an atomic offensive, there was no unified or wholly coordinated effort regarding the execution.

In the postwar years, the focus of American military strategy regarding the production, development, and employment of the atomic bomb languished. Confusion regarding atomic weapons reigned, not only among military planners and decision makers, but also among civilian leaders. This lack of a unified view was not the fault of any one organization or entity. Many federal entities, both civilian and military, failed to grasp fully the nature of the new technology or how to plan, produce, and organize atomic capabilities into a credible military force that adequately expressed national objectives. Even if the nation was going to use atomic weapons as a means of military or diplomatic discourse, it would have been hard-pressed to employ this ordnance. While Americans and many of their national leaders thought the nation had an ample supply of atomic bombs, the reality was very different. After the war, the nation's stockpile of atomic weapons was so meager that the head of the Army's nuclear weapons assembly training team said, "President Truman and the State Department were plain bluffing ... the Russians. We couldn't have put a bomb together and used it. [Fortunately] The Russians ... never called our hand."[70]

After the war, control over America's atomic stockpile passed from military authority to civilian control. While many Americans initially wanted atomic authority to reside in the hands of the military, public opinion slowly swung the other way.[71] An amalgamation of legislative proposals led to the 1946 Atomic Energy Act (McMahon Act), which established the Atomic Energy Commission (AEC). The newly formed AEC assumed responsibility for all atomic materials, research, and development originally established during the wartime Manhattan Project. While the AEC assumed control of fissionable materials and established new policies, the military still had a voice in the atomic dialogue. The Atomic Energy Act included the establishment of a Military Liaison Committee (MLC) that was a joint organization with representatives from the Army and Navy. The MLC's role was to provide input and advice to the AEC regarding military priorities and concerns regarding atomic weapons.

However, the relationship between the MLC and the AEC was not always cordial or cooperative. The balance of civilian-military control created a tension between the National Military Establishment (NME) and the civilians overseeing the development of atomic energy. Personal agendas, ideas, and philosophies made policy development and execution a difficult process. Many in the AEC viewed the military with a suspicious eye and jealously guarded their authority regarding atomic weapons. This tension had strategic implications for the nation's atomic military capability in the years following the war and remained well into the 1950s.

Furthermore, with the war over, the AEC had its work cut out in maintaining, and in some cases rebuilding, the atomic energy program. After the explosions of the "Little Boy" and "Fat Man" bombs over Hiroshima and Nagasaki and the surrender of Japan, the MED under Leslie Groves was transferred to the AEC, but the physical plants and facilities associated with the war effort had their own problems. Reactors were worn out, facilities needed upgrading, and a revitalization of the atomic endeavor was required to develop, build, and maintain a nuclear stockpile. More importantly, much of the exceptional intellectual talent of the MED left government service and returned to the private sector or academia.

Along with the AEC, Congress established a Joint Committee on Atomic Energy (JCAE) that controlled the budget and direction of AEC activities. This committee was one of the most powerful in Congress and shared responsibilities regarding atomic decisions with the president. The chairman of the Joint Committee for most of the postwar years was Senator Brien McMahon, a Democrat from Connecticut and a fierce advocate of American atomic power. The power of the JCAE was a significant factor in atomic weaponry and production and also had a role to play in the tension between the AEC and MLC.

While the MLC served as the military's conduit to the AEC, the military had its own responsibilities in determining postwar atomic requirements, strategies, and potential organizations. In late 1945, outgoing USAAF Chief Arnold directed a study to determine the employment, size, organization, and composition of the postwar atomic air force. The study was headed by future USAAF Chief of Staff General Carl Spaatz and included another future Air Force Chief of Staff General Hoyt Vandenberg, and the future Supreme Allied Commander-Europe, General Lauris Norstad. Known as the "Spaatz Board," the study outlined a rather simplistic idea of the future of air force strategic bombardment and failed to fully appreciate the nuances of atomic weaponry.

In their analysis, Spaatz Board members argued that atomic weapons do not alter the nature of a strategic air offensive "but [merely] given us an additional weapon."[72] These men envisioned a future air campaign that included a combination of both conventional and atomic bombing. Toward this end, the board argued that the atomic bomb did not require a material change to the "employment, size, organization, and composition of the postwar Air Force."[73] In this assessment, members of the board merely continued supporting Air Force doctrine of the time. It was not just the Spaatz Board members who echoed this sentiment. In the Fall 1947 issue of AUQR, famed aircraft designer Alexander de Seversky argued that it was a mistake to see atomic power as something new.[74] In Seversky's mind the atomic bomb was "simply a vastly improved explosive" and "it will remain simply a more efficient weapon at the disposal of air power."[75] The idea that it was "just another weapon" eventually lost validity, as atomic weapons ultimately became more important and served not just as the foundation of American bombing strategies but also as the basis for overarching military strategies. Future war plans during the era focused largely upon the use of atomic weapons and their effects. While conventional bombing still had a place in Air Force strategic missions, the atomic bomb served as the anchor point for military approaches.

Despite their rather simplistic ideas regarding atomic weaponry, Spaatz Board members did, however, envision the conduct of warfare changing with the advent of long-range strategic bombers. In their final report, members thought that major conflicts lasting years were a thing of the past. Entire wars would be fought in days, weeks, and months, not necessarily in years. They also estimated that mass destruction on an apocalyptic scale might be in store for the future. They articulated these ideas by stating that mankind might not "see another war so mild and so slow as World War II, or one with as little destruction of life and property."[76] The idea that American military might consisted largely of a series of strategic bombing raids played a significant role in military planning following the war. Furthermore, these air leaders envisioned a requirement that the United States have a standing military that was ready to strike from the initial onset of war, arguing in their final report "a premise necessitated by the recent failure of isolationism and unpreparedness and by the fact that never again will we be able to prepare after war starts. Unless we stand in split-second readiness we will lose a future war."[77] In fact by winter of 1947–1948, the Air Force began playing with the idea that it could "kill a nation" by developing a comprehensive list of industrial targets based upon their experiences from the global conflict and including atomic weapons.[78] In this effort, bombing would focus not just on industrial capabilities but also on the governmental control mechanisms and ability to mobilize. While many in Air Force circles opposed the idea of nation-killing, the possibility of doing it was now real.

In an article written for *Collier's* magazine in December 1945 and entitled "Airpower in the Atomic Age," Spaatz described a vision indicative of the USAF's thought regarding future conflict. In the piece, he wrote that war in the future "would be aimed at smashing the enemy's whole organism and would counter his offensive incidentally in the process."[79] As Spaatz anticipated, an effective air offensive would "pulverize" the adversary's industrial centers, and with "immediate blows against [enemy] means of civilization and military support, his industrial and economic areas would make his continuance of the struggle pointless and bring a quick surrender."[80] Spaatz suggested a wholesale change in American military thinking. With this vision of a new type of war, Spaatz argued that atomic weapons meant America must be on the offensive from the very start. In the nuclear world, with improvement in aircraft and missiles, Spaatz concluded that the "offense has a crushing advantage" and "our habits of strictly defensive thought must be weeded out. We need a national psychology of offense."[81] He argued further, "For the world's greatest democracy to remain in its traditional defense minded rut during this time of military revolution would be an historic calamity."[82] Obviously, this idea represented a radical shift in American military thought.

Despite the wholesale change that atomic weapons potentially brought to warfare, Air Force leadership had yet to come to grips with the employment of these weapons in future conflicts. Without recognizing the unique aspects atomic weapons brought to war, most Air Force planners thought that air strategy in the next war would resemble the one that preceded it—protracted and total and aimed at national infrastructure and production capabilities.[83] However, this protracted effort with atomic weapons might last only one to three months, as opposed to one to three years, and would be conducted with perhaps 300 planes.[84] The execution of the atomic air offensive was a centerpiece of Air Force rhetoric, but the plans, assets, and doctrine behind such an effort was sorely lacking. Coordination between federal legislative and executive entities and other military services was at best tenuous.

In speeches by various members of the USAAF leadership immediately after the war, the constant theme was that America needed an Air Force ready to retaliate against any aggressor with large-scale nuclear destruction from the air. In both the tone and intent, their words laid the foundations for what eventually became "massive retaliation" and the deterrence policy adopted by subsequent administrations. Fears over an "atomic Pearl Harbor" underscored the importance of preparedness and the ability to attack immediately

Introduction 19

with nuclear weapons if required.⁸⁵ Representative of this thought was another AUQR article written in 1948, arguing, "If bombing is required to enforce our will, let it be atomic bombing.... We can concentrate our energies on the super air blitz which will force an unqualified decision within a month.... A ready fighting team, a true atomic-bombing-force-in-being, can win the game without ever making a substitution."⁸⁶ This same sentiment was consistently expressed throughout the postwar era, as nuclear confrontation was considered almost inevitable. When asked by a naval officer visiting SAC headquarters about the command's capability to conduct strategic bombing if atomic weapons were outlawed, LeMay replied, "Foolish question. It is inconceivable to me that this situation will ever arise."⁸⁷ Shortly after taking command of SAC, LeMay testified to a senior Air Force panel determining bomber requirements that "the fundamental goal of the Air Force should be the creation of a strategic atomic striking force capable of attacking any target on Eurasia from bases in the United States and returning to the points from take-off."⁸⁸

The other services also had their hands in the discussion. What role were the Army and Navy to play regarding atomic weapons? The recent war had seen carrier aviation mature and become the primary striking power of the American fleet. As a result, naval aviators now believed they had a role in the atomic offensive. Both of the other branches (excluding the Marine Corps) felt that they had a part to play despite the Air Force's perceived monopoly on atomic delivery. These debates within the NME also had implications for the development of the atomic offensive. This argument would come to a head in the fall of 1949, with results reverberating for years.

In addition to the Air Force's ideas regarding postwar bombing methodologies, early American war plans developed during the period were also problematic. Planners at the Joint Chiefs of Staff (JCS) level and below were completely unrealistic about American military abilities in both nuclear and conventional bombardment and could not translate the atomic monopoly into any realistic plan as an expression of national policy.⁸⁹ In the period after the war, military planners were scarcely aware of the power of atomic weapons and its potential effects. Information about atomic weapons was "close hold," with strategic planners only estimating what effect they might have without having much actual data about their overall result. Furthermore, for a period of time, the number of potential targets in early war plans far outstripped the number of nuclear weapons stockpiled. As atomic weapons production slowed to almost a standstill after the war, target lists began to grow. While production would eventually ramp up by 1950, early atomic target planning did not reflect the actual inventory of bombs available.

While the atomic bomb was viewed as the primary weapon for the Air Force, a significant part of planned aerial offensives included the use of conventional munitions. As much as the U.S. atomic air fleet was unprepared for a sustained offensive, so too was the conventional bombing force. The available strategic bombing fleet after World War II was too small and unprepared to conduct an extensive bombing campaign of the Soviet Union. Not only was the Soviet Union a vast country with thousands of square miles in which to hide military infrastructure and capabilities, but its integrated air defense capability was largely unknown to Air Force planners. Furthermore, planners suffered from a lack of detailed and current information on targets located in the interior of the Soviet Union. Much of the information regarding potential target areas came from eyewitness accounts or word of mouth from veterans of the Eastern Front during the war. In addition to a lack of information regarding the threat, a paucity of recent intelligence on potential targets, and a relatively small strategic bombing fleet, during this time SAC also had to deal with poor morale, insufficient maintenance support, and temperamental equipment. Conventional or atomic, the Air Force strategic bombing fleet was insufficient and unprepared to conduct a sustained wholesale attack on the Soviet Union. War plans such as PINCHER, BROILER, HALFMOON, and OFFTACKLE developed after the war all failed to appreciate the limitations of the strategic bombing force existing under the Truman administration's paltry defense budget.

Additionally, these plans failed to align national goals and objectives as to the use of atomic weapons. At the strategic level of war many unresolved questions remained. Toward what end should atomic weapons be used? What did we hope to achieve with the atomic bomb? What constituted victory in a nuclear war? What were we to do after the end of hostilities: Were we to just leave the Soviet Union "a smoking irradiated ruin?"[90] When LeMay assumed command of SAC, his operations officer, General J. B. Montgomery, asked to see the war plan. What was presented was "very sketchy, very weak ... [with the officer having] it in his pocket."[91] As one SAC pilot recalled, "We had a list of targets, but apparently someone was going to assign us [which] targets we were to attack before take-off."[92]

A comprehensive national strategy comprises three interrelated elements, the "Ends-Ways-Means," that should neatly nest together. National strategy begins with an envisioned end state or objective that supports the nation's best interests and goals. Once the "end" has been defined by the national authority, then supporting concepts, policies, and programs are developed and built that serve as the foundation for the envisioned "end." These supporting concepts, policies, and programs outline the "way" in which the national goal or objective will be achieved. The "way" outlines the methodology, practice, and approach used to obtain the stated national objective. The third part of a national strategy includes the mobilization of the "means" or resources mobilized to shape the environment. The means provide the tools and assets to exercise control over circumstances that achieve the overall objectives.[93]

As a result, a comprehensive national strategy properly aligns the "Ends-Ways-Means" of the state in a coherent and properly resourced manner. From 1945 to 1950, American strategies centered on atomic capabilities and resources (means), war plans (ways), and envisioned goals (ends) were clearly misaligned, uncoordinated, and dysfunctional. The nation had very little idea of what its end state was with regard to atomic weapons. What did the nation hope to achieve with the atomic bomb? Supporting national policies NSC 30 and NSC 20/4 provided very little in the way of guidance. Furthermore, the ways in which the NME planned to execute an atomic offensive were neither realistic nor properly resourced. The AEC, charged with both the production and maintenance of the atomic stockpile, was struggling with an exodus of talent, failing facilities, and was overly suspicious of military influences. Lastly, the means to conduct an atomic air offensive were paltry at best and woefully unprepared and equipped to carry out the task assigned. SAC's atomic bombing aircraft were far too few and their performance limited, its knowledge of Soviet targets was speculative at best, and its crews were alarmingly ill-trained to conduct the enormous task assigned to them. In all, America had very little idea what to do with atomic weapons, how they would translate into national goals and objectives, and failed to properly produce and maintain the stockpile and delivery means.

While the "American Pax Atomica" was seemingly a foundation of international discourse, the nation's atomic resources and organizations in the period following the war lacked vision within the legislative, executive, and military segments of the federal government. An intellectual, doctrinal, and organizational void existed after the war regarding America's atomic weapons production, development, planning, and use. From 1945 until 1950, American nuclear strategy was adrift and uncoordinated despite the public's belief that the United States was secure with its atomic monopoly. This void had direct military results—especially for the USAF's Strategic Air Command. Plagued by its own internal problems regarding the strategic bombing fleet, the Air Force was tasked with missions that were ill-conceived and were not necessarily nested with national strategic goals. However, fault does not lie solely with the Air Force, but rests to a degree with the myriad of competing ideas, agendas, arguments, and politics of the immediate postwar era.

As a result of these issues and others, America's "atomic shield" during this period was little more than a "paper tiger." This book will look at the incoherent nature of American atomic weapons development, ordnance production, war planning strategy, and strategic bombing capability. The development of American early atomic strategy is not necessarily a military history, but one that speaks to the function of disjointed federal action, uncoordinated joint operations, unilateral military planning, and poor national resource management. The inability to clearly align American ends-ways-means reflects the broken nature of national security policy regarding atomic weapons during this time and provides a lesson in dysfunctional civilian-military relations.

PART I. THE BOMB

1

Mr. X and the Fiscal Year (FY) 50 Debate

A starting point for the American government's perspective regarding the postwar international environment is George Kennan's "Long Telegram" message from Moscow on February 22, 1946. In this transmission, Kennan, the deputy chief of mission of the U.S. embassy in Moscow, provided the intellectual cornerstone for American military and political policy for the next few decades.[1] In his message Kennan outlined a mistrustful view of the Soviet Union and explained, "At the bottom of the Kremlin's neurotic view of world affairs is the traditional and instinctive Russian sense of insecurity."[2] He further claimed that "world communism is like a malignant parasite which feeds only on diseased tissue."[3]

The message was popular reading in the Truman Administration and eventually appeared in the academic journal *Foreign Affairs* under the pen name "Mr. X." The most important aspect of the Kennan "Mr. X" article came from one of the last passages, as it suggested that the United States embark "with reasonable confidence upon a policy of firm containment, designed to confront the Russians with unalterable counter force at every point where they show signs of encroaching upon the interests of a peaceful and stable world."[4] Kennan's ideas quickly gained traction, and American foreign policy strategy obtained a new name: "containment."

While Kennan's opinion took a dim view of Soviet intentions, he seemed to ignore the Russian experience in the 20th century. It had been attacked twice and suffered horribly in both world conflicts. Cold War scholars have refuted such alleged intentions on the part of the Soviet Union and see Stalin more in a defensive mode following the war. Historian John Lewis Gaddis identified Stalin's postwar goals specifically as "security for himself, his regime, his country and his ideology precisely in that order."[5] Furthermore, Gaddis argued that Stalin was betting that another capitalist crisis would occur following the war and that the United States would lend money to the

USSR for reconstruction in order to keep markets open for American manufacturers.[6] In keeping with Marxist ideology, Stalin thought that capitalism would eventually sow its own seeds of destruction and the countries of Western Europe would ultimately turn to communism for a solution.[7] According to Gaddis's interpretation, there was no need for offensive military action on the part of the USSR, as time would provide the eventual victory of communism.

Regardless of Gaddis's opinion of Stalin's intentions, most Americans in the late 1940s saw the USSR as a nefarious agent in world affairs, bent upon global expansion. Despite the fact that the Soviet Union cut the size of the Red Army from 11.5 million men to 3 million and that its defense expenditures were half of America's, polls taken at this time overwhelmingly reflected the suspicious mood of Americans toward the Soviets.[8] In August 1946, 60 percent of Americans surveyed thought that Russia "was trying to build itself up to be the ruling power of the world," while only 26 percent thought that the USSR was merely trying to protect itself from another war.[9] A year later, another poll found that 71 percent of Americans believed that one nation was trying to dominate the world, and of that 71 percent, a full 78 percent believed that the one country attempting to dominate was Russia.[10] Six months later, in February 1948, 73 percent of those polled believed that Russia would start a war with the United States to "get something she wanted."

On November 23, 1948, National Security Council (NSC) Memorandum 20/4 officially reflected the growing concern over Soviet actions and echoed the sentiment expressed by Kennan in his 1946 telegram and "Mr. X" article. NSC 20/4 argued that the Soviet Union was bent upon the ascendency of global communism with the USSR as the dominant power and that in support of this endeavor, Russia was "building up as rapidly as possible the war potential of the Soviet orbit in anticipation of war, which in the communist thinking is inevitable."[11] Furthermore, the document argued that the Red Army was capable of taking over all of Europe and strategically important parts of the Middle and Near East in as little as six months.[12] NSC 20/4 also speculated that by 1955 the Soviet Union would have an intercontinental bombing capability that could reach the continental United States with a host of nuclear, biological, and chemical weapons.[13] However, the memo argued that the Soviets were not deliberately looking for a conflict with the United States and were trying to achieve their aims by political means backed by military intimidation. While armed conflict was always a possibility, the State Department estimated that the Soviet leadership "probably did not intend deliberate armed action involving the United States at this time."[14] However, U.S. planners did not discount war by miscalculation and thought that the two powers might easily stumble into conflict.

While Kennan's observations served as the foundations for ideas articulated in NSC 20/4 and NSC 68, during the late 1940s a number of competing interests at the federal government level precluded the development of a coherent atomic military strategy. Fiscal concerns intermixed with debates regarding civilian/military control over the atomic stockpile and arguments over roles and missions for the NME all contributed to the discombobulated nature of U.S. military atomic strategies. Various competing agendas, some personal and others organizational, precluded effective development of a comprehensive vision for the American atomic arsenal. For the first five years, American atomic power, strategy, and organization were a model of dysfunction.

The FY 50 Debate

Flush from victory, after World War II most of America turned inward for economic and domestic prosperity. To deal with a huge debt incurred during the Great Depression and the war, the Truman Administration sought to balance the federal budget and curb government costs, especially defense spending. A smaller military reflected the mood of the nation, as it maintained only a cadre force despite the apparently growing threat of communist incursions. In line with American tradition, the military downsized following the war, and the priority of effort, for both the nation and the Truman administration, turned to the economy and postwar prosperity. Both citizens and corporate America saw a bright future ahead and looked to the government to reform many of the essential wartime economic policies. Industry sought an end to price controls, and Americans looked forward to the end of rationing with the hope that the peacetime economy would not yield a huge rise in inflation.[15] As the basis of the economy shifted from wartime to peacetime, fears over inflation and another depression served as reminders to Truman that a balanced federal budget and the amelioration of the wartime national debt was the priority.[16]

While many feared that the U.S. economy would slide back into a depression following the war, this concern failed to materialize. Instead, the nation prospered for the first time since before the 1920s.[17] However, some economic fears did manifest, as inflation steadily rose in the postwar years. The consumer price index in 1945 was 76.9 but steadily grew a quarter in three years and by 1948 was 102.8.[18] As inflation grew, so too did the occurrence of labor strikes that resulted in the loss of over 116,000,000 working days.[19] Truman remained concerned with balancing the federal budget and vetoed any tax cut forwarded by the Republican-controlled 80th Congress. As the nation transitioned to peacetime, Truman also ensured that defense expenditures were slashed. During his annual State of the Union address in January 1946, he outlined a plan for a reduction in military expenditures by dropping them from a planned figure of $70 billion for fiscal year (FY) 1946 to $49 billion. For the following year he planned to reduce the figure again to a mere $15 billion and sought to keep military spending around this level for future FYs.[20] While military expenditures rose to a wartime height of 37.4 percent of the GNP in 1944, they began to fall steadily to 20.7 percent in 1946 and by 1948 represented a mere 4.4 percent.[21]

Instead of depending upon a large standing military, Truman saw that economic solvency provided the best bet for national security in the postwar world. In the same 1946 address, he said further, "National security does not consist of an army, a navy, and an air force. It rests on a much broader basis. It depends on a sound economy of prices and wages, on prosperous agriculture, on satisfied and productive workers, on a competitive private enterprise free from monopolistic repression...."[22] As Truman saw it, the capitalistic system of finance and its economic viability would serve as a bulwark against communist influence and deter the spread of Soviet influence.

Truman's ideas were not erroneous and had positive effects for domestic life. After the war, U.S. prosperity grew significantly, as Americans had more discretionary funds than ever before. Between 1947 and 1961, national incomes rose 60 percent and consumerism grew as Americans increased spending on household furnishings, luxury items, and appliances.[23] Americans purchased millions of cars, stoves, televisions, and refrigerators. This consumerism underpinned the idea that a prosperous lifestyle in a capitalist system was a symbol of its superiority over communism and its associated ideals.

In his effort to ensure economic well-being and general security, Truman sought to balance the federal budget after the nation had incurred a combined wartime and depression era debt of over $241.8 billion.[24] Planned cuts in military spending were one of Truman's primary methods of restoring long-term financial solvency. While holding the opinion that the military always requested more money than it needed, Truman began applying the "remainder method" of fiscal policy to the defense budget.[25] This methodology considered all expected civilian governmental expenses and balanced them against the federal government's projected income.[26] Once the civilian expenses were subtracted from the federal revenue, the "remainder" served as the budgetary limit for the military.[27] This system of budgeting obviously placed defense funding as the lowest priority and the state of the postwar Army, Navy, and Air Force reflected such frugality. Fiscal conservatism served as the foundation for many Truman administration policies and actions. Ironically, this same frugality led Truman to rely—implicitly at least—more upon atomic weaponry for defense than large, standing conventional forces.[28]

The military, much like the average consumer, increasingly found its purchasing power reduced as inflation rose. The services increasingly depended upon more expensive weapon systems that exacerbated the already austere financial situation. While a wartime four-engine B-17 Flying Fortress bomber cost $218,000, the price of a postwar B-36 Peacemaker and its 10 engines (6 propellers and 4 jets, starting with the "D" version) was more than $3.6 million.[29] Fighter aircraft costs also soared. The cost of the war's most famous fighter, the P-51 Mustang, was $54,000, compared to one of its successors, the F-89 Scorpion, with a price tag of $855,000.[30] As a result, the military was strapped with a smaller budget and rising inflation, while desiring more expensive equipment.

The FY 48 budget allocated just over $10 billion for national defense and for the next few years would remain just above that level.[31] According to Truman, his paltry FY 49 budget was designed for "only the minimum [military] requirements."[32] The total military obligation that year was divided fairly evenly among the three services. The Army received $4.6 billion, the Navy $3.6 billion, and the Air Force 1.47 billion.[33] (The allocation between the services is deceptive, as half of the Army's allocation was designated for the Air Force as it separated into its own service.[34]) Additionally, personnel manning was set at a ceiling of 1,423,000, a reduction of 13 percent from the FY 48 level.[35] Ironically in the same budget, Truman proposed an increase in the budget for the AEC, which was separate and distinct from the NME, from $456 million to $660 million.[36]

The even distribution of funds to each service had become a staple of Truman's defense expenditures. While Air Force officers saw strategic bombing as the nation's "Sunday punch" in offensive action, the equitable budgeting drew the ire of Secretary of the Air Force Stuart Symington, who in July 1948 complained about "ax-grinders dedicated to obsolete methods [of warfare]."[37] In the mind of strategic bombing advocates, allocating the meager defense budget piecemeal to all the services wasted resources that could best be used where they really counted—the strategic bombing fleet. For the Air Force, the requirement was a 70-group air force, and in a 1949 memo, Symington declared that the service was woefully deficient not only in the number of groups but also in modern aircraft designs.[38] Furthermore, as Symington and the Air Force saw it, "the only consideration which could keep the Soviet Union from making this attempt [to attack] is the fear of a retaliatory atomic attack by the Air Force against the Soviet Union."[39]

With all the advances in technology and the growing importance and increasing relevance of the airplane, on July 18, 1947, the president established an Air Policy Commission to help define the role of aviation in America's future. In his guidance, he told the appointed members, "There is an urgent need at this time for an evaluation of the course which the United States should follow in order to obtain, for itself and the world, the greatest possible benefits from aviation."[40] The commission considered both the civilian and military applications of aviation and looked beyond the contemporary environment. Philadelphia lawyer Thomas K. Finletter, who became Secretary of the Air Force in 1950, served as chairman. He and four other prominent businessmen, most without aviation experience, were tasked by Truman to report their results by the beginning of 1948.[41]

During the commission's six-month deliberations, it conducted both closed- and open-door meetings, interviewed over 150 officials and executives, and visited 17 civilian and military aircraft establishments.[42] The commission also received testimony from the chiefs of the respective military departments and Defense Secretary James Forrestal. At the end of 1947 the "Finletter Commission," as it was known, completed its investigation and submitted its findings to the president in a report with the ominous title "Survival in the Air Age." The commission placed great emphasis upon the airplane in national defense. During the commission's study, Secretary of War Robert Patterson testified, "I believe in air power, without if, buts, or howevers.... I believe that our national defense should be centered on air power ... to a far greater degree than is the case at present. It is my opinion that we will not need the strongest army in the world or the strongest standing navy in the world, but we will need the strongest air force in the world."[43] Even the Army secretary reported "air power is our first line of defense in the event of war."[44] Critical of the current state of U.S. air power, the commission reiterated a requirement for a 70-group air force that its leaders had requested since the end of the war.

The commission membership echoed the USAF's arguments that America needed a robust deterrent military power so strong that "other nations will hesitate to attack us or our vital national interests because of the violence of the counter attack" and stated that such a capability required a "force in being."[45] This "force in being" needed to be present during phase one of any war. A 1946 work written by a veteran of the strategic bombing campaign over Germany specifically addresses the issue of military preparedness for nuclear war in light of a democratic form of government. William Borden's *There Will Be No Time* argued that democratic governments were at a disadvantage to dictatorships in preparing for war, as the focus of effort was different.[46] While democratic citizens focus upon jobs and economic domestic concerns, dictatorships were able to prepare for war because they did not answer to a constituency.[47] Borden concluded that in the nuclear world, a standing military force ready to strike back at an aggressor was an imperative, despite the democratic foundations of the country. He further warned that the penalty for not supporting such preparation was not just a longer casualty list but "certain national death."[48] During the war, the United States had the "luxury" of time to ramp up its industrial base to make the tanks, ships, and planes needed to fight the Axis powers. However, in the postwar world, with the advent of intercontinental bombing and atomic weapons, the nation would

1. Mr. X and the Fiscal Year (FY) 50 Debate 29

not have time to build a military as it had done previously. The specter of a potential "atomic Pearl Harbor" was an underlying concern. Borden and others believed that the nation needed a strong air arm in existence at the very start of a conflict to preclude national catastrophe. Symington too agreed with Borden's dire prediction and argued that "in this air-atomic age, there is no 'time' to buy: and therefore how can we stay free unless we stay strong?"[49]

Furthermore, while still envisioning a requirement for an army and a navy, the commission stressed that the nation's military security needed to be focused on air power. Recognizing that the Russians would eventually develop the atomic bomb, the commission reported that any future attack with weapons of mass destruction would likely come from the air, and the only method to counter such a threat was a robust air force.[50] Much as Churchill had argued in his MIT speech, the committee emphasized the primacy of air power over other forms of warfare.

The commission also stipulated that the "force in being" be built around a fleet of bomber aircraft and that these planes would attack an enemy who would have its "cities destroyed and its war machine crushed."[51] In order to conduct this wartime mission, the commission suggested that the 1947 USAF strength of 55 groups be increased to 70 groups, with 700 very heavy bombers, and that this growth be completed by January 1950.[52] To support this increase in the size of the USAF and build the additional bombers, the commission recommended an increase in defense expenditures for the USAF. While the JCS saw the importance of a well-funded air arm, it argued for an equitable and even-handed approach to military expenditures.[53] Each service, especially the Air Force, claimed relevancy in the modern age, but Truman's fiscal conservatism precluded large sums for defense expenditures that might imperil the president's goal of economic solvency.[54]

In addition to the Finletter Commission, Congress established its own investigative body to review air-power requirements for the future. This investigation, published as the Hinshaw-Brewster Report, reiterated many of the same conclusions from the Finletter Commission, including the need for a 70-group air force. However, this recommended increase in the size of the USAF and its budget did not mean that the argument for building a larger nuclear bomber fleet was finished. With Truman's defense spending limitations, all the services were feeling the fiscal restraints, and the two reports only exacerbated inter-service rivalries.

According to the report, during FY 1947, the Navy was funded at over $4 billion, with the Air Force budgeted at only $2.8 billion. In order to build the required air power, the commission recommended an increased USAF appropriation of over $4.1 billion in FY 1948, while keeping the Navy and Army budgets at approximately $4 and $3.2 billion respectively.[55] This increase in Air Force budget allocations was to continue under the commission's plan into FY 1949 and in subsequent FYs.

The commission's request for increased budgets flew in the face of Truman's fiscal conservatism. In 1948, events in Eastern Europe raised international security tensions and seemed to validate Kennan's observations. Regardless, Truman was determined to limit defense expenditures to $15 billion, with atomic bombs being the most obvious fiscally sound answer to any potential Soviet threat.[56] American leaders increasingly looked to the ill-equipped and poorly trained SAC to thwart any potential Soviet attack. In FY 48 appropriations, the Air Force received an influx of money totaling $4.5 billion, with SAC as the priority.[57] However, this influx of funds fell far short of what the USAF leadership required. FY 49 provided no relief to the NME and the services continued to struggle with insufficient funds.

The struggle of the FY 50 budget process demonstrated the national disconnect regarding atomic strategy and the NME. On May 13, 1948, Truman announced his decision to limit FY 50 defense expenditures to $15 billion on the same day he limited the services to a mere $3 billion in supplemental funds for the FY 49 NME budget.[58] He was resolute in his intent as he expected his orders "to be carried out whole-heartedly, in good spirit and without mental reservations."[59] Of historical significance is that the NME FY 50 budget submission was the first unified military budget. With this in mind and in preparation for the FY 50 budgeting process, Secretary Forrestal argued that existing international tensions required a revision in military spending and an increase in the federal allocation.[60] Despite political challenges in Europe, the secretary was chagrined to hear Truman tell him "that he [Truman] was preparing, not for war, but for peace. He was basing his military policy on the assumption that there would not be war."[61] Despite the Finletter and Hinshaw-Brewster findings and the increase in global tensions, the debate regarding the FY 50 budget fully illustrated a disconnect between policy and strategy.

By May 1948, the JCS had approved an emergency war plan called HALFMOON. The plan was a short-range proposal that outlined courses of action for the first year of a global conflict with the Soviet Union.[62] While the plan had a number of shortcomings, it served as a basis for military requirements during the FY 50 budgeting process. However, Secretary Forrestal was faced with perplexing questions: What was his budget supposed to reflect? What were the nation's national security goals and objectives? Should it maintain the current military structure or should it reflect a wartime requirement as specified in HALFMOON?[63] On July 10, he forwarded a request to the National Security Council arguing that military planning, in this case fiscal planning, needed to reflect U.S. national objectives based upon potential enemies and international commitments. Toward this end, Forrestal was tasking higher authority to spell out what the NME should be planning for and how that would affect the manning, training, and equipping of the military. Both he and the JCS were unhappy with the guidance in the existing NSC 7, "The Position of the United States with Respect to Soviet Directed World Communism." Looking for guidance to underpin the defense budget and substantiate an increase in expenditures, he took the issue to George Kennan at the State Department, who was equally opaque about United States policy.[64] Kennan and the planners at the State Department began drafting what would eventually become NSC 20/4, which outlined more specific guidance for Forrestal and the NME. However, NSC 20/4 provided little help during budget development, as it was not approved until 24 November 1948, only a week before the Secretary of Defense was to submit his FY 50 proposal to the president.[65] Regardless, even when NSC 20/4 was published, it failed to spur defense allocations as Forrestal had hoped.

Kennan believed that if war were to come, it would be accidental and that the Soviets were not looking to conduct a deliberate offensive against the West. While some attempt was made to establish such guidance by the State Department, the thrust of Kennan's guidance to Forrestal was fairly ambiguous and was of little help to the Defense Secretary. In Kennan's mind, war was a possibility but not a certainty, and as a result, the NME should not look for a dramatic increase in the budget based upon the presumption of conflict. In fact, NSC 20/4 tacitly warned against overspending on defense, arguing that the nation should "maximize its economic potential."[66] With no help from the State Department, Forrestal had few options. In a memo from Truman regarding the NME limit of $15 billion, the president told his defense secretary "It seems to me that the proper thing for you to do is get the Army, Navy, and Air Force people together and establish a program within budget limits which have been allowed. It seems to me that is your responsibility."[67] Despite Truman's guidance and advice, the Defense Secretary had no authority to force a compromise among his service chiefs.

In mid-July, Forrestal directed the services to draft their respective budgets by the end of the month. Pressed for time and still unable to determine specific roles and missions regarding atomic warfare, the services submitted their individual proposals, which, when added together, totaled $29 billion—$14 billion over the Truman allocation.[68] However, some agreement was reached regarding the role of the Navy and Air Force in the atomic mission. This agreement was rare, as the Army Air Force and the Navy had been at odds during the war, and with the creation of an independent air service, naval aviators looked suspiciously at the new branch. Navy leadership anticipated Air Force missions eclipsing the carrier navy and believed that airmen might make a power grab for unity of air power under one service. Such concerns were not altogether unfounded. A similar situation occurred in interwar Great Britain as the Royal Navy's Fleet Air Arm became subservient to a national Air Ministry staffed largely by Royal Air Force officers. As a result, the Fleet Air Arm languished and was wholly unprepared for the upcoming global conflict. The U.S. Navy feared the same eventuality happening in the United States—even before the war—and fought the Air Force over its expansion in roles and missions.

Concurrently, with the budget debate ongoing, a discussion regarding the custody of atomic weapons between the AEC and the NME was coming to a head. This too became part of the inter-service rivalry regarding roles and missions. The Navy and Forrestal believed that carrier aviation had a role to play in an atomic offensive, at least against naval targets. The Air Force took exception to this suggestion, arguing that strategic bombing was still an exclusive Air Force mission. This debate would come to a very public hearing in October 1949 and then reemerge with the advent of nuclear submarines and ballistic missiles. For the time being, the Air Force jealously protected its strategic bombing mission and its supporting budget.

Eager to reduce the total dollar amount, Forrestal appointed a Budgetary Advisory Committee (BAC) in August to help pare down the military's budget request. Using HALFMOON as a baseline, the BAC reduced the figure to $23.6 billion. While the services worked jointly to determine costs, their analysis found that even to maintain the military at its current configuration, $3.6 billion more was required than the FY 49 allocation.[69] The services needed at least $18.6 billion just to maintain their existing capabilities. Furthermore, since inflation needed to be considered, the BAC recommended an additional $5 billion; hence the $23.6 billion total.

In October 1948, the BAC met again in an attempt to further reduce the $23.6 billion figure. However, in these deliberations, inter-service rivalry appeared in earnest. The Army and the Air Force argued that the Navy's aircraft carrier requirements were excessive and proposed a reduction. As a result, two sets of figures were presented to the secretary, with the joint Air Force/Army figure at $15.8 billion and the Navy's at $16.5 billion. Chief of Naval Operations (CNO) Admiral Louis Denfeld decried the attack on the Navy's carrier requirement and countered that the "unpleasant fact remains that the Navy has honest and sincere misgivings as to the ability of the Air Force [to] successfully deliver the [atomic] weapon by means of unescorted missions flown by present day bombers deep into enemy territory in the face of strong Soviet air defenses, and drop it on targets whose locations are not accurately known."[70] While sharp in his rebuke of the Air Force's strategic bombing capabilities, he was not at all inaccurate or far from the truth. A full year later, the Air Force and the Navy would be at loggerheads regarding the efficacy of carrier aviation compared to strategic bombing. This issue eventually manifested itself in the "Revolt of the Admirals," forcing Denfeld from his position as CNO in October 1949.

Days later, on October 5, 1948, Forrestal briefed Truman on the fiscal impasse at the Pentagon. Interestingly, Truman's tightfisted military budget guidance occurred during the same year that the Soviets backed the Czechoslovak coup d'état in February, fighting raged in the Greek Civil War, and the Russians blockaded Berlin. Despite the aggressive actions of the Soviets and the prevailing American sentiment regarding Communist intent, Truman still clung to the idea of fiscal solvency throughout the election season. During the October 5 meeting, Truman told Forrestal that he did not want to give the appearance that the nation was rearming for war and exacerbate international security tensions.[71] In Truman's view, the perception of rearmament would potentially goad the Soviets into conflict by giving them a casus belli. Truman did hint at the idea of supplemental budgetary requests to the NME budget, but the FY 50 mandated figure would remain.

The next day Forrestal informed the JCS of the president's stance regarding the $15 billion defense limit and that they would have to budget based upon that figure, equitably distributed, but also stated that supplemental funding might be a requirement.[72] Slowly Forrestal realized that the defense budget required more than what Truman was willing to give. Again the secretary had the BAC meet, using HALFMOON as a baseline for planning, a calculation that developed a budget of $17.5 billion. Forrestal eventually argued that in order to push for a budget larger than $15 billion, the NME was going to have to show the president that "we have taken every drop of water out of this thing that we can find—we can't catch it all—but I have got to be able to say we have gone into this thing from the ground up."[73] On 15 October Forrestal told the JCS that he would approve a budget between $14.4 billion and the $23.6 billion (the figure the BAC proposed).[74] Even this level, in his opinion, would not see to the defeat of the Soviets but was merely a start if war came.[75] He also tasked the JCS to develop a budget that fit within the president's guidance.

Eventually, on November 8, the JCS submitted a budget that fit the president's mandate. The division of funds gave the Army $4.8 billion, the Navy $4.6 billion, and the Air Force $5 billion. The services arrived at this second budget by haggling over carrier numbers and using services' draft force requirements based upon a $16.9 billion figure. Forestall now had two budget figures to present to Truman. Again, seeking support from the State Department, Forrestal contacted George Marshall to help validate an increase in defense spending and possibly recruit an ally in the budget debate. Forrestal posed three questions to his State Department counterpart to help frame NME budget requirements:

1. Had the international situation improved sufficiently in the past year to warrant a substantial reduction in military forces [that was] planned for and the end of the current fiscal year?
2. Had the situation worsened so that there should be an augmentation of the planned forces?
3. Or was the situation about the same?[76]

Marshall, having just returned from Europe, was sympathetic to Forrestal's predicament but offered no real help and seemed less alarmed with the international security situation.[77] In his response to Forrestal on 8 November, the Secretary of State wrote, "We must expect from the current fiscal year a situation which is neither better nor worse than that which we have faced in 1948 insofar as it affects the ceiling of our military establishment."[78] Marshall had faith in the Truman Doctrine and initiation of the European Recovery Plan (Marshall Plan) as a hedge against open conflict with the Soviets and did not provide the justification Forrestal wanted for a higher NME budget figure.

Truman's come-from-behind victory over Thomas Dewey on November 2 bolstered the president's confidence and faith in his existing policies. As a result, Forrestal was not optimistic about changing Truman's mind.[79] Much as before, the State Department was no help weeks later when NSC 20/4 was published. While it identified a nefarious Soviet threat, it still fell short of advocating a huge increase in defense expenditures in case of an accidental war.[80] NSC 20/4 specified that the Unites States should maximize its economic potential and strengthen its peacetime economy. This statement seemed to underpin Truman's fiscal policies and frugal defense expenditures. Furthermore, the document stipulated that if war was to come, the United States should not have a "predetermined requirement for unconditional surrender."[81] The ambiguity of this statement calls into question an envisioned end state should conflict occur. What was expected from the military if war came?

Eventually the Secretary of Defense submitted three proposed budgets to the president: The $15 billion (Truman's limit), $16.9 billion (JCS compromise), and the $23 billion (BAC-HALFMOON submission).[82] On December 9, Forrestal, the service secretaries, and the JCS briefed the proposed budgets to Truman. After a meeting that lasted less than an hour, and much to the military's chagrin, Truman chose the smallest figure. Days later Forrestal wrote, "He [Truman] is a hard money man if ever I saw one, and believing as I do that we can't afford to wreck our economy in the process of trying to fight the 'cold war,' there is much to be said for his thesis of holding down spending to the absolute minimum of necessity."[83] While the dollar figure appeared to be on par with previous allocations, with rising inflation, the figure reduced military purchasing power and eroded military capability. On January 10, 1949, Truman forwarded his budget to Congress with an NME allocation of $14.24 billion.[84]

Truman attempted to sugar-coat the military budget by claiming the figure focused on modernization and an increase in the reserves, but the JCS saw things differently. A secondary effect of the FY 50 budget battle was an increase in inter-service quarrels over money that would continue for the foreseeable future. When the budget arrived in Congress, it was subject to more scrutiny. Testifying before the House Subcommittee on Armed Forces Appropriations, Forrestal argued that the budget was one that maintained the force and was not indeed a "war budget."[85] However, Congress would enact its own changes to the president's proposed budget, with a focus on air power. With the Finletter and Hinshaw-Brewster recommendations in mind, in April 1949, changes to the budget included a reworking of allocations in order to increase the Air Force from 48 groups to 58 in the upcoming FY. With this increase it would seem that the atomic air offensive was gaining some traction on Capitol Hill. However, the increase did not substantially change the ability of the United States to sustain such an effort. Since the end of the war, Air Force advocates had requested the 70-group structure. But this request was never realized until after the start of the Korean War.

Throughout 1948, Truman lost confidence in Forrestal. Issues regarding custody of atomic weapons, inability to get consensus over service roles and missions, and poor leadership regarding the budget caused the president to question Forrestal's decision-making ability. At one point Truman quipped to an aide, "I am the Secretary of Defense. Jim calls me several times a day asking me to make decisions on matters that are completely within his competence, but he passes them on to me."[86] In January 1949, the president summoned the Defense Secretary to the White House and asked for his resignation. Forrestal was out by the end of March and replaced by a major fundraiser from Truman's reelection bid, Louis Johnson. Johnson firmly supported the president's parsimonious defense spending.

Eventually the FY 50 budget was passed with $14.69 billion allocated to defense. In the end, Congress authorized supplemental spending for the USAF, including an additional $851 million to support a 58-group air force. However, this allocation occurred on 18 October 1949, after the fall of China to Mao and his communist forces and, more importantly, the unexpected explosion of a Soviet atomic bomb in August. Other events would take place in 1950 that would reshape not only American foreign policy, but its military tradition and subsequently the defense budget.

The submitted military budget for FY 51 was not altogether different from the previous submission, although it did at least recognize the increasing relevance of the atomic air offensive. The budget for the USAF was some $400 million more than the Army's and $600 million more than the Navy's.[87]

In the end, Congress apportioned an additional $200 million for the Navy and $100 million more for the Army. However, final congressional approval of the FY 51 budget occurred on August 28, 1950, after the start of the Korean War and around the same time the new fiscally aggressive NSC-68 policy was signed by Truman. When the FY 51 budget was approved, it was largely done with the understanding that both fiscal and military policy changes were well on their way.

As Truman was exercising fiscal restraint, he was implicitly placing more of the national security requirements on atomic warfare. While defense monies declined, expenditures on atomic research rose and would eventually become a centerpiece of American defensive thought. However, while research monies increased, the Air Force, and more specifically Strategic Air Command, remained under-manned and ill-equipped to perform the mission assigned—even with supplemental allocations. Truman eventually had to come to the conclusion that the economic strength of America in peacetime could not, by itself, change the international security situation. However, this did not happen overnight and would require international events in Asia to finally persuade the president to change his mind regarding defense expenditures. The Air Force and atomic offensives would take center stage and be funded accordingly, but only after the approval of NSC-68.

2

The Atomic Energy Commission and the Fight Over Custody

As World War II progressed, it was understood that the nation's atomic energy effort, under the auspices of the Army's Manhattan Project, would fall under an organization other than the military. Wartime expediency mandated military control of atomic materials and secrets, but after the war, Congress needed to make a determination on how the nation would govern its atomic resources. In the waning months of the war, Truman relied upon the ad hoc "Interim Committee" to provide advice regarding the use and implications of atomic weapons. The term "Interim" was deliberate, as it expressed the organization's temporary nature until a more permanent structure was established. Following the Allied victory, the newly formed United Nations deliberated the merits of the Baruch Plan regarding the sharing of atomic technology, while the United States moved forward with organizing its national resources in the field. The Baruch plan was a U.S.-sponsored proposal that would place atomic technology under an international organization and hopefully control the proliferation of such weapons. In the plan the United States would slowly phase out control of its atomic stockpile and transfer it to international control only after a universal agreement was reached. However, the Soviets demanded that atomic weapons be banned before such negotiations could even take place. Unveiled in a speech at the UN on June 14, 1946, the Baruch plan evolved from an earlier paper supporting the idea of international control of atomic technology. For Brigadier General Leslie Groves, head of the Manhattan Project during the war, the Baruch Plan was a danger to national security and to the existence of America's atomic energy program. In his mind, many in the State Department were "more concerned about the momentary good will of other nations than about the welfare of the United States."[1] However, the Soviet Union refused to support the plan and, jealous of the American monopoly, blocked any counter proposals. By the end of the year the Pollyannaish idea of global control of atomic energy was dead. America was then free to pursue atomic technology, as were the Soviets.

To organize America's postwar atomic energy program, two key pieces of legislation were submitted in Congress in late 1945. In October, the May-Johnson bill was forwarded and proposed a committee of nine commissioners, five civilian and four military, to oversee and control the atomic materials and production. Critics charged that the proposed structure could end up marginalizing the civilian members despite the minority representation of the military. Many civilian scientists decried the bill, claiming it gave too much power to the military and would preclude further atomic research.[2] Conversely, Groves, as one of the more visible experts regarding atomic technology, thought the legislation minimized military influence regarding atomic matters. While Truman initially supported the bill, his support began to wane as arguments mounted over the proposed structure. However, the president was still a proponent of civilian control, arguing, "It is a mistake to believe that only the military can guard national security. The full responsibility for a balanced and forceful development of atomic energy ... should rest with the civilian group directly responsible to the President."[3]

However, the chairman of the Senate's Special Committee on Atomic Energy, Brien McMahon (D–CT), submitted an alternative to the May-Johnson bill, attempting to address the more controversial elements of the earlier bill. Under the McMahon proposal, an Atomic Energy Commission would be composed of five civilian representatives, all working on a full-time basis. While the AEC would be fully controlled by civilians, for military input the McMahon bill made provision for a Military Liaison Committee (MLC) that would advise AEC commissioners on military concerns regarding development, manufacture, use, and storage of weapons.[4] These military representatives were also charged to consult the AEC commissioners on the allocation of fissionable materials for military research and the control of information relating to the manufacture or utilization of atomic weapons.[5]

In addition to the MLC, the McMahon submission proposed the creation of a General Advisory Committee (GAC) composed of prominent scientists to also advise the commissioners. The GAC's mission was to provide information regarding scientific and technical matters relating to resources, production, and research and development of fissionable materials.[6] Initial members of the GAC included some members of the old Manhattan Project, such as Enrico Fermi, Cyril S. Smith, and Robert Oppenheimer.

Lastly the bill established the Joint Committee on Atomic Energy (JCAE) that gave Congress a direct role in the atomic decision-making process and, more importantly, a hand in confirming AEC commissioners. This organization became one of the most important assignments within Congress as it controlled funding for both the military and civilian use of

2. The Atomic Energy Commission and the Fight Over Custody

Harry Truman signing the McMahon Bill, August 1, 1946, establishing the Atomic Energy Commission. The Commission would inherit all Manhattan Project assets and resources. Behind the president, left to right: Senators Tom Connally, Eugene D. Millikin, Edwin C. Johnson, Thomas C. Hart, Brien McMahon, Warren R. Austin, and Richard B. Russell (U.S. Government photograph).

atomic energy. The JCAE was composed of representatives from both houses of Congress. Members played a significant role, as they could enact decisions regarding atomic matters separate from the executive branch.

The legislation establishing the AEC mandated that the new organization be established on January 1, 1947. Congress approved the Atomic Energy Act, and Truman signed it into law on August 1, 1946, with the AEC assuming "control over the production, ownership, and use of fissionable material to assure the common defense and security and insure the broadest possible exploitation..."[7] Concurrently, the Baruch Plan was gaining no traction in the UN, and it appeared that the United States would retain, temporarily at least, its monopoly on atomic technology.

While the AEC was officially created with the new year, candidates for the AEC were not announced until October. Moreover, selecting commissioners did not get under way until January 31, 1947. Scrutinizing commissioners for the AEC was the assignment of the JCAE, headed by Senator Bourke B. Hickenlooper (R–IA).[8] Working from a list of presidential nominees, the committee identified David E. Lilienthal as a candidate for chairman of the AEC. A lawyer by trade, and having no formal training in nuclear matters, Lilienthal was not new to the world of technology management. Having served as the chairman of the Tennessee Valley Authority (TVA), he was familiar with large technical endeavors.[9] While desiring the position as chair of the AEC, he also understood the enormity of job. He wrote in his journal, "If they ask me if I consider myself 'qualified' I am tempted to say 'Hell no ... and any man who thinks he is really qualified for such a fantastic responsibility proves by that admission that he isn't qualified.'"[10] When asked about his views regarding the role of the AEC, Lilienthal argued that its primary role was to make atomic energy a weapon of war but that he kept in mind that the technology had peaceful uses too.[11]

However, this statement addressing the peaceful purposes of the atom was indicative of Lilienthal's key underlying objective; to reduce the amount of military influence on atomic technology and especially the influence of General Groves. In his memoirs, Lilienthal made note of the "military mind" and viewed the military with great suspicion.[12] His distrust of the military was clearly illustrated, as he wrote, "It is extraordinary ... how freely the Armed Services make the most bloodthirsty statements about their preparations with no one so much as raising an eyebrow."[13] A firm believer in civilian control of the military, Lilienthal would parry any attempt by the military to gain control of atomic weapons. Regarding the "military mind" and its influence with the "dangerous atom," Lilienthal clearly saw himself as a hedge against the abuse of the new technology as he feared the use of atomic weapons would "[make] Attila the Hun seem like a Piker."[14]

With Lilienthal nominated as chair, the other candidates for AEC membership included Robert Bacher, Lewis Strauss, Sumner Pike, and William Waymack. At the core of the confirmation process was an underlying concern over the amount of military influence in atomic energy decision-making and its balance with civilian control. Furthermore, political posturing was also a part of the confirmation process, as Republicans accused Lilienthal of being part of a large communist cell at the TVA and sympathetic to Soviet causes.[15] For weeks Senator Kenneth McKellar (D–TN) delayed and attempted to derail the appointment.[16] Little could be done in the way of atomic development until the leadership of the new organization was confirmed.

In mid–February 1947, as the political theater was still unfolding, delaying the confirmation process, Undersecretary of State Dean Acheson warned newly appointed Secretary of State George Marshall that delays in the AEC confirmation process damaged our national security.[17] Marshall forwarded

2. The Atomic Energy Commission and the Fight Over Custody   41

Major General Leslie Groves, head of the Army's Manhattan Project, with his civilian nemesis, David Lilienthal, chairman of the Atomic Energy Commission. Lilienthal inherited Grove's Manhattan Project assets when the AEC was established on January 1, 1947. Each man held a low opinion of the other (U.S. Government photograph).

these concerns to the president. Finally, on Monday March 10, the JCAE confirmed all the nominations. However, the nominations were then forwarded to the Senate for final confirmation. Debate continued regarding the dubious charges made against Lilienthal, with little success in proving them. The formal confirmation vote occurred April 9, but for the first four months of the AEC's existence, efforts largely focused on the confirmation process, with little headway being made on other issues.

Once the AEC members were confirmed, they could finally get to work on the issues before them. The tug-of-war regarding custody of atomic weapons was a chief concern between the AEC and the military. Military service chiefs were in favor of retaining custody of atomic weapons.[18] Even before the AEC was established, Groves was concerned over the availability of atomic weapons and feared that civilians would preclude military access to the bombs in time of national wartime emergency. Groves remained in Washington as a member of the MLC but also commanded the Armed Forces

Special Weapons Project (AFSWP) at Sandia Base, with USAF General Lewis Brereton as chair of the MLC. The AFSWP was the military component coordinating with AEC elements in New Mexico. While Brereton at the MLC served at the strategic and policy level, Groves's AFSWP worked with AEC organizations at the operational level.

Originally built from the 2761st Engineer Battalion (Special) and then renamed the 38th Engineer Battalion (Special), the AFSWP started to develop rudimentary competence with atomic weapons during the first year of its existence.[19] Initial classroom instruction began in early 1947, with field exercises starting later that year. AFSWP's first endeavor to exercise its newly developed capability occurred in November in an exercise named Operation AJAX.[20] AJAX not only evaluated the military's ability to assemble MK IIIs competently but also simulated the task of conducting the exacting work at a forward location. Working with the 509th Bombardment Group, the AFSWP tested its ability to handle and assemble the weapons. The AJAX exercise utilized Wendover Field, Utah, as the simulated forward location. A Rear Assembly Team (RAT) at Sandia made the initial bomb assembly; then the weapon was ferried to Wendover for final preparation. At Wendover, a Forward Assembly Team (FAT) assembled an expeditionary building and completed the weapons assembly process. While the operation did not require the actual movement of fissionable materials, the exercise did simulate the requirement to fly three atomic missions. A problem with one of the bomb's alternators required a quick delivery of replacement parts from Sandia. Regardless, AJAX went relatively well and validated the RAT-FAT concept, but it did identify some glaring problems. There remained issues regarding poor communication between the forward and main assembly locations, issues with a reliable power supply at the forward location, and a lack of logistical support from the AEC.[21]

AJAX also identified a lack of quality control on the part of the AEC regarding bomb components.[22] The exercise revealed what was described as an "appalling" condition in the state of electrical components coming

Armed Forces Special Weapons logo (U.S. Government photograph).

from the AEC.²³ For years afterward, the military had to conduct inspections of weapon components to ensure that they met high military specifications, not just the AEC minimums.²⁴ That the military found components in a substandard state only led to the continued distrust between the military and the civilians.

The initial relationship between the AFSWP and the civilian AEC "Z Division" at Sandia Base, near Albuquerque, New Mexico, was an acrimonious one. Z Division was formed in 1945 and named after its first leader, Jerrold Zacharias. He and the division were given the responsibility of ordnance engineering and assembly of the first Los Alamos–based designs.²⁵ Reorganization of weapons development responsibilities and the testing required, as well as to make room at the crowded Los Alamos Scientific Lab (LASL) location, saw the movement of Z Division from the Los Alamos and Wendover Field locations to the old Oxnard Municipal Airfield, known as Sandia Base, in September 1945. The site was a convalescence center for injured airmen and a salvage center for some 2,000 surplus aircraft for the Reconstruction Finance Corporation.²⁶ After the war, the site became the repository for unused atomic weapons components and eventually the location for developing, stockpiling, and assembly of atomic weapons.²⁷ It was initially a rather unremarkable base with little infrastructure and few amenities. When Groves visited in spring 1947, he apologized to the wives for the lack of proper living quarters.²⁸

As the civilian personnel left the program with the war's end, Groves saw the need to put regular commissioned officers at Sandia to handle atomic ordnance. Groves sent Colonel Gil Dorland to assess the situation at Sandia, and upon return he reported that the current commander of Sandia was "a highly qualified technician" but that long-range planning was poor and controls lax.²⁹ By the summer of 1946, more military personnel were posted at Sandia for weapons assembly training, but many of the remaining civilian staff believed that atomic weapons assembly was still too complex for military personnel to handle.³⁰ To address this situation, Groves sought the best and brightest officers for atomic assembly duties—as he put it, "hot-shot officers ... the best the Army had [and] the greatest single collection of abilities in one small unit that ever existed in the history of the Unites States Army."³¹ Despite the assignment of high-quality officers to the program, many civilians looked upon the military personnel with antipathy. George Kistiakowsky, a key designer for explosive lenses used in the implosion device, reportedly had a poor opinion of the mental agility of military officers.³² When one of these new "hot shot" officers arrived at Sandia, he recalled seeing a memo advising the civilian scientists that "these people are going to ask all kinds of stupid questions, be patient with them."³³

Instead of having a few broadly trained technicians, Dorland broke the assembly process down into parts and had narrowly trained teams work concurrently on separate subcomponents of the bomb. Once the subcomponents were cleared and tested, then the crew would test the overall assembly.[34] Still, the number of these highly trained weapons assembly teams remained limited for the next few years. By the end of 1947, military competency regarding weapons assembly had risen appreciably, and in December, a 24-week individual weapons assembly course at Sandia was established. Once this course was completed, the service member required further follow-on team training in order to be fully qualified. A report by the Joint Strategic Survey Committee estimated that three teams would be available by June 1948 and seven by July 1949, with seven more teams by 1950.[35] By December 1948 it was reported that five teams were trained with a sixth available later in the month and a seventh team being established in January 1949. While training was taking place, a July 1948 memorandum by the Air Force Chief of Staff reported that the requirement to assemble 100 bombs per day was not feasible with the current MK III design and associated trained assembly team. Furthermore, the current estimated goal of having ten teams was insufficient for Air Force requirements.[36] However, with the introduction of the newly designed MK IV bomb in 1949, the assembly of atomic weapons was not considered to be limiting factor.[37]

On November 12, 1947, after the AJAX exercise, Brereton forwarded a proposal to the AEC stating that the military required instant access to atomic weapons "to insure interested agencies of the Armed Forces are prepared to use the available bombs, [and] it is necessary that they have actual custody of the completed weapons."[38] This request came about because of the proven military competency regarding bomb assembly and evidence that the AEC was not maintaining bomb components in a satisfactory manner. Lilienthal was less than supportive and parried the requests, arguing that any change in the current arrangement required presidential action. Despite the ongoing military training and increased quality of servicemen assigned to the AFSWP, the AEC chair was convinced that the military lacked the competency to conduct such complex actions.[39] The situation created a kind of farcical arrangement. Because the military planned to use atomic weapons in the future, it would need familiarity with the munitions. However, the AEC was not willing to let the armed forces train with the munitions, so then how could the military plan on employing them? Aside from the military competency issue, Lilienthal's concern regarding the "military mind" precluded effective preparation of a potential atomic offensive. Furthermore, Lilienthal's suspicion of the military filtered down to the AEC's organization at Sandia that supposedly coordinated with Grove's AFSWP. The mistrust and wariness between these two operational organizations reflected the larger relationship between the military and civilians regarding atomic custody.

2. The Atomic Energy Commission and the Fight Over Custody   45

This issue regarding custody was more than just a contest of egos between the military and the AEC. Up until March 1949 the only atomic weapon in the U.S. arsenal was the MK III, an implosion device of the same design as the "Fat Man" bomb dropped on Nagasaki. However, the MK III was more a science experiment than an actual weapon system. Assembly was a cumbersome affair that required skill and patience. One scientist called it "[A] Rube Goldberg affair that took an assembly team of scientific experts a week's worth of effort to assemble."[40] As an example, the lenses that focused the initiating blast on the plutonium core, resulting in fission, were hand-cast and had to be glued into place with a slow-drying adhesive.[41] The MK III required approximately 40 men working two to three days to assemble; then once completed, the bomb's active life span was little more than a week.[42] After that time, the bomb's batteries had to be replaced. Additionally, the bomb's plutonium core emitted so much radiation that it caused damage to the high explosives and detonators that initiated the implosion resulting in atomic fission.[43] Both of these replacement actions required the entire disassembly and reassembly of the bomb—again requiring two to three days. Having the skilled and qualified personnel to conduct the replacement actions as well as availability of the assembly teams was problematic. According to one Los Alamos scientist regarding the weapon's design, "We had, to put it bluntly, lousy bombs."[44]

In addition to assembling the weapon, loading it was also a cumbersome event. The MK III weighed some 10,300 pounds and could only be carried by specially configured B-29 "SILVERPLATE" bombers. Because of the weapon's size and weight, it could not be loaded like conventional munitions. The aircraft had to be towed to a 12' × 14' × 8' loading pit near the parking ramp with its bomb bay over the pit. Once the bomber was in place, the weapon was hoisted into the aircraft's specially modified bomb bay. Once loaded, the bomb required monitoring and was then fused in flight by a trained weaponeer. As a result, not having the logistical capability organic to the unit to assemble and load the weapon would cause problems for any military commander tasked with conducting a sustained atomic air offensive. Additionally, a transfer of custody from the AEC to the military might preclude quick use of the weapon if the situation required. Members of the MLC were keenly aware of those issues. In a December 16, 1947, letter from the MLC, the services argued that national security required the "instant use" of all "possible means of defense."[45] Highlighting the clumsiness of the current arrangement, the memo stated that "[to] launch an attack with atomic bombs under existing conditions, would require a complicated procedure involving the dual responsibility of the AEC and armed forces."[46] That precedent and its associated procedures had yet to be established or tested. Others in Congress were also aware of the potential dangers of the clumsy

Crew loading a MK III weapon from a bomb pit into the bomb bay of a SIL-VERPLATE B-29 bomber (U.S. Government photograph).

arrangement, as six separate bills were submitted mandating a repeal of the McMahon Act and return of the atomic program back to the military.[47]

However, Lilienthal's position was strengthened when in February 1948 the GAC assembly of scientists supported his stance by arguing that the military lacked the technical expertise to maintain the weapons and that the AEC should retain custody.[48] The AEC did not respond to the MLC's December 16 letter until four months later and then merely reiterated its previous position. At the beginning of March and after Groves retired, Major General Ken Nichols took command of the AFSWP and hoped to increase military influence regarding atomic weapons custody.

On March 5, Secretary of the Army Kenneth Royall attempted to open the dialogue between the AEC and NME by hosting a dinner party. Lilienthal was invited, as well as other top NME civilians. During the course of discussion, Lilienthal stated that improving Sandia was a priority, as it was where the military and AEC "must fit closely."[49] Royall, who had just visited Sandia, agreed with the AEC chair's assessment and stated, "I saw it was a mess ... and something had to be done ... and that we are moving that way."[50]

2. The Atomic Energy Commission and the Fight Over Custody   47

On March 13, 1948, a joint memorandum to Forrestal signed by all the service secretaries argued that "further delay in the resolution of this question of custody will be to the grave detriment of the national defense."[51] The tension between the AEC and NME was not lost on the chief executive. Days earlier, Truman had summoned Lilienthal, Royall, and Nichols to the While House, on March 11. In the meeting, the president told both Nichols and Lilienthal, "I know you two hate each other's guts ... but I expect you two to cooperate."[52] Truman went on to tell Nichols, "If I instruct Mr. Lilienthal that the primary objective of the AEC is to develop and produce atomic weapons, do you see any reason why you cannot cooperate with fully with Mr. Lilienthal?" To this Nichols replied, "There is no problem if that is the primary objective."[53] Turning to Lilienthal, Truman directed him to "get down to the business of producing atomic weapons."[54]

Illustrating the disconnected nature of atomic policy, after Nichols's meeting with Truman, the general went to the Director of the Joint Staff to discuss the possibility of scheduling AFSWP–AEC–Air Force joint exercises. Expecting cooperation and support, he was met surprisingly with a warning. The Director informed Nichols that the aims of his exercises were violating a presidential order and not to plan the use of atomic weapons.[55] Nichols asked the director if he was telling him to stop. To this the director replied "No, I am not telling you to stop, I just want you to know that you are not in accord with the present presidential policy."[56]

The issues regarding the small pool of skilled weapons assembly teams and atomic competence were highlighted during the SANDSTONE atomic test held in April and May 1948 as the Berlin Blockade crisis emerged. At the end of March, in a meeting at Forrestal's office with the service chiefs, Secretaries Royall and Symington, and retired General Dwight Eisenhower, the issue of atomic capability came to the fore. Eisenhower inquired about American atomic capability given the growing tensions around the German capital. The response to Eisenhower's question was an alarming one. Nichols answered that the United States could not prepare or assemble any bombs for delivery at the time because all the qualified personnel were at Eniwetok preparing for the SANDSTONE tests.[57] In subsequent meetings the issue was raised of returning some of the assembly personnel back to Sandia in case the atomic bomb was required during the early part of the crisis, but the idea of returning the teams was eventually nixed by the AEC.

In a May meeting of the AEC and MLC at Kirtland Air Force Base, a few miles north of the AEC's Sandia location, the stalemate continued. Regarding custody, AEC representatives, namely Norris Bradbury, continued to argue that the weapons were too sophisticated and complex for military personnel. Nichols again contended that the weapons needed to be under control of a military command at a time of war and that the services required competency regarding weapons assembly and operation.[58] Admiral William Parsons, the weaponeer for "Little Boy," sided with the military, arguing that "it was time to dispel the belief that only an Einstein could assemble or test an atomic weapon."[59] By June the AEC's General Advisory Committee concluded that the services were indeed capable of competent stewardship of the stockpile. The new chair of the MLC, Donald Carpenter, who replaced Brereton, attempted to allay the commission's fears over quality control; he promised that the armed services would allow the AEC regular access to weapons in military custody in order to inspect and service bomb components.[60]

The Kirtland gathering resulted in yet another special meeting of the MLC and AEC on June 18 in Washington. Despite Carpenter's optimism on the possibility of a compromise, Lilienthal remained obstinate and Nichols argued that "emotion rather than reason was the basis of his [Lilienthal's] position."[61] For Lilienthal, the issue was more about control over the military than it was about the mechanical aspects of atomic weapons and technical competence. While steadfast in his opposition, the AEC chair did agree to forward the issue to the president for consideration.

Days later, at a meeting between Forrestal, Lilienthal, and Carpenter, and with the Berlin Blockade crisis unfolding, the AEC chair at least admitted that his commission could not support atomic missions that were staged from overseas bases.[62] With B-29s at forward based in Europe, getting MK III bombs ready for delivery would cause significant logistical problems if that course of action was selected. Additionally, there were no special "SILVERPLATE" B-29s located in Europe even to drop the weapon on a Soviet city. Similarly, there were no facilities in Europe to support the building and loading of the weapon, although some preliminary plans were being developed by the AFSWP. Regardless, Lilienthal and other members of the AEC remained resolute in their stance on civilian control.

As a result of the custody impasse, Forrestal requested a meeting with Truman to discuss the matter directly. Forrestal's case for military custody was based upon four points: (1) that a surprise attack could expose the United States to unreasonable risk of mistake, confusion, and failure to act with necessary speed and precision… (2) that the military needed to learn in peacetime how to maintain and operate atomic weapons… (3) that giving custody to the NME will facilitate the storing of the … components in the most favorable strategic locations … and (4) that delivery of the weapons to the NME should further the research and development activities in weapons design.[63]

On a tip from presidential advisor Clark Clifford, Lilienthal learned that Truman already supported continuing AEC custody. Hoping to preclude a standoff, the AEC chairman informed Forrestal of this information.[64] Despite learning of Truman's inclination, Forrestal continued to press for

2. The Atomic Energy Commission and the Fight Over Custody 49

the meeting. In preparation for the custody discussion, Truman asked Budget Director James Webb to provide written comments on the issue. In Webb's response, he argued for AEC retention based upon a number of rationales: First, the public demanded civilian control; second, the AEC was doing an excellent job in its custodian responsibilities; third, the inter-service squabbles over roles and missions created jurisdictional issues between the Air Force and Navy; and fourth the current international situation (Berlin Crisis) might upset the delicate balance of diplomacy and send the wrong message.[65] On the third point, Webb placed his rationale firmly in the lap of Forrestal and the NME's inability to resolve issues over roles and missions—especially strategic bombing.

When the showdown began on July 21, Truman was already in a grim and solemn mood.[66] The Oval Office was packed, and almost from the beginning the session went badly for the NME. When MLC chair Carpenter read a prepared statement that was identical to a document the president had in his hands, Truman curtly responded "I can read."[67] Later the president hinted at his inclinations as he stated, "I don't think we should use this thing unless we absolutely have to. It is a terrible thing to order something like that ... that is so terribly destructive, destructive beyond anything we ever had. You have got to understand that this isn't a military weapon. It is used to wipe out women and children and unarmed people ... and not for military uses. So we have to treat this differently from rifles and cannon and ordinary things like that."[68] Ironically, this statement was contrary to what the Spaatz Board suggested in December 1945. The tone of the meeting did not get any better. Frustrated by the debate, at one point Army Secretary Royall replied, "We have been spending 89 percent of all the money for atomic energy for weapons. Now if we aren't going to use them, that doesn't make any sense."[69] His extemporaneous statement unintentionally supported the very argument Lilienthal and the AEC membership were making.

Truman's inclinations were again shown when he stated, "You have got to understand that I have got to think about the effect of such a thing on international relations. This is no time to be juggling an atom bomb around."[70] After this statement, the meeting then broke up. In Truman's mind, moving the bomb into military hands with the Berlin Crisis looming might have secondary and tertiary effects on the international diplomatic front and be interpreted as an escalation.

Two days later, at a cabinet meeting, Truman told Forrestal that the weapons were to stay in the hands of the AEC. The president did provide the armed services some hope as he mentioned that he might be willing to revisit the situation at a later date. In Truman's official response to Forrestal on August 6, he stated: "I do not feel justified in exercising my authority under the Atomic Energy Act of 1946 to order the transfer of the stockpile to the armed services. This decision is based on considerations of public policy, the necessarily close relations between custody and weapons research, the efficacy of existing methods of custody and surveillance, and the general world situation."[71] Adding insult to injury, the president did not even provide the Secretary of Defense an advance copy of his public announcement of the decision. The gulf between the AEC and the NME remained. As MLC chair Carpenter observed, "The members of the AEC thought all military officers were damn fools and the officers thought all AEC people were damn crooks."[72]

However, there was a silver lining to the president's decision for Forrestal and the military. With the weapons squarely in the hands of the civilian authorities, Carpenter suggested that the NME start drafting procedures to exercise transfer authority of the atomic munitions in case of emergency. Additionally the Berlin Blockade spurred the increased training of assembly crews, but the AEC could only provide so much training support, as they controlled most of the materials required for the course of instruction.[73] Starting in 1948, the Air Force and AFSWP conducted a number of field operations to test the transfer of materials. Operations BANJO, COWBOY, WHIPPOORWILL, and NUTMEG exercised the military's ability to support, store, move, and load the atomic bomb. The Navy also conducted an exercise named EASTWIND to test bomb assembly on aircraft carriers in anticipation of having a role to play in an atomic offensive.[74] Furthermore, the AFSWP was directed to begin training military crews to assume full custody whenever the president authorized a transfer of weapons.[75]

While individuals were trained, the equipping of various crews designated to assemble the weapons was still a problem. As trained personnel became available, assembly teams were created and designated as "Special Weapons Units" (SWU), composed of 77 specially trained individuals. There remained a shortage of supporting personnel and equipment for the individual SWUs. Three SWUs were created, one of the three put on 24-hour alert to deploy anywhere in the world. The SWUs rotated alert duty on a monthly basis, the designated crew remaining within one hour of Sandia.[76] However, equipment sets were short, and no one SWU was with its full kit. In order to create a fully manned and equipped SWU, the two other SWUs, not on duty, had to provide selected items of equipment to the alert crew.[77] In a crisis, therefore, the United States could assemble bombs at only one location.

In November, the AEC and NME came to an agreement regarding guiding principles for the transfer of atomic weapons from one agency to the other. On December 14, 1948, Operation UNLIMITED was the first test of these new procedures between the AFSWP and the AEC and validated the existing arrangement.[78] UNLIMITED started with a simulated coded message

2. The Atomic Energy Commission and the Fight Over Custody 51

from Washington and utilized dummy weapons to go through the complex transfer procedures. Despite Nichols's misgivings about the ability of the AFSWP and the AEC to coordinate the transfer, the exercise proved useful. Nichols still had concern over the transfer procedures if required in an emergency, but he admitted it was "the best arrangement that could be made under the present custody decision."[79] Changes to the 1946 Atomic Energy Act and AEC reorganization were required to refine the transfer procedures and the relationship between the military and its civilian masters. For the next year, exercises similar to UNLIMITED continued, and by May 1949, both the AFSWP and AEC were working together for better transfer and storage procedures.

Furthermore, a better-designed MK III Mod 1 and the new MK IV bombs entered the stockpile, facilitating easier assembly. In 1949 the improved coordination and better-designed weapons began to ameliorate the situation. Nichols assumed that by July the AFSWP could assemble 20 MK III and 30 MK IV weapons per day, and by December that number would increase to 30 and 50 respectively.[80] However, by September the AFSWP claimed it could assemble 63 bombs (MK III and MK IV) per day and by December, 100.[81] Additionally, training of assembly crews grew and more qualified personnel became available. In 1948 the USAF had only two assembly teams, but by the end of 1949 there were 12, with three more in training.[82] Additionally the Army remained at four with the Navy growing by one and having a total of three.[83]

By March 1950, the AEC had agreed that the NME should stockpile non-nuclear components of atomic weapons and delegated responsibilities for maintenance of these items. Additionally the AFSWP competency grew appreciably and the AEC became increasingly comfortable with the military's ability to store and assemble atomic ordnance. Once the Korean War broke out, the AEC's grip on atomic weapons began to loosen. In July 1950 the president authorized the transfer of bomb capsules, without the atomic components, to the Air Force and Navy for possible deployment overseas. Eventually, as the nuclear stockpile grew, the AEC's ability to control the larger inventory suffered. Once NSC-68, followed by NSC-162/2, became policy, military custody of the larger, more refined weapons became a requirement as delivery methods too grew in capability.

However, for the first five years of American Pax Atomica, the military had little access to the weapon it was supposed to deliver. Even analysts who were trying to develop potential damage assessments on Soviet cities if attacked with atomic weapons had little information from which to plan. The best data they could obtain came from the U.S. Strategic Bombing Survey (USSBS) review on the atomic effects on Hiroshima and Nagasaki—and that was little more than a 43-page pamphlet with pictures and maps.[84] The

AEC was so "close hold" with atomic data that it precluded effective strategic war planning. The tension between the civilian AEC and the NME was a problem. Lilienthal's distrust of Groves and the NME precluded military proficiency with atomic bomb assembly, and the AEC's jealous ownership of the munitions was problematic if the United States found itself in a position to again use them. While Truman argued that the atomic bomb was not a "military weapon," his smaller defense expenditures tacitly put national defense directly into the nuclear realm. As a result, the NME found itself not only under-funded but also unfamiliar with one of its primary weapons.

Other factors also affected American atomic capability. With the demise of the wartime Manhattan Project following the passage of the McMahon Act, the nation's ability to manufacture atomic weaponry languished in the immediate postwar era. While the AEC succeeded the Manhattan Project, the new civilian organization had its work cut out regarding atomic production, organization, and facilities. Wartime expediency and motivation were no longer driving factors in the atomic community. Directed to reduce the size of the Manhattan Project, Groves quipped that he needed to "get rid of five million dollars' worth of facilities each week."[85] Deteriorating facilities, declining resources, and, more importantly, the loss of prominent physicists and scientists crippled postwar atomic production and research. As a result, the very structure of the American atomic effort during this period suffered. According to Edward Teller, chief proponent and designer of the hydrogen bomb, "In the period between 1945 and 1949 we didn't get anywhere in our atomic production program in any direction. We didn't expand our production of Uranium very much. We didn't really get going on any reactor program."[86] While Teller omits some of the efforts made to get atomic production revitalized, his point regarding the actual manufacture of required materials was accurate.

Prior to their confirmation in April, in January 1947 AEC nominees visited Los Alamos and thought they would see a stockpile of atomic weapons ready for delivery. However, the reality was something very different. Instead of seeing dozens of neatly stored bombs ready for use, Lilienthal recalled, "we [the AEC nominees] had just discovered ... this [atomic] defense did not exist. We did not have a stockpile."[87] Years later Lilienthal quipped, "It was assumed we had a stockpile. We not only didn't have pile, we didn't have a stock."[88] Another AEC candidate saw that "we had a lot of nuclear capsules—nuclear cores—I guarantee you. But we didn't have weapons, we had lots of pieces."[89] The best the United States could do in June 1946 was stockpile parts and components that could be pieced together to make a total of nine bombs.[90] That same year Truman opined that the U.S. arsenal was about a "half-dozen ... but that was enough to win a war."[91]

However, during this time, no formal procedures were in place to report

2. The Atomic Energy Commission and the Fight Over Custody 53

the inventory to the president. At a White House meeting with Truman on April 2, 1947, Lilienthal and members of the AEC briefed the president on the status of the existing atomic stockpile. The formal report to the president emphasized the "serious weakness in the [atomic] situation from the standpoint of national defense and security; 1. The present supply of atomic bombs is very small. The actual number for which all necessary parts are available is ____."[92] (The official document left the actual number blank, as Lilienthal orally briefed the quantity.) Starting with the figure of nine bombs, then subtracting the two CROSSROAD explosions of July 1946 at the Bikini Atoll, the available figure briefed to Truman would likely be reduced to seven. The chairman went on to inform the president that none of the bombs was assembled and that no military training for the handling of the bombs was completed. Upon learning that America had no atomic weapons at the ready, Lilienthal reported that the president looked grey.[93] In fact it was the first time Truman was officially apprised of the nation's atomic stockpile since the war. As the United States became more dependent on atomic weapons for its national defense and was beginning to draw the line regarding containment and its supporting policies, the country was only producing components for one MK III atomic bomb every two months.[94] Furthermore, national leadership was blissfully unaware of the feeble nature of the atomic capability. One of the first war plans in the postwar era was named BROILER and published in November 1947. Members of the Joint Strategic Planning Group (JSPG) that put the plan together did not even know how many weapons were available to support the plan or what the American atomic bomb production capacity was. They merely assumed that the nation had enough on hand to complete the plan.[95]

JCS report 1745/1, dated February 25, 1947, articulated the concern over the paucity of atomic bomb production and the small stockpile. The report argued that the developing war plans "emphasize the importance that atomic weapons will play" and went on to express the concern that the "present methods of producing fissionable material for atomic bombs preclude the possibility of increasing the production rate after an emergency arises."[96] The report further states, "It appears that the atomic bomb and future military requirements of fissionable material cannot be met for a number of years."[97] The report continued that the number of bombs on hand was inadequate, that the current supply of fissionable materials would fall short of the military requirement, and that current capacities should be maximized or expanded to serve the military defense and security interests of the United States.[98]

The bulk of the American atomic production capacity during the time was in three locations. Built during the war years, these locations required upgrade and refurbishment after the war. The biggest facility, located at Oak Ridge, Tennessee, housed the Y-12 electronic isotope separation plant and the huge K-25 gaseous diffusion plant. The Y-12 and K-25 plants at Oak Ridge were the key facilities that produced the uranium for the "Little Boy" weapon dropped on Hiroshima. The cutting-edge intellectual work on atomic technology and design was done at the laboratories at Los Alamos, New Mexico. The third major location was the Hanford Engineering Works (HEW) at Richland, Washington. This site produced plutonium in three of its resident reactors. This plutonium was used in the "Fat Man" implosion device used on Nagasaki. These reactors became even more important after the war, as plutonium-based weapons served as the basis for U.S. atomic defense. Wartime expediency and military necessity mandated the isolated location of these disparate centers. Now with the war over, what was to be done with these locations and their respective products? What was the strategic direction of the atomic production capability?

In order to keep the facilities functional, Groves ordered small, short-term research projects and assistance to the Navy's 1946 CROSSROADS atomic tests.[99] However, with wartime immediacy absent, the atomic production and design efforts languished. At the lab in Los Alamos, the poor living conditions and, more importantly, a lack of strategic direction caused many scientists to return to civilian academia. Not only was Los Alamos lacking focus and purpose following the war, but the physical state of the world's foremost atomic laboratory was sorely lacking. In 1947, personnel at the lab were still living in ramshackle "temporary" wartime buildings that had spartan amenities. Many buildings were just Quonset huts in need of basic maintenance.[100] Buildings and cars were mud-caked as paved roads and sidewalks were rare, private telephones did not exist, the local school consisted of a single wooden building, and church services were held at the post theater.[101] The remoteness of the lab added to the gloom, as a single dirt road leading to the lab cut through the small Indian town of Espanola.[102]

Not only had the physical state of the Los Alamos post deteriorated, but the intellectual and managerial talent dwindled as people began to depart at the end of the war. During the war, the cutting-edge nature of the Manhattan Project and the challenges of the task at hand made Los Alamos an attractive posting for both aspiring and established scientists. Peace was enough of an incentive for many "long hairs" (a tongue-in-cheek term used by military personnel to describe the civilian scientists) to return to civilized academia. Even the wartime director, J. Robert Oppenheimer, left the program to return to California Institute of Technology and eventually became director for the Institute of Advanced Study at Princeton.

Along with the departure of much of the intellectual brain trust, the remaining staff at Los Alamos did not inherit a coherent or complete process for the development of atomic weapons. The atomic weapons created during the war were largely experimental affairs hand-made by the exceptional

2. The Atomic Energy Commission and the Fight Over Custody   55

intellectual talent assembled in the remote location. The empirical "trial and error" nature of the Manhattan effort left few formal or uniform procedures that could be used to develop or help establish mass production of atomic weapons.[103] Furthermore, no large-scale production facilities existed to produce bombs en masse in the years following the war. After the CROSSROADS tests, even more of the civilian technicians who assembled the "Able" and "Baker" bombs also left the program, leaving very little corporate knowledge behind. For about a six- to eight-month period following the Bikini test, one officer said grimly about the U.S. assembly capability, "We were plain bluffing. We couldn't have put the bomb together and used it."[104] The civilian head of Sandia, Dale Corson, echoed this sentiment. "If the personnel situation continues to deteriorate ... there will not only be no personnel trained in bomb assembly and testing, but there will be no one capable of teaching the art to new personnel."[105] While Z Division would survive, it was not until 1947 that a standardized method of weapons assembly was developed, and it was two more years before assembly-specific buildings were in place for the operation.[106]

After the war, Norris Bradbury succeeded Oppenheimer as the director of the Los Alamos laboratory and sensed the uneasiness and the flagging morale among the staff. Bradbury tried to create a better working environment and brought in bands, entertainment, and even professional wrestlers, but these efforts could only go so far.[107] Those who remained attempted to record and document all they had learned during the Manhattan Project and also provided assistance to the Navy's CROSSROADS tests. According to one Manhattan scientist, "wartime development yielded nothing more than a laboratory version of everything: weapons, test units, field kits, drawing manuals. Any operation [in the assembly of the bomb] was very strongly dependent on technical knowledge of individuals; there was no time to write down more than the absolute minimum."[108]

The lack of formalized procedures and manuals created a crisis in late 1946 as plutonium supplies became scarce. Given a lack of plutonium for MK IIIs, Groves thought he might need to rely on the less efficient "Little Boy" design of uranium weapons if the need arose.[109] However, those who remained at Los Alamos had no exact record of the design for "Little Boy," as it was such an experimental design.[110] In order to solve this problem, some of the original machinists were located to find out a particular component's specification. In one instance, the machinist confessed that he had no drawing for the specific part they were asking about. He admitted that he determined the size of the part by winding it around a Coke bottle![111] Furthermore, remaining Los Alamos technicians were also the inheritors of various parts and subassemblies built either for the bomb or its test designs. But no one knew which parts were used in which designs.[112]

CROSSROADS tests provided no real progress regarding scientific development of atomic weapons and were largely military experiments used to measure blast effects and other data.

The main purpose of this series of explosions included obtaining information regarding ship design, observing atomic blast effect on tactical formations, and determining safe anchoring distances in port, damage to aircraft, and consequences upon living beings.[113] With the fading idea of international control, use of atomic defense became more and more accepted, and the idea that there was no defense against an atomic attack became largely recognized.[114] The results of the CROSSROADS test were summed up in the Compton Report and published in June 1947. The report reinforced the idea that no defense against the bomb was possible and that "the loss of atomic dominance might be fatal to our national life and can be retained only by unflagging effort to hold that leadership in science and engineering which made the atomic bomb possible."[115] The report went on to state that "so long as the world lacks such acceptable guarantees of permanent peace, the manufacture and stockpiling of atomic weapons and fissionable materials [must] be continued ... in quantities ... [that will] overwhelm swiftly any potential enemy."[116]

Up until the SANDSTONE tests of April/May1948, the United States did not conduct any atomic explosions involving research or refinement of bomb design. From the period 1946 until late 1948, atomic weapons production was largely focused on the cumbersome MK III plutonium weapons that were very difficult to produce, assemble, and maintain.[117] During the postwar period, the American atomic effort was in a state of limbo, awaiting direction and guidance.[118] Outside establishing the AEC and supporting the failed Baruch Plan on international control of atomic technology, Truman provided little guidance regarding the atomic program.[119]

In the summer of 1947 after the establishment of the AEC, the pace at Los Alamos picked up as the staff found a sense of purpose. Personnel were busy trying to standardize procedures, improve the quality of existing MK III weapons, and develop new designs.[120] In the attempt to document the efforts of Manhattan and capture the development of the original designs, the remaining staff at Los Alamos framed a number of questions that were key elements in developing large-scale production processes. "X Division" addressed questions regarding lens design that helped focus the initial imploding blast on the atomic components to cause critical mass.[121] In "M Division," scientists worked on specifications standardizing the atomic cores of the weapon and developing manuals for AFSWP and AEC Sandia assembly teams. They were also busy developing the MK IV weapon, which included a new core design.[122] Scientists at Los Alamos understood that the "Little Boy" and "Fat Man" designs were inefficient devices in the use of scarce

2. The Atomic Energy Commission and the Fight Over Custody 57

fissionable materials and were looking for better yields from the precious materials they had.[123] "CMR Division" focused on requests for chemical support and the supply of uranium and plutonium to meet the demand for fissionable materials. Lastly, "Z Division" continued developing production/assembly capacities and establishing methods of maintaining weapons.[124]

While Los Alamos eventually found purpose and direction, all the designs and experiments in the AEC were dependent upon an ample supply of fissionable materials. One of the key materials after the war was plutonium, which was produced only by the HEW reactors in Washington. While plutonium served as the core of the implosion design, HEW also produced the polonium-beryllium centers that served as neutron initiator for the "Fat Man" implosion. However, on 18 June 1947, the general manager for the MLC, Carroll Wilson, reported that the existing reactors at Hanford were starting to show their age. Since polonium had a short half-life of some 138 days, a continuous supply of neutron initiators was required if the small stockpile of atomic weapons parts were used. If the HEW reactors failed, the stored plutonium cores would be worthless as weapons, because without the viable neutron initiators, the fissionable reaction would fail to start. As a result, the reactors would eventually need to be replaced to maintain the supply of initiators and also supply Los Alamos with materials to experiment with. Due to the cutting-edge technology of atomic science, no one was sure when the reactors would fail, but it was clear that replacement or refurbishment was now a requirement.

The scarcity of fissionable supplies was a consideration as early as the 1946 CROSSROADS tests. While a third explosion was scheduled for CROSSROADS, Groves and others advised Truman to cancel the test, code named "Charlie," scheduled for March 1947. The cancellation was based upon the concern that using plutonium for actual explosions expended the precious material that could be used for research and design of better bombs. Since CROSSROADS was a military test, not a scientific one, using part of the small supply might frustrate future development of better weapons.[125]

HEW's "B reactor" was the only location where weapons-grade plutonium was made. "B" reactor held 64,000 rods of Uranium-238 (U-238) fuel elements inserted into a core of graphite and bombarded with neutrons for weeks at time. After this period, the U-238 fuel elements changed composition and yielded a small amount of Plutonium-239 (P-239).[126] However, having gone "active" two years earlier, by 1946 the graphite core of the reactor was beginning to warp and bend the fuel tubes that held the uranium. Corrosion of the fuel tubes was also occurring and threatened to leak cooling water into the core of the reactor.[127] To protect it from further damage, in March 1946, "B" reactor was shut down, coinciding with a reduced demand on the remaining two reactors, "D" and "F." Production capacity on these

Front face of the B reactor at Hanford Engineer Works, Richland, Washington (U.S. Department of Energy photograph).

two reactors was reduced to approximately 20 percent per unit in order to reduce wear on the structures and prolong their useful life.[128] Despite worries over reactor condition, the required supply of the short-lived Polonium initiators demanded continued reactor operation. As a result of the shutdown and reduced demands on the HEW reactors, the only production facility for plutonium during the immediate postwar era was now operating at around 40 percent of its original capacity.

Conversely, the Oak Ridge gaseous diffusion plants were functioning well beyond expectation, but the unexpected quantities of uranium produced did not necessarily add to the nuclear weapons stockpile. The gun-type "Little Boy" device, based entirely on Uranium 235 (U-235), was not stockpiled subsequent to the war. The gun-type design used three times the amount of fissionable material used by the more efficient plutonium-based implosion design.[129] The supply of U-235 during the war was very scarce. When the Interim Committee suggest that the United States might want to demonstrate the atomic bomb to the Japanese in an effort to seek surrender, Groves

2. The Atomic Energy Commission and the Fight Over Custody   59

answered that it would take another six months to produce enough fissionable material to make another weapon. While the United States did again have components for the gun-type assemblies starting in 1948, no nuclear components were on hand for the design.[130] However, the U-235 produced by Oak Ridge was very useful outside the gun-type assembly design and adapted for use in future iterations of the implosion device. In 1947 the United States produced eight times as much U-235 as P-239. Making use of this material, physicists added U-235 to the implosion core design, thereby reducing the amount of plutonium required. Furthermore, this blending of materials for the implosion design improved the yield-to-weight ratio of the core itself.[131] As a result, the small, precious stockpile of plutonium could be stretched further with the incorporation of U-235, a process that had the added benefit of making more efficient use of the neutrons inherent in the materials.

With the failing state of the HEW reactors, the AEC was faced with the dilemma of building new facilities or focusing upon a new method of plutonium production called "reduction-oxidation" or "redox." The more efficient redox process promised to produce much less waste with irradiated fuel rods and would eventually consolidate the plutonium processes.[132] While Groves advocated the development of "redox," in October 1947 the AEC decided to build two new reactors at Hanford and tacitly lowered the priority of redox. Construction of new reactors "DR" and "H" began in the fall of 1947 and was in full swing by spring 1948. The "DR" reactor went active by October 1950 and "H" became operational a year earlier. However, while the construction of the new reactors was under way, the supply of plutonium remained a constant worry.

Following the slowdown and shutdown of the existing HEW reactors, in 1947 General Electric engineers began renovating the failing structures. Crews replaced various components of the reactors and made improvements to the original structure. Fuel tubes for irradiation were replaced and new fuel slugs were designed to handle higher radiation levels.[133] In the interim, P-239 production remained, at best, meager. It was not until March 1948 that sufficient renovation work on the existing reactors was completed and the reactor restarted. After the upgrade of the older reactors and with the ever-present demand for uranium still valid, MLC manager Wilson reported that neither "B" nor "D" reactors would fail suddenly and could still operate for a few more years.[134] As a result, until summer 1948 when AEC had three full-time reactors operating with two more under construction, American production of P-239, a key component of its atomic weapon arsenal, remained basically at a standstill.

During the postwar years, the use of the composite core, which consisted of both U-235 and P-239, was incorporated with a new "levitated core" design. This levitated design had the fissionable pit suspended within the

The building in the right center, between the water towers, is the B reactor at Hanford Engineering Works that made plutonium. It began to show wear from use after the war and had to be shut down in March 1946. Reactors D and F were reduced in capacity (U.S. Department of Energy photograph).

tamper high-explosive assembly.[135] The space between the core and the tamper created better compression of the core. However, this development and design work occurred over a three-year period and was not tested until the SANDSTONE tests in April–May 1948. SANDSTONE validated what became the MK IV design and represented the only major advancement in atomic weapons prior to the Korean War. Formal work on the MK IV started in October 1945, although ideas regarding the more efficient use of fissionable materials started earlier that year. Z Division of Los Alamos Labs during this time was looking at improving the MK III design and in 1946 incorporated a 60-point high-explosive implosion system that would replace the older 32-point arrangement. Simultaneity of the blast was a key component for a uniform compression of the fissionable core. By increasing the amount of initiating explosions and creating a more spherical blast, compression of the fissionable materials produced a higher-yield blast.[136]

The idea of using the 1946 CROSSROADS test as a platform for testing

2. The Atomic Energy Commission and the Fight Over Custody 61

the MK IV design was considered. However, Los Alamos declined the opportunity to test the new bomb and recommended using the MK III design for a number of reasons. Since CROSSROADS was a military test designed to evaluate and determine blast effects, scientists thought for comparison purposes that the same bomb ought to be used that had been used previously (in this case "Fat Man" at Nagasaki). Furthermore, using an unproven design was a liability. If the CROSSROADS test of a MK IV failed, the military would be faulted for not using a "proven" design for the "effects-centric" experiment. Lastly, since this was an experiment to evaluate effects and not the weapon itself, Los Alamos was unwilling to use the MK IV design, as the weapons performance might be hard to determine given the focus of the test.[137]

In January 1948, before the SANDSTONE test had even begun, the joint chiefs were already requesting bombs with better explosive yields given the amount of fissionable material available. Information from the MLC suggested that with the fissionable material on hand, it might be more efficient to build bombs with 100 kilotons (KT) yields rather than just 20KT.[138] The report was very calculating in that it surmised that if the material was used to create ten 20KT weapons, the explosions in total would create 3.4 square miles of destruction per bomb, hence a total of 34 square miles. However, if the AEC built seven 100KT bombs with the same amount of fissionable material used to build the ten 20KT, the larger-yield bomb would destroy 10 square miles per bomb for a net total of 70 square miles destroyed.[139] In essence, the AEC might be able to build more efficient bombs based upon the precious stockpile. This of course assumed that there were targets worthy of such attack and that a yield of that size was warranted.

The newer design innovations were successfully tested via the X-Ray, Yoke, and Zebra shots during SANDSTONE at Eniwetok. Once these tests were completed, the AEC was in a position to start mass-producing and stockpiling atomic weapons. After the SANDSTONE tests, MLC chair Nichols believed that "we should be thinking in terms of thousands of weapons rather than hundreds."[140] The new MK IV weapon had many improvements other than efficiency in design. The first test of the MK IV yielded a blast of 37 kilotons (KT), almost twice as much as the "Fat Man" and "Little Boy" explosions of ~20KT. The second explosion produced a burst of 49KT. In addition, the MK IV was easier to assemble, using less manpower, it was safer to load and carry, and was more robust in the surrounding climate.[141] More importantly, the MK IV with the composite cores promised a 63 percent increase in the number of available bombs and a 75 percent increase in bomb yield.[142] However, production of this new weapon did not begin until March 1949, almost four years after the original MK III design was used over Nagasaki. In May 1948, Los Alamos began designing the MK V lightweight version of the bomb that weighed only 3,000 pounds, whereas the MK III and IV weighed some 10,000 pounds each.

Part of the Atomic Energy Act included provisions for determining annual production of fissionable material. The act placed this authority under the purview of the president. In this regard, the president determined the number of atomic weapons and associated components that were to be built each year. One of the first actions of the newly formed AEC was to recommend to the president the production requirements for 1947. While the AEC was working on the new design and refurbishing and building reactors, the military was still looking forward to having these weapons as tools of national military might. However, if the AEC was responsible for the manufacture and storage of atomic weapons, how many bombs were required by the NME? What amount of fissionable material needed to be produced by the facilities Oak Ridge and HEW to support national security objectives? Throughout this period the answers to these questions were few and far between. Up until 1947 very few military officers at the national level had any idea about the characteristics or potential of atomic weapons. During the war, Groves kept such information very close, on a "need-to-know basis." Joint staff planners and the Joint Strategic Survey Committee were not authorized access to atomic weapons capabilities until late 1947.[143] How could the JCS and associated planners reasonably design a bombing campaign if the relevant personnel were unfamiliar with the capabilities and limitations of the ordnance used?

In October 1947, the JCS submitted to the AEC its schedule of production goals through 1953. The Joint Strategic Survey Committee developed a requirement for "400 atomic bombs of destructive power equivalent to the Nagasaki type bomb [~20 KT]."[144] Furthermore, the document specified interim production requirements but stated that the weapons were to be ready by 1 January 1953.[145] However, in light of the SANDSTONE tests and the increased capabilities of the MK IV design, the MLC suggested that the JCS review weapons requirements. Taking the MLC's advice, the JCS forwarded a request to Forrestal in December 1948 and subsequently passed it to new MLC chairman William Webster. In Webster's request to the AEC in January 1949, he wrote, "The current established military requirement for scheduled bomb production should be substantially increased and extended.... You will be advised at a later date of the number of bombs ... required by the NME."[146] This submission also coincided with a request to increase the budget of the AEC from $632 million to $725 million. When the request for an acceleration of the atomic energy program made its way to the AEC, Lilienthal was not receptive to the request. In his suspicious mind, the chairman saw the request merely as a way for the military to try to reassert its influence in the atomic arena by making arbitrary demands.[147] Lilienthal suspected that production

2. The Atomic Energy Commission and the Fight Over Custody 63

requirements from the military were based largely upon what the military envisioned the AEC could produce, rather than thoughtful, critical analysis of what we required to defeat the Soviet Union.[148]

To reconcile the differing views, on July 26, 1949, Truman appointed a special committee to review the request and validate requirements. In his guidance to the committee, Truman charged them to review the request based upon four considerations—adequacy of the current stockpile for national defense in light of current production, relative gain in national security, effect the increase might have on the budget, and potential of offsetting costs in other elements of national defense.[149] However on 1 September, an American WB-29 reconnaissance plane flying a routine surveillance mission from Misawa Air Base, Japan, to Eielson Air Base, Alaska, took air samples over the Kamchatka Peninsula. In the plane's specially designed filters, it captured radioactive particles that provided evidence of a nuclear detonation. Further analysis confirmed that the particles were residue from an atomic event. This discovery had significant repercussion on not only American military posture, but also foreign policy.

Taking the international situation into consideration, the special committee submitted its formal report in October 10, 1949. The report overwhelmingly supported an acceleration in atomic production, arguing that the "intrinsic scarcity [of atomic weapons] must be eliminated as the predominant consideration of atomic weapons use in war…[and] allow the JCS greater flexibility to plan as desirable the employment of atomic bombs for operations where they could be employed more economically than other military measures."[150] In its concluding analysis, the committee stated that "the proposed expansion is not untimely from the viewpoint of possible international repercussions, particularly in view of the recent atomic explosion in the USSR."[151] The report further specified that the program was "in consonant with paragraph 21-a of NSC 20/4 … [and would serve] as a source of encouragement to nations resisting Soviet political aggression and as a basis for immediate military commitments for rapid mobilization."[152] The committee also found that the acceleration was feasible, given the AEC's growing production capabilities. As a result, the decision was more a fait accompli, given the Soviet explosion, with Truman authorizing the acceleration on 19 October.

Once he had approved the acceleration, Truman asked Secretary Johnson to outline the goals of the effort and how it would affect existing strategies. When the JCS reported back to the president on January 10, 1950, they lauded the increase but still had not developed plans that fully leveraged the acceleration. In this response the JCS reported that the military use of atomic weapons was still "in its infancy."[153] This was an ironic answer given the fact that almost every existing war plan up to that point was founded directly upon atomic weapons. The JCS surmised that until they had a better idea of what the higher production levels were, they were not able to change or alter established plans. However, they did believe that more weapons increased flexibility and created a more effective deterrent.[154]

This increase in the atomic arsenal also coincided with the arguments over the development of what was referred to as the "super bomb." The Soviet atomic weapon caused reconsideration of weapons technology that utilized hydrogen as the primary source of explosive force. A few days before the Special Committee submitted its report to the president, Truman was initially briefed on the concept of a hydrogen bomb (H-bomb), which promised an explosive yield in megatons (MT) rather than KT. This exponential increase in destructive power was accomplished by use of fusion, instead of fission, but was still just a theoretical concept in 1950. However, if a technological design could leverage a fusion reaction, a weapon could now possibly destroy hundreds of square miles of a city as opposed to the paltry four square miles seen at Hiroshima.

Senator Brien McMahon of the JCAE argued in favor of the new weapons, writing to the president, "There is no moral dividing line that I can see between a big explosion ... and many smaller explosions causing equal or still greater damage."[155] Debate ensued for months between the AEC commissioners, the JCS, the GAC, and the JCAE. On January 31, 1950, Truman finally directed the AEC to investigate the technological feasibility of the H-bomb and supposedly barked, "What the hell are we waiting for? Get on with it."[156]

By 1950, the stockpile had grown to 298 atomic bombs, and by 1953 the number increased more than threefold, to 1,161.[157] However, having an "adequate" supply became problematic. What constituted adequate? Truman speculated that the JCS would probably request a number that would ensure more than enough were available for a given war plan. Demand from the military would come, not from careful analysis, but merely based upon what the AEC's resources could produce.[158] With the stockpile finally growing and teams available to assemble the weapons, there came more questions. Toward what end should the weapons be used? What should be targeted and where was it? How would an atomic air offensive serve national goals and objectives?

3

Inter-Service Squabbles

The National Security Act of 1947 significantly changed the landscape of America's military establishment. The legislation created the NME and united the Department of the Navy and the War Department under a Secretary of Defense, while also realizing air power advocates' desire for an independent Air Force. While it was thought that the new structure would streamline functions and enhance planning, the act fell short of expectations. Differing slightly from the legislation, Truman's Executive Order 9877 directed:

> The United States Army ... is organized, trained and equipped for prompt and sustained combat incident to operations on land.... The United States Navy [to include naval aviation] is organized, trained and equipped primarily for prompt and sustained sea combat.... The United States Air Force ... is organized, trained and equipped for prompt and sustained air offensive and defensive operations.[1]

Under the Secretary of Defense were secretaries of the Navy, Army, and Air Force, with each military service chief subordinate to his respective civilian superior. While the language of the order appeared simple enough, bitter arguments ensued between the services over roles, missions, and, as a result, budget allocations. Even at the end of the war, Eisenhower recognized the changing nature of warfare and the requirement for interoperability, arguing that science and technology had "scrambled" the traditional service domains and that the era of separate warfighting functions was "gone forever."[2] Nevertheless, inter-service rivalry regarding air power was a key point of discussion in the postwar era. This discussion was a continuation of a doctrinal argument that existed during the interwar years, as the Navy jealously guarded its mission to defend the nation from seaborne attack, while the Army Air Force argued it could interdict enemy ships before they appeared off the American coastline. With William "Billy" Mitchell's 1921 sinking of the *Ostfriesland* and his call for an independent air service, lines were beginning to appear between naval aviation and its land-based counterpart even before the war began.

The war saw the rise of the aircraft carrier as a decisive component in warfare, especially in the Pacific, as the carrier began to replace the battleship as the primary "ship of the line." For strategic bombing advocates, the combined bomber offensive and the advent of atomic weaponry changed the nature of war and how future wars would be fought. With the end of the war and the advances made in aviation technology, the peacetime rivalry between the services began anew—this time between the new independent Air Force and its old rival, the Navy. In the Air Force's opinion, the inherent offensive capability of the airplane and its ability to deliver nuclear weapons at the heart of an enemy's war-making capability made other forms of warfare obsolete. For the Air Force, aviation combined with atomic weaponry gave America a "Sunday punch" capability to knock out a potential adversary with strategic nuclear attacks. In this effort, the Air Force believed that it single-handedly could end any war in a matter of a few days, if not hours.

As early as 1945, Spaatz, who soon became the first Air Force Chief of Staff, argued that the nature of war had changed and wrote, "It must be total in every way, designed to destroy an enemy's home base and spare him nothing."[3] Toward this end, strategic bombing was the primary means of attaining national military objectives by destroying enemy infrastructure, production capacities, and military forces. In light of this vision, the Air Force viewed the other military services as appendages, relegating them to secondary and supporting roles. In a 1947 speech, General LeMay argued, "US defense requirements in light of the modern situation [were]:

    A. Overall air supremacy in being.
    B. Regular land, sea and tactical air forces strong enough to contain any possible enemy.
    C. Strategic air power in being strong enough to accomplish the strategic air mission.
    D. Facilities for producing the necessary main reserve land, sea and tactical air forces in time for the final blow.[4]

Despite shortcomings in the initial design of the newly fielded B-36 Peacemaker bomber, the Air Force asserted that the aircraft provided a unique capability to deliver bombs throughout the globe. To the air-minded, the only need for an Army was to hold and guard air bases for the Air Force to wield its "big stick." As for the Navy, it protected the U.S. shoreline from invasion. In the new air age, only air power could deter an attacking enemy force.[5]

The other services, chiefly the Navy, took a dim view of this Air Force vision. While initially afraid of losing their sea-borne air armadas to the Air Force, naval aviators believed that aircraft carriers with their accompanying air wings provided a unique capability that could not be matched by land-based aircraft. This idea applied to the new atomic realm, as the Assistant

Chief of Naval Operations, Rear Admiral Daniel Galley, argued that "the Navy can become the principal offensive branch of the national defense system, one that will actually deliver the knock-out blows."[6] The Navy thought that large land-based bombers were vulnerable to enemy air defenses and in addition argued that wholesale nuclear attack had severe moral implications contrary to American ideals. As the Air Force pushed for more bombers, the Navy envisioned a new, larger aircraft carrier fleet with its accompanying air wings to meet America's future defensive needs. To meet this need, the Navy argued for an aircraft carrier design that had a flush deck, an array of fighters, and attack aircraft capable of delivering atomic ordnance.[7] To the Air Force, this naval platform offered an inferior and less effective means of striking the enemy and posed a threat to the building of an Air Force strategic bombing fleet. More importantly, in light of Truman's fiscal frugality, a new carrier was a challenge to fit into the overall defense budget.

Within six months of Truman's executive order, in December 1947 outgoing Chief of Naval Operations (CNO) Admiral Chester Nimitz argued, in what became known as his "valedictory," that carrier aviation had a unique capability, one that was especially relevant given the new security environment. Because it was assumed that the United States would own the sea lanes, American carriers could stay at sea for months and launch sustained air attacks, atomic and conventional, against vital elements of enemy infrastructure. Nimitz also argued that "if we are to project our power against vital areas of an enemy across the ocean before beachheads on enemy territory can be captured, it must be by air-sea power."[8] To the Navy mind, the Air Force's strategic bomber fleet was too dependent upon overseas bases controlled by foreign nations, and heavily laden land-based bombers were too vulnerable to enemy defenses. To the Navy, the development of the huge B-36 bomber was a mistake. The large six-engine bomber was essentially a "white elephant" that would easily be shot down by defending Soviet interceptors. In Nimitz's opinion, the inherent flexibility of carrier aviation to strike from the sea against inland targets was a better choice than the Air Force option. Conversely, the Air Force argued that carriers were too vulnerable to enemy attack, were unable to operate close enough to an enemy to be effective, and lacked the striking power and range of a land-based air force.[9]

While the National Security Act and Truman's Executive Order 9877 seemingly laid out the responsibilities of the services, the two documents contained differences that required further reconciliation/refinement. In February 1948, Forrestal ordered a complete review of the services' respective roles and appointed a joint committee to draft a revision. Once it was completed, Forrestal planned to publish the revision as a directive from the secretary and have the president rescind the earlier executive order.[10] In support of this effort, on February 11 an ad hoc committee began outlining the services' various roles and mission. From the beginning, debate ensued between the Navy and Air Force regarding strategic bombardment and the air campaign. Recognizing that carrier aviation could play a role in strategic air operations, the Air Force (supported by the Army) offered that Navy strategic missions were permissible but needed to fall under the purview of the Air Force for coordination and targeting purposes. As Air Force officers saw it, since their service was tasked with "primary responsibility for strategic air," Navy operations in support of an air campaign needed to fall under the Air Force to avoid unnecessary waste and confusion.[11] The Navy took umbrage with granting the Air Force what appeared to be "veto power" regarding air naval operations and rejected any Air Force oversight of carrier operations.[12] Much as in the interwar years, the two services were again at a doctrinal impasse.

Hoping to end the standoff, Forestall called a meeting of the services at the Key West Naval Base in Florida from March 11 to 14, 1948. During the conference, it was agreed that naval aviation would retain its autonomy. However, as a limiting factor, the Navy was not to use this authority to create an independent strategic bombing fleet.[13] While recognizing the capabilities of naval aviation, Forrestal did not intend to give the Navy carte blanche authority to develop a wholly new aviation component that duplicated a strategic bombing capability. Both the Chief of Staff of the Air Force, General Carl Spaatz, and the new CNO, Admiral Louis Denfeld, agreed to Forrestal's restriction. While the conference drew some limitations for the Navy in strategic bombing, these discussions also helped expand the role of naval aviation in terms of atomic weapons. Forrestal came away hopeful that the two services had reached agreement over their respective roles and also with an understanding that both services would have access to the atomic inventory. When briefing Truman on the results of the conference, Forrestal reported that the Navy was "not to be denied use of the A-bomb."[14]

Subsequently, the service chiefs drafted what became known as the "Functions Paper" and forwarded the document to Forrestal for approval. The Secretary approved the submission, sent it the president, and asked him to revoke his earlier Executive Order 9877. On April 21, Truman agreed, and the document was forwarded to the service secretaries. In addition to the primary functions of the services, the Key West agreement made provision for "collateral duties" that allowed one service to support another in carrying out primary functions. This was supposed to facilitate a "one-team-one-fight" joint camaraderie of U.S. military forces. Toward this end, the Navy claimed its collateral functions included "carrier based strategic air operations, close air support, and aerial photography."[15] With this in mind, the Navy saw its air wings participating in the strategic air campaign regardless of the Air

Force's primary mission. Hence the lines regarding these issues remained blurred, and wariness still existed between the two services.

The suspicion between the two services also expanded to disagreement over the authority of the AFSWP. On March 23, Spaatz forwarded a recommendation to the Joint Chiefs that the Air Force serve as the executive agent for the AFSWP. This argument arose as the atomic arsenal remained relatively small, around 50 bombs in the spring of 1948, and Spaatz worried that confusion "could result in the AFSWP receiving individual uncoordinated and even conflicting requests and instructions."[16] Of course, CNO Denfeld took issue with Spaatz's request, as it would potentially interfere with the Navy gaining access to atomic weapons, especially if the Air Force retained a monopoly regarding weapons assembly. While the B-29 SILVERPLATE bomber was the only aircraft capable of delivering the atomic weapons in 1948 (with the higher-performing B-50 coming online), the Navy was in the process of developing the AJ-1 Savage and modified P2V Neptune aircraft that were capable of carrying atomic ordnance from carrier flight decks. Furthermore, the Navy was in favor of stockpiling more of the smaller "Little Boy" bombs that weighted some 1,300 pounds less than the MK III. The issue of Air Force sponsorship was forwarded to the MLC for consideration. MLC chair Don Carpenter believed that the issues surrounding the AFSWP were "merely a symptom of fundamental disputes of strategic bombing. This question must be settled first before any organization can be satisfactorily accepted."[17]

However, the rising tensions of the Berlin Crisis may have influenced Carpenter, as he recommended that the Air Force have temporary authority until the matter could be reviewed thoroughly.[18] In addition, the emergency war plan entitled HALFMOON included the potential use of carrier aviation in an atomic offensive against the Soviets. With HALFMOON and AFSWP issues at the fore, the Air Force and Navy debate continued, forcing Forrestal to again assemble the service chiefs for discussion. From August 20 to 22, the JCS again met, this time at the Naval War College in Newport, Rhode Island. An interim agreement was reached in which the Air Force would not block Navy access to atomic weapons or exclude the service from atomic planning efforts. In return, the Navy would agree to Air Force stewardship of the AFSWP until the MLC concluded its own study. But with the HALFMOON plan, the Navy had at least a doctrinal wedge in the atomic strike mission and some satisfaction that it would have access to atomic weaponry.

Animosity between the two services continued, not just in the walls of the Pentagon and in government offices, but in the public domain. In order to garner support for air power, the Army Air Forces began planning a deliberate public-affairs campaign before the war was even over.[19] Air Force public-relations offices began proclaiming that the "air age" of the 20th century had arrived and was eclipsing sea power, which had been the dominant realm during the 19th century.[20] Hence, the Air Force was the future, and the Navy was the past. However, Navy Secretary John Sullivan was not convinced that a navy-centric public-relations campaign was sufficiently important to counter the air force effort and wanted to support the spirit of unification under Forrestal and the National Security Act. While CNO Denfeld understood the value of public support, Navy public relations was not under his charge—it was the purview of the Navy secretary.[21] Despite Sullivan's reluctance to counter Air Force claims on a departmental basis, Navy officers and their supporters took this issue into their own hands and began disputing Air Force claims individually. Meanwhile Secretary of the Air Force Symington was publicly pushing the air-power agenda. In a speech made on July 27, 1948, in support of the proposed 70-group Air Force, and at the expense of carrier aviation, the secretary posed the question, "Can the country afford to spend the many billions of dollars additional required for unnecessary duplication? That is what must be decided if America is not to destroy itself through debt."[22] Without a comprehensive and coordinated public-relations effort, the Navy could not compete with the Air Force's determined endeavor. As a result, support within the public realm, and more importantly in the halls of Congress, began to wane for naval aviation.[23]

While these doctrinal arguments between the services took place in the halls of the Pentagon and other government spaces, a very public argument over roles and missions between the Air Force and the Navy began forming in April 1949. Even before the war ended, the Navy looked to expand the capability of carrier aviation. In fighting the Japanese, U.S. aircraft carriers were equipped with planes of relatively short range. World War II carriers and their crews were often within striking distance of enemy land- and sea-based attack aircraft. In order to help keep the ships out of harm's way and increase striking capability, the ship's air wing needed aircraft that could fly farther with increased payloads. As a result, the Navy needed a bigger platform to launch and recover heavier and more capable aircraft. Toward this end, the Navy was interested in "exhausting ... all possibilities of carrier aviation" and looked to building an entirely new class of carrier platform.[24] This naval aviation atomic mission would also necessitate the development of aircraft to deliver atomic ordnance. Given Truman's fiscal austerity, this idea of building a new, bigger, and better carrier was problematic. Not only was the proposed aircraft carrier, named the USS *United States*, expensive to build, with a cost around $43 million in the FY 50 budget, but the platform also required associated logistical and tactical support. Along with the carrier, other support ships and the accompanying carrier air wing ballooned the cost of the proposed capability to a whopping $1.265 billion (in 1949 prices).[25]

3. Inter-Service Squabbles

Supposedly looking to curb costs, the new Secretary of Defense, Louis Johnson, who replaced James Forrestal, cancelled the USS *United States* on April 23, 1949, a mere five days after the keel plate for the ship was laid.[26] Adding fuel to the inter-service fire was Secretary Johnson's termination of the program without first consulting the Secretary of the Navy, Sullivan. Sullivan resigned in protest.[27] New to the position of Secretary of Defense, Johnson was looking for an opportunity to establish himself as a strong, decisive leader following Forrestal's weak example. Furthermore, Johnson's pro–Air Force leanings were designed to preclude the Navy from getting into the strategic bombing realm. In an interview given weeks after the cancellation, Johnson reportedly felt that the new carrier was competing with the Air Force and that as long as he (Johnson) was the secretary (of defense), the Navy would have no part in long-range or strategic bombing.[28] Furthermore, the Secretary underscored his position by arguing that he was willing to allow an increase in carrier aircraft combat radius for 530 miles to 750 miles, but that was all they were going to get.[29]

Although the Navy was losing ground in the atomic strategic bombing fight, the Air Force had its own problems. In light of the emerging controversy, the director of the Bureau of the Budget, Frank Pace, sent a memo to Truman the same month regarding atomic warfare and the procurement of the B-36. The director's memo called into question American nuclear defense posture and presidential authority. Pace expressed his concerns regarding atomic weaponry, writing, "I do feel, however, that it is one thing to hold a substantial atomic stockpile in readiness for possible use, but a wholly different matter to base war strategy upon an uncritical acceptance of the idea of atomic warfare on what may amount to an unrestricted scale." The memo warned that a commitment to B-36 production and atomic re-armament might "put the president in a most awkward position if he desired to alter the strategy in the midst of the intense pressures of the hour."[30] The director also posed a significant question regarding presidential authority, asking, "Does the present strategy, implemented by the B-36 program, take out of the president's hands the final decision, in time of war, as whether atomic bombs are to be used?"[31] In conclusion, the memo recommended that the B-36 program be evaluated based upon what the program might mean regarding presidential nuclear authority.[32]

As a result of Pace's memo and concern, Truman asked his Air Force aide, Brigadier General R. B. Landry, whether the nation was placing too much emphasis on strategic bombing and "putting all its eggs in one basket?"[33] Landry replied that the Air Force was merely trying to respond to an enemy threat as fast as it could "as distinguished from forces to become available later through mobilization."[34] While Landry's response was balanced and gracious, considering the other military services, it masked the

B-36A in flight. First delivered to SAC in June 1948, the B-36A was not designed to carry atomic ordnance. Retrofit through the SADDLETREE program was required to make many of the B-36s atomic capable. A later version of the bomber had two J47 jet engines installed in pods near each wingtip. Questions remained about the survivability of the bomber given the advent of jet fighters (U.S. Air Force photograph).

underlying thought of the Air Force as an organization and its views on future conflict. The stage was being set for a public debate on the nuclear bombing strategy.

Dubious claims surfaced against Symington and others in the Air Force over the development of the B-36 bombers. During May 1949, an anonymous letter, written by pro-navy interests and sent to Congressman James E. Van Zant, charged that procurement irregularities existed in the B-36 program.[35] The letter claimed that Symington and Secretary Johnson had a vested, personal monetary and political interest in the expensive bomber project.[36] These charges led to a congressional investigation, and the inquiry provided a venue for a debate regarding the prospect of naval aviation vis-à-vis the emerging Air Force roles and the larger issue of the U.S. commitment to nuclear bombardment as the first line of defense.

The charges against Symington, Johnson, and Vultee Corporation President Floyd Odlum, maker of the B-36, were summarily dismissed in August when former Navy Commander Cedric R. Worth, a special assistant to the Secretary of the Navy, admitted his part in the authorship of the anonymous letter. Furthermore, in his testimony before the congressional committee, Worth retracted his statements accusing Air Force leadership of wrongdoing and was subsequently suspended from his job at the Department of the Navy.[37] Others were also implicated in writing the anonymous letter. The list of those implicated included the famous war hero Arleigh "31 Knot" Burke who was currently serving in the OP-23 office (Organizational Policy and Research Division—tasked with defending Navy roles, missions, and the budget). While Burke was removed from the posting and grilled in the press, his career recovered and he eventually became the CNO. While the charges against Air Force officials were no longer valid, the battle over nuclear bombing and the primacy of the Air Force still loomed as naval officers still argued to present their case regarding the importance of carrier aviation.

In October the issue of strategic bombing was rejoined as Navy officers testified in front of the House Armed Services Committee, arguing their case against the B-36. Naval officers claimed that the "atomic blitz" the Air Force proposed did not provide a deterrent effect and that the B-36 was "a billion dollar blunder."[38] Admiral Arthur Radford argued, "The B-36 has become, in the minds of the American people, a symbol of a theory of warfare—the atomic blitz—which promises then a cheap and easy victory if war should come."[39] Naval officers also thought the World War II design origins of the B-36 made the plane too slow for the nascent jet age and therefore vulnerable to an effective enemy air defense.[40] Additionally, these officers believed that fast-attack carrier aviation had a role to play in an atomic offensive and that the value of a naval campaign had been proven during the Pacific war. In his testimony during the congressional hearings, Admiral Radford expressed concern that the nation had placed too much emphasis on strategic bombing.[41] Radford went on to argue that "[he did not] believe that the threat of atomic blitz will be an effective deterrent to a war or that it will win a war ... and that we must have a much more capable and efficient weapon than the B-36."[42]

Not only did the Navy question the practicality of the B-36 in an upcoming war, but it called into question the morality of the nuclear offensive. Radford went on to argue the whole theory of "atomic annihilation" and that this application of power "would be politically and economically useless ... [and] morally reprehensible."[43] Additionally, Rear Admiral Ralph A. Ofstie, a contributing author to the CROSSROADS atomic test report, questioned the efficacy of strategic bombardment and asked, "Does the concept of strategic bombing effectively support the policies, objectives and commitment of the United States?"[44] He also claimed that "strategic bombing, as now accepted, unavoidably includes mass slaughter" and that "the moral force of the people of this country is in strong opposition to military methods so contrary to our fundamental ideals. It is time that strategic bombing be squarely faced in this light; that it be examined in relation to the decent opinions of mankind."[45]

Ofstie went on further to classify strategic bombardment as a "ruthless and barbaric policy."[46]

Near the end of the October deliberations, CNO Denfeld was the last to testify. Despite being a subordinate of Secretary Johnson, the admiral now defiantly broke with his civilian superior and contradicted Johnson's ideas regarding strategic bombing and the role of naval aviation. In his testimony, Denfeld stated, "As the senior military spokesman for the Navy, I want to state ... that I fully support the conclusion presented to this committee by the Navy and Marine officers who have preceded me."[47] Denfeld went on further to argue Navy grievances regarding the Department of Defense (the Department of Defense was the successor name applied to the National Military Establishment. The official name changed in October 1949) policies and its efforts to downsize the Navy. He stated that DoD "limitations are imposed without consultation" and the only guidance the Navy received was to decommission ships and organizations.[48] Regarding strategic bombing, Denfeld argued that he could not accept the idea that the "initial air offensive is ... solely a function of the United States Air Force."[49]

Following the naval contingent, Secretary Symington and Chief of Staff Hoyt Vandenberg gave their testimony supporting the B-36 and expressing their opposition to the building of USS *United States*. When JCS Chairman General Omar Bradley testified, he also supported the Air Force argument and reinforced the importance of the strategic air offensive. As a result, the Navy position vis-à-vis the other services was eroded. As a result of his defense of his Navy brethren, advocacy of carrier aviation, and defiance of his superior's position regarding strategic bombing, Denfeld was fired as CNO by Navy Secretary Francis Matthews. The basis for his removal was the admiral's "inability to conform" to DoD policies. Admiral Forrest P. Sherman replaced him on November 2, 1949.[50]

In the end, the B-36 controversy and the inter-service squabbles helped to at least air the festering grievances of the services. However, the competing priorities regarding defense roles and mission continued to preclude a coherent and well-organized atomic strategy. Instead, arguments ensued over equipment and individual material solutions rather than a comprehensive review of atomic strategies and the best way to collectively carry out such an offensive. Budgets and allocations drove atomic planning as well as the pet projects of the various service components and the civilian contractors that supported them. In determining postwar arrangements, the United States had not established firm peacetime missions and commitments for the Air Force; therefore aviators lacked political guidance and made their own assumptions.[51]

During the postwar period, the Navy and the Air Force fought each other for influence and budget allocations rather than developing an integrated atomic war plan that leveraged the best attributes of the services.

3. Inter-Service Squabbles

At the federal level, the United States failed to adequately organize, source, and plan atomic strategies, associated organizations, and required capabilities during the first few years of the Cold War. Truman's steadfast devotion to a parsimonious defense budget had reverberations that affected the nation's ability to effectively leverage its monopoly. Furthermore, the fight over defense spending allocations merely reflected the larger inter-service fights over roles and missions. The inability to properly budget defense allocations and coordinate both civilian and military organizations undermined America's atomic monopoly. Throughout this period the United States bluffed on the atomic hand it was holding and was fortunately never called on it. While the crisis in Berlin figured prominently in some of the decisions made regarding atomic weapons, no real consensus existed at the highest levels of the federal government over how this weapon was to be resourced, allocated, or delivered. Production capacities were also an issue for years, as the AEC had to reinvigorate various labs and reactors required to produce fissionable materials. The atomic "science project" the AEC inherited from the MED was not prepared to produce the quantity and quality of weapons thought to be needed in a future conflict. Fights over vision, both civilian and military, proved a stumbling block to effective inter-service coordination and precluded an "all of government" approach to the issue.

PART II. AMERICAN WAR PLANNING

4

The Postwar World and the USSBS

With the surrender of the Axis powers, America needed to refocus its military efforts and war plans based on the postwar security environment. With the advent of strategic bombing and atomic weaponry, the American plans for the future looked very different from the "color" or "rainbow" plans that were drafted by the Joint Army and Navy Board prior to the war. While the "color" plans looked at war against specific countries, the "rainbow" plans drawn up just before World War II looked at war in more of a geographical perspective. However, war plans subsequent to 1945 were focused on the Soviet Union and reflected Kennan's suspicion of the expansionist nature of Communism. As early as 1944 the JCS were already looking at the postwar environment regarding the Soviet Union. By February 1945, the United States began analyzing Russian war intentions and anticipating the geo-political tension that would result after the Allied victory.

The American relationship with the Soviet Union had always been one of suspicion and mistrust. The United States loathed the establishment of communism in Russia beginning with the October Revolution in 1917 and attempted to thwart the effort with the ill-fated Archangel and Vladivostok expeditions of 1918–1919. Following World War I, fervent anti-communist sentiment became part of the national fabric and remained a foundation of American patriotic ideals. As a result, the pattern of the U.S.-Soviet relationship was already well established before World War II and continued after the Allied victory.[1]

Despite U.S.-Soviet cooperation in the war against Hitler, neither side completely trusted the other, and the marriage of convenience quickly deteriorated after V-J Day. While there is no definitive start date to the beginning of the "Cold War," many largely accept the end of World War II as the event precipitating the ideological struggle.

As Truman succeeded FDR, the anti–Soviet sentiment within the U.S.

government continued in earnest. Truman held deep-seated hatred of both communism and the Soviet Union and reportedly believed that the "Russians were as untrustworthy as Hitler and Al Capone."[2] Adding to the political dichotomy was Truman's steadfast belief in American "moral superiority" and the observation that Russians mistook generosity as a sign of weakness.[3] Furthermore, he believed that the USSR needed to be "taught how to behave in the civilized world" and that the world depended upon American economic, political, and liberal values.[4] The establishment of the "Truman Doctrine" on March 12, 1947, clearly drew the line between the two powers, as the president stated, "It must be the policy of the United States to support free peoples who are resisting attempted subjugation by armed minorities or by outside pressures."[5] There was no doubt in anyone's mind to whom "outside pressures" referred.

Throughout the postwar period and well into the 1950s, the issues regarding the apparent appeasement of Soviet expansion served as rhetorical fodder for domestic discussion and for the political positioning between the Republican and Democratic parties. Charges of being "soft on communism" served largely political ends in domestic arenas as both parties used this accusation to sway voters. In this same vein, political leaders argued that the high standard of the American way of life proved the superiority of capitalism over communism. The contemporary "zeitgeist" in America wove economic prosperity with patriotic overtones and connected consumerism and the conventional values of the family unit as part of a safeguard against communism.[6] The ideological and political lines between the superpowers had clearly been drawn. Hanson Baldwin, the military editor for the *New York Times,* argued in 1947, "The United States and Russia are face to face in a struggle for the world, a conflict short of war, but a conflict nonetheless."[7]

Eager to offset the Republican gains in the 1946 midterm elections, Truman set out to firmly establish his anti-communist stance and bolster the Democratic Party's public image as champions of democracy. In 1947, Truman signed Executive Order 9835, which established the Employee Loyalty Program that held hostage anyone with a communist connection.[8] This program allowed federal civilian employees to be dismissed from their jobs if "reasonable doubt" of their loyalty was found.[9] This program facilitated the subsequent communist witch hunts of McCarthy and the House Un-American Activities Committee (HUAC).[10] In addition to the Truman Doctrine, on April 3, 1948, Truman initiated the Marshall Plan in Europe as another effort to stem growing communist influence. As the Soviets exerted their influence in Poland, Romania, Hungary, Bulgaria, and Czechoslovakia, America sought to establish capitalist trading partners in Western Europe.[11] The Marshall Plan not only provided reconstruction opportunities to a war-torn Europe for humanitarian purposes, but also served as an economic bulwark against further communist gains. By encouraging capitalism and sowing the seeds for future markets, the Marshall Plan was a direct attempt to prevent further communist influence in Western European political arenas. The Marshall Plan served in concert with the Truman Doctrine, as the president claimed they were "two halves of the same walnut."[12]

On the domestic front, Truman's policies were bearing some political fruit. In his close election campaign against Thomas Dewey in 1948, the challenger stated that he lost because "the [Russian] bear got us."[13] Dewey concluded he was not sufficiently critical regarding Truman's "tough on communism" stance, but historian Arnold Offner argues, "Truman appeared to be doing what the public wanted him to do, namely, sustain a tough policy—short of war in Berlin and elsewhere."[14] The domestic political agenda not only shaped American postwar foreign policies and agendas, but helped to drive defense policy and practices.

During this same time the United States developed war plans purportedly designed to ensure the defense of the free world from communist expansion and protect the American way of life. In the effort to contain the Soviet Union, these plans were supposed to be expressions of national policy that underpinned the envisioned "ends" of American national objectives. Developed by the Joint War Plans Committee (JWPC), later titled the Joint Strategic Plans Group (JSPG), these plans represented the "ways" in which the U.S. military would achieve a desired end state by use of armed force. The combination of strategic bombers and atomic weapons served as the foundation for military expression of national goals and objectives. But just how was a strategic bombing campaign with atomic weapons supposed to meet those envisioned end states? At an even more fundamental level, did the American experiment with strategic bombing during the war provide the validation of this new dimension in warfare? What targets needed to be hit with atomic weapons and what was the desired effect from such raids? Did the plans developed by JWPC/JSPG outline courses of action that turned atomic war into a coherent expression of national political goals and objectives?

U.S. Strategic Bombing Survey as a Baseline

Following the war, the USAAF leadership was convinced of the superiority of the air arm in modern war and firmly believed that their efforts had been the decisive factor in the Allied victory.[15] The charred remains of German and Japanese cities stood as testaments to the destruction wrought by America's air armadas and were harbingers of the potential of air power.

The Allied Combined Bombing Offensive (CBO) dovetailed the capabilities of the Royal Air Force's (RAF) bomber command with the USAAF's strategic bomber effort. While the Americans bombed, purportedly with precision, by day, the RAF bombed area targets at night. This combined offensive was specifically aimed at German production capacity, its factories, infrastructure, and the morale of the population. On September 3, 1944, President Roosevelt directed that the Secretary of War, Henry Stimson, study the effects of the strategic bombardment of Germany and on August 15, 1945, made the same request regarding the Pacific bombing campaign. This desire to capture and record the effects of strategic bombing, done at the behest of the USAAF, resulted in the establishment of the U.S. Strategic Bombing Survey (USSBS). The USSBS was a combined organization with some 300 civilians, 350 officers, and 500 enlisted men with the primary purpose of "establishing a basis for evaluating the importance and potential of airpower as an element of military strategy...." The intent was to get an unbiased and accurate assessment of the CBO and analyze its overall effectiveness.

The USSBS easily serves as a baseline for comparative analysis regarding postwar strategic bombing ideas and envisioned methodologies. Many of the same targeting strategies utilized by the Air Force subsequent to the war were based upon what transpired during the CBO over Europe and the strategic bombing of the Japanese home islands in the Pacific. Taking experiences from the recent global conflict, air planners targeted much of the same kind of infrastructure in the Soviet Union as they had previously with the Axis powers. However, according to the USSBS, USAAF strategic methodology alone did not force the Axis capitulation. Much of the USSBS analysis hints that the CBO effort was, at best, marginally effective and was merely a factor in the Allied victory and not the decisive factor. Why didn't the CBO effort work as promised by the interwar air advocates? The reasons for this are complex and arguable. In order to evaluate the potential of postwar planning methodologies, a review of the USSBS finding is required.

In light of American prewar doctrine, the USSBS analyzed the actual execution of the CBO and weighed its effectiveness. When the USSBS finally ceased operations in 1947, it had produced some 300 highly detailed reports regarding the effects of strategic bombing of both Germany and Japan. USSBS efforts should be lauded as members sifted through the shattered infrastructure and societies of Germany and Japan to find relevant data, with some reports hidden in homes, barns, caves, once in a henhouse, and twice in coffins![16] As a testament to their diligence, the USSBS staff also suffered a number of casualties during their study and sustained four deaths in obtaining data.[17]

Expecting a validation of the CBO, USAAF officers looked forward to seeing the results on paper. While many air leaders believed that the USAAF's effort proved the value of air power and the prewar doctrine of daylight precision bombing, the USSBS was not the definitive validation some expected. The Allied victory in the air was total, complete, and a factor in the victory over the Axis. However, the survey's findings were not necessarily the ringing endorsement some air-power advocates anticipated.

During the interwar years, at the Air Corps Tactical School (ACTS) at Maxwell Field, Alabama, U.S. officers began to outline the doctrinal precepts of daylight precision bombing. By 1935, ACTS solidified ideas regarding the use of strategic bombing by arguing "the principle and all important missions of air power when its equipment permits is the attack of those vital objectives in a nation's economic structure which tend to paralyze the nation's ability to wage war and thus contribute to the attainment of the ultimate objective of war, namely the disintegration of the will to resist."[18] However, while targeting the production facilities of an enemy nation, ACTS doctrine did not subscribe to the idea of wanton killing of civilian populations. In trying to maintain the moral high ground, USAAF doctrine argued that the "direct attack of civilian populations is most repugnant to our humanitarian principles and certainly it is a method of warfare that we would adopt only with great reluctance and regret."[19] As a result, for the Americans, the strategic bombing of the enemy nation did not need to be wholesale, but aimed directly at the key components of the industrial base. With the destruction of the production capacities and infrastructure of a modern industrial state, the enemy's armed forces would be devoid of equipment, unable to sustain forces in the field or employ an effective defense. Additionally, the bombing effort would destroy the enemy's economy while having the secondary effect of demoralizing the national populace.

In support of this precision bombing effort, the USAAF largely utilized the Norden MK XV bombsight that could place 90 percent of the bombs dropped from an airplane within one mile of the aim point, with 40 percent landing within 500 yards. When the United States finally entered World War II, the USAAF was eager to test its new strategic bombing doctrine and provide proof of the efficacy of air power. The 8th Air Force began flying strategic bombing missions out of England in August 1942 and was accompanied in the role by the 15th Air Force flying out of bases in the Mediterranean by November 1943.

However, once the USAAF bomber fleets appeared over Europe, the execution of strategic bombardment failed to meet expectations. Overcast skies and weather often precluded precision bombing as the USAAF bombardiers could not see their targets and high-level winds affected bombing accuracy. Bombing from altitudes of 20,000 feet, early raids placed an average of only 20 percent of bombs within 1,000 feet of the target area.[20] Furthermore, effective enemy flak and fighters frustrated the Allied bombing effort, inflicting an early loss rate of about 8 percent per mission. During the early part of the CBO, aircrews were required to complete 25 missions before they could return home. With a loss rate of 8 percent, men quickly realized that statistically they would not complete their full tour of 25 missions and would be killed, missing, or captured around their eleventh mission. In assessing the prewar doctrine against the conditions over war-torn Europe, one USAAF leader stated, "There is a lot of difference between bombing an undefended target and running a barrage of six-inch shellfire while a swarm of pursuit [fighters] are working on you."[21] Indicative of this aerial bloodletting was the October 14, 1943, raid to the German ball bearing plant at Schweinfurt. In this follow-up to an earlier August raid, 228 bombers flew without fighter escort and into German Flieger Abwehr Kannone (FLAK) guns. The 8th Air Force lost 62 planes with another 138 damaged, some beyond repair. This equated to an overall loss rate of 27 percent of the bombing force. Both the Air Force and the USSBS concluded that the losses experienced by deep penetrations without escort could not be sustained.[22]

This issue of bomber losses was not really addressed until January 1944, when the VIII Fighter Command changed its doctrine to "ultimate pursuit" and allowed fighter escort to aggressively attack Luftwaffe fighters instead of staying with the bombers. Additionally, at the same time USAAF fighter units were increasingly being equipped with the new P-51 Mustang aircraft. The P-51 not only had the range to escort the bombers to their objectives, but once engaged with Luftwaffe fighters, its superior maneuverability and speed tipped the scales in favor of the USAAF. By the fall of 1944 the Luftwaffe was only a shell of its former self.

With all the challenges encountered by Allied aircrews in the European skies, the "'round the clock" bombing of Germany's cities changed the very nature of the urban landscape. In all, the CBO dropped 2,700,000 tons of bombs in over 1,440,000 bombing sorties, costing the USAAF 79,265 airmen and the RAF 79,281.[23] In addition to the human costs, both Allied air forces lost over 40,000 airplanes. For all this effort the CBO damaged or destroyed some 7,200,000 homes, killed 300,000 civilians, wounded 780,000, and made 7,500,000 homeless.[24] While the effect on the German populace was significant, for the Americans the effect on German production capacity was the overriding objective of the bombing campaign.

However, the targeting of factories in Germany did not necessarily validate the USAAF's prewar doctrine, as German production of wartime equipment actually rose in the later stages of the conflict, especially when the bombing was at its most intense. Hitting armament and aircraft factories did not materially restrict military operations until very late in the war, when Germany's defensive perimeter had already shrunk appreciably. But until

1945, the Nazi state increased production in many war-supporting industries despite Allied attack. How could the Germans thrive materially while the Allies constantly bombed their factories? The answers to this question are complex.

The Germans started the war with an ample supply of machine tools and factory space and did not fully mobilize their industrial capacity until 1942, but by then it was too late to affect the war's overall outcome.[25] By late 1942, the fortunes of war had turned against the Third Reich, and it could no longer keep pace with Allied industrial capacity. The USAAF assumed the German industrial base was already at 100 percent capacity; however, the Nazi state still had plenty of underutilized production capability. In its analysis, the USSBS found that dispersed German production methods in concert with phenomenal wartime improvisation mitigated the effects of much of the Allied bombing effects. The targeting of German aircraft production in spring of 1944 did not result in a drop in production but forced the Germans to be more efficient in the factories and double their efforts. Despite the more efficient use of their available resources, the Germans still suffered from the absence of raw materials and labor.

USAAF bomb damage assessment also exaggerated the effects of the aerial assaults on manufacturing plants. Hitting a building or a plant did not necessarily render the machine shops and lathes housed in the damaged structure inoperable. Much of this machinery remained intact or could be moved to other locations and used again. In January 1944, the German aviation industry produced some 1,316 single-engine fighter aircraft, and the figure dropped to only 1,016 for the month of February as a result of the "Big Week" raids of 20–26 February.[26] The "Big Week" was a concerted effort by both the 8th and 15th Air Forces to target as much of the German aircraft industry in one week as possible. But even with this concerted effort, by March the figure again rose to 1,377 and continued to rise about 300 additional aircraft per month to a peak of 3,031 in September![27] In fact, the USSBS reported that the German aircraft industry produced 39,000 aircraft of all types in 1944 and that the strength in units at the end of the year was almost unchanged from the January figure.[28]

Additionally, despite the efforts of the CBO, at no time in the war did the German war machine suffer from a lack of armored vehicles, U-boats, ball bearings, machine guns or most artillery pieces or suffer from a paucity of ammunition and various other sinews of war.[29] While the German economy did eventually collapse, for a myriad of reasons, the USSBS noted that "the recuperative and defensive powers of Germany were immense; the speed and ingenuity with which they rebuilt and maintained essential war industry in operation clearly surpassed Allied expectation."[30] Furthermore the USSBS found that no indispensable industry was permanently destroyed by a single raid.³¹ This is not say the CBO did not have an effect; it certainly did. But the strategic bombing effort did not produce the single-handed blow that the framers of precision daylight bombing doctrine had hoped.

The survey also found that USAAF targeting strategy, initially, was less than effective. The targeting of ball bearing factories, submarine pens, or aircraft factories had little or no effect on the overall German war capacity. Only after the USAAF focused its efforts on the German petroleum industry, starting in summer 1944, did the CBO start having the strategic effect it hoped in its prewar doctrine. German oil supply was already tight when the war began, but when refineries were systematically attacked by the USAAF, the effects of a petroleum shortage cascaded throughout the Nazi state. Obviously the shortage of gasoline affected Luftwaffe sortie generation and overall operations, but the lack of petroleum was also a key consideration in Wehrmacht ground actions, as evidenced in the Battle of the Bulge in December 1944. Apart from the direct shortage of gasoline for combat units, German industry also suffered in areas that were dependent upon oil. The rubber, nitrogen, and methanol supplies began to dry up as a result of the oil shortage, and that had dire consequences for other industries. Nitrogen was a key ingredient in explosives and for agriculture, while rubber had key applications in both military and civilian uses. While no evidence was found that rubber was a limiting factor in German military operations, had the war continued for another six months the Wehrmacht would have had to curtail operations.³²

As for the morale effect the bombing was expected to have on the enemy population, the USSBS found that the Germans continued to work as long as the means were available.³³ The idea that aerial bombardment would cause widespread panic and a drop in national morale was largely a fallacy developed during World War I. The Zeppelin raids over London, Ipswich, and Yarmouth had caused localized panic and concern and served as an impetus for the birth of the Royal Air Force. But over time, populations became accustomed to aerial bombardment and the dread and panic among the masses eventually abated or at least were significantly reduced. This decrease in the shock value of bombing civilians was seen during the interwar years in Spain, Ethiopia, and China as populations became accustomed to the aerial assaults. However, early air-power advocates still subscribed to this idea.

The prewar doctrine held that enemy populations would capitulate as a result of the destruction of infrastructure and services, and not necessarily because of the deliberate targeting of the population. The Air War Planning Documents (1 and 42) avoided the deliberate targeting of civilian populations, but still implied that the German nation's will to support the war effort might wane as a consequence of the bombardment. However, the USSBS found little to support this supposition. Germans workers, many enslaved or

4. The Postwar World and the USSBS 85

coerced, still reported to the factories, repaired damaged infrastructure, and produced armaments. Regarding the nature of Nazi Germany's totalitarian regime, the USSBS reported, "the power of a police state over its people cannot be underestimated."[34]

In the Pacific, the firebombing efforts against the Japanese were certainly destructive and affected the national infrastructure and forced the evacuation of urban areas, but the USAAF did not start these raids until March 1945. By that time, the U.S. Navy had already sunk much of the Japanese merchant fleet in its interdiction campaign and isolated the home islands from their sources of war materials in Southeast Asia and the East Indies.[35] Short on natural resources, Japan relied upon sea lines of communication to keep its factories stocked with supplies and raw materials. For example, oil, as in Germany, was an important element in the Japanese war machine. However, oil imports from the south began declining in August 1943 and were eliminated by April 1945.[36] Japanese crude oil stocks were exhausted, resulting in the cutting of aviation training programs and even some combat operations.[37] By 1944 many Japanese factories were devoid of the raw materials needed to continue production of war items. Even without the destructive firebombing, the overall production in Japan would have dropped by some 50 percent solely as a consequence of the naval interdiction campaign.[38]

In the end, the survey found that air power was a factor in the Allied victory, but not the decisive cause of the Axis defeat. The USSBS executive summary for the Pacific war went so far as to conclude that "the role of air power cannot be considered separately ... from the roles of ground and naval forces nor from the broad plans and strategy from which the war was conducted."[39] The synergy of air, naval, and ground campaigns underpinned by an abundance of war material collectively defeated the Axis war machine. Many other factors also played into the Allied victory. Unfortunately for most air-power advocates, the USSBS did not definitively state that air power was the decisive factor for victory.

The USSBS also argued that strategic intelligence was a key element, especially in the opening stages of the war.[40] At the start of World War II, USAAF knowledge of German infrastructure was inadequate, as there was no process to share information between the military, government, and private/corporate organizations.[41] Knowing the nature of a given target, where it is, and how it contributes to the enemy's economy and war-making production is a key component for a strategic bombing campaign. The USAAF attempted to hit and destroy ball bearing plants, U-boat shipyards, and aircraft factories, with very tepid or slight results. Not until the CBO targeted the synthetic oil production in mid–1944 did the strategic bombing have a noticeable effect on the German war machine. However, by the time oil became a primary target, the fate of Nazi Germany was already becoming apparent on both fronts. As a result of the CBO experience, a robust intelligence effort and knowledge of enemy critical vulnerabilities was paramount for a successful strategic bombing campaign. This element was sorely lacking in postwar targeting strategies.

Although the results of strategic bombing in World War II were equivocal, airmen in the postwar era were steadfast in their advocacy of air power and the belief that it could single-handedly bring victory. In one of the first highly regarded books about atomic war, entitled *The Ultimate Weapon*, author Bernard Brodie argued that along with atomic bombs came a wholesale change in warfare. Analysis conducted by Brodie during the 1950s echoed the USSBS findings and argued that the strategic bombing campaign was but one element in a combination of forces that defeated the Axis and that air power alone could not have secured victory.[42] While Brodie saw some merit in the USAAF conventional wartime bombing efforts, he also believed that atomic weaponry significantly changed the mission of armed forces. Furthermore, with the advent of the atomic bomb and improvements in aviation technology, many believed that air power was now the decisive force regardless of the USSBS findings. The salient message of Brodie's book was that "the chief purpose of our military establishment has been to win wars. From now on, the chief purpose must be to avert them. It can have no other useful purpose."[43] Furthermore, because of the airplane's destructive potential with atomic weapons, Brodie believed that war in the future would be a short affair lasting only a few days.[44] These ideas regarding war in the future also permeated throughout the USAF and served as the foundation for American defensive strategies during the Cold War.

However, the polemics regarding the findings of the USSBS in its Pacific War analysis led Major General Orvil A. Anderson of the Army Analysis Division to dispute formally the findings of the USSBS. In submitting a minority report to the secretary of war, Anderson argued that the survey distorted the worth of air power in the recent conflict and undervalued its promise for the future. His minority report called into question the value of the USSBS and argued, "As a broad evaluation of the report, I consider it an instrument which perceives the truth but has not pointedly developed fundamental issues as working thesis. For this reason it lacks the focus, strength, and impact required to make it a compelling instrument...."[45] While the USSBS considered all naval, ground and air aspects, Anderson thought it diluted the impact of air power. He argued that despite the survey's findings, leaps in aviation technology and the development of long-range air weapons provide an "effective means of striking directly at the enemy's sustaining resources and his will to wage war."[46] This idea was supported by another AUQR article in late 1948 stating that with atomic weapons, the air power was now 200 times as effective as it was in the past.[47] As a result, Anderson and his ilk believed that morale and destroyed enemy production capacities were elements worthy of targeting, despite the survey's findings on the matter.

Furthermore, the general stated, "Surface forces need be opposed and neutralized only as required in acquiring and/or defending necessary air bases [and] ... in the future, the range of air weapons and their ability to penetrate enemy air defenses will be fundamental considerations in the development of a nation's primary striking force."[48] Anderson boldly stated that "the mission of airpower has ceased to be ancillary. It has become primary...."[49] Anderson thought that the very nature of war had changed. The idea of ground combat being the decisive element in war was no longer nearly as relevant. Seizing and holding terrain was to take a back seat to the destruction of enemy production facilities and infrastructure. Armies were needed merely to secure the air bases for strategic operations.

Echoing the primacy of air power, this same sentiment was expressed by Stuart Symington, future Secretary of the Air Force who told a crowd in Detroit, "Our strength in the air will decide the destiny of America."[50] Regardless of what the survey reported about the effectiveness of the strategic air effort in World War II, it did not shake the Air Force's opinion of its pivotal role in any upcoming conflict.

5

National Security Objectives?

In February 1948, international tensions rose as the Soviet Union backed the Czechoslovakian Communist Party in a coup d'état that helped solidify Russia's hold on Eastern Europe. Tensions continued to rise when on March 25 the Soviets begin restricting Western military and passenger traffic to the traditional German capital of Berlin. Days later the Soviets upped the ante and forbade the movement of trains running out of Berlin for the Western-occupied zones without Red Army approval. Furthermore, the Red Army also mandated that Allied truck transportation could not leave the city without Soviet inspection. Finally, on June 24, the Soviet Union shut off all ground and water transportation to and from the non–Soviet zones, resulting in a full blockade. In response, the next day the Western Allies began the Berlin Airlift and continued the aerial lifeline for the next thirteen months.

While the U.S. Air Forces in Europe under Curtis LeMay began the airlift effort, Truman was looking at options with a determination to keep the Western presence in Berlin. In addition to the airlift, Truman also ordered the forward deployment of three B-29 bomb groups as a show of force to the Soviets. The 301st Bomb Group was already deployed, with one squadron on a rotational basis at Furstenfeldbruck. The 28th and 307th Bomb Groups were also deployed to bases in the United Kingdom and Germany by mid–July.[1] While none of these aircraft were versions capable of delivering atomic ordnance, it is doubtful that the Russians knew of this limitation. The mere presence of strategic bombers may have been enough of a show of force to deter the Soviets from further action. However, the 509th Bomb Group, the only unit with SILVERPLATE bombers at the time, was put on alert status with preliminary coordination with the Royal Air Force in England. While SILVERPLATE bombers remained in the United States, planners looked at energizing the AFSWP and the AEC regarding the transfer of custody of atomic ordnance and looking at possible staging of facilities in England or other locations. Although the United States made some minor mobilization preparations, the Central Intelligence Agency (CIA) found no evidence of large-scale deployment on the part of the Soviets.

The deployment of B-29s and show of force by Truman was one of the first overt acts of deterrence in the Cold War. The idea of having a military force so strong and capable that it would cause any potential aggressor to think twice about offensive action became the cornerstone of Cold War doctrinal precepts. The use of the word "deterrence" first appeared in U.S. military circles as early as 1946 and was quickly adopted by planners in the Army Air Force.[2] The idea received official approbation with regard to the Soviet Union on August 25, 1948, in NSC 20/2, as the document specified that "the U.S. defense effort must be based on the principle of deterrence."[3] While the United States adopted the word in 1948, it had no real capability, militarily at least, to back up the concept.

Despite the lack of Red Army movement, Truman was, for the second time in his presidency, considering the use of atomic weapons. However, he was adamant that the decision to use atomic ordnance remain in the president's hands alone. Simultaneously, while the crisis was unfolding, the issue of custody of the stockpile was also coming to a head. Concerned that the military might overstep its authority regarding authorization, on July 15, six days before the Oval Office showdown between the AEC and NME regarding atomic custody, Truman expressed to Forrestal that he didn't want "some dashing lieutenant colonel" making the decision to use atomic weapons.[4] The international exigency over Berlin no doubt reinforced in Truman's mind that the atomic stockpile should remain in civilian AEC hands—much to the chagrin of Forrestal and the rest of the NME.

In response to Truman's concerns over atomic authority, and after his discussion with Forrestal, the NSC drafted a document that outlined guidance in the use of such weapons. The result was "NSC 30 United States Policy Regarding Atomic Weapons." While approved by the council on September 16, 1948, it was never signed by the president. The letter provided little guidance regarding the actual use of atomic weapons, but it did address Truman's concern regarding "some dashing lieutenant colonel" acting on his own. His taking no formal action on the policy letter was curious, considering Truman's concerns at the time. By providing only tacit approval of the document, the president may have been giving his military advisors sufficient leeway and flexibility regarding bombing methodologies and target sets.[5] This was consistent with his approach regarding the "Little Boy" and "Fat Man" drops.

The target list for those two bombs dropped in the war was developed by a military panel that was then scrutinized by Secretary of War Stimson. Truman's only input into the targeting process was the removal of the city of Kyoto. The deletion of Kyoto came as a result of Stimson's service in the

Far East before the war. He appreciated the cultural significance of the city to the Japanese people. Once he saw Kyoto on the target list, Stimson took the issue to Truman and pleaded his case to have it removed. In response to the targeting of Kyoto, Truman reportedly said, "Even if the Japs are savages, ruthless, merciless, and fanatics, we as the lead of the world for the common welfare cannot drop this terrible bomb on the old capital or the new. [Stimson] and I are in accord. The target will be a purely military one...."[6] But given the context of the time, Truman may have figured that NSC 30 established enough precedent to preclude a premature use of atomic weapons without his authority. However, this is an unusual assumption given Truman's inherent suspicion of military officers.

Whatever Truman's rationale was for providing only tacit approval, paragraph 12 of NSC 30 specified that atomic weapons were indeed a part of the American arsenal and that the "NME must be ready to utilize ... all appropriate means available, including atomic weapons, in the interest of national security...."[7] As a result, the use of atomic weapons was now official policy despite discussions in the United Nations over the Baruch Plan. The next paragraph articulated the real nature of the policy letter, stipulating that "the decision as to the employment of atomic weapons in the event of war is to be made by the Chief Executive when he considers such decision to be required."[8] The policy reserved this decision for the president alone.

Outside this, NSC 30 provided no further guidance on what to target in support of national goals or towards what end. Questions remained as to what events might require an atomic response, and if approval was given, what target sets needed to be hit and when?[9] NSC 30 did not articulate under what circumstances the president would allow atomic weapons to be used. Could atomic weapons be used preemptively or just in a retaliatory action? If only in a retaliatory mode, did the initial aggressor have to use unconventional weapons (gas, chemical, biological, and possibly atomic) first or could the initial U.S. salvos include atomic ordnance? Or were atomic weapons merely a "silver bullet" used for special targets and effects? There was no guidance to these lingering questions.

Almost a year before NSC 30 was approved, in November 1947 future USAF Chief of Staff General Hoyt Vandenberg already sought guidance regarding the use of atomic weapons and the goals of an American bombing campaign against Russia, asking:

> In a war with the USSR is our purpose to destroy the Russian people, industry, the Communist party, the communist hierarchy, or a combination of these? ... Will there be a requirement to occupy, possibly reconstruct, Russia after victory, or can we seal off the country, letting it work out its own salvation?[10]

Due to the high level of secrecy surrounding the stockpile and the associated technology, American planners had only a semblance of knowledge of what atomic weapons might provide in a given conflict. With much of the nuclear test information kept from strategic planners, most of them had little idea what these weapons' strategic effects might be. Furthermore, they did not fully understand what these weapons could actually do to a given target location or how they might best be used to reach national war objectives. Similarly, W. Walton Butterworth, Director of the Office of Far Eastern Affairs at the State Department, echoed a comparable sentiment regarding atomic weapons. In a memo dated September 15, 1948, shortly after NSC 30 approval, Butterworth asked "when and how [should] such weapons be used? Should we ... begin bombing major centers of population ... or start with smaller centers important for transportation or specific industries? This question should be answered not so much on the basis of humanitarian principles as from a practical weighing of the long-run advantage of this country."[11] The lack of specific guidance left military planners with a wide latitude regarding use of atomic weapons, which provided planning flexibility but simultaneously failed to make any real connection to an envisioned end state.

New York Times editor Hanson Baldwin echoed these same sentiments earlier than Vandenberg in a March 1947 article regarding the new role America played in securing the future of western civilization. In the piece, Baldwin argued that America was now the West's sole protector from the encroachment of Russia and stood as the most important factor in preventing a "reversion to nihilism and the dark ages."[12] While America was the bulwark against communist aggression, Baldwin was concerned that the United States still had "no finished, over-all military policy [and that] our fighting forces are handicapped not only by the demands for economy but by lack of legislation and by piecemeal legislation. There is no rounded and complete policy to guide them in organization or development of post war forces."[13] While the piece was addressing military applications as a whole, he was obviously concerned about both conventional and atomic strategies.

In addition to the concerns over national strategy and alignment of "Ends-Ways-Means," the morality of the atomic air offensive was called into question—and not just by the civilian community opposed to atomic weaponry, but in some cases by military leaders. In September 1947 the first commander of SAC, George Kenney, stated, "It has not been morality but expediency that has governed the use of new weapons."[14] Given the nature of the Pacific war, Kenney's observation certainly had merit. In an undated memo to Secretary Symington, the first Air Force Chief of Staff, Carl Spaatz, also raised the morality question. Knowing that a wholesale strategic bombing effort with atomic weapons was being planned, Spaatz queried his boss regarding the legal and moral aspects of the aerial campaign, asking, "Do you realize that in accepting our new jobs and in the event of war with Russia we will be hanged as war criminals if we lose? There had better be some real hard honest-to-God thinking about what we need to avoid being on the losing side. The U.S. has already set the pace for the atomic bomb, strategic bombing, and hanging war criminals."[15] While Spaatz argued in 1945 that the atomic bomb did not change the nature of strategic bombardment, he at least began to recognize that the moral implications were becoming a salient issue and required a discourse.

While the framers of precision bombing during the interwar years specifically tried to avoid civilian casualties, planned bombing methodologies in the postwar Air Force were no longer constrained by such considerations. Results in the CBO, firebombing of Japanese cities, and the atomic attacks were direct evidence of this change in application—despite what the doctrine mandated. Indicative of this thought, in 1947 the USAF Directorate of Intelligence forwarded a study of target sets in the USSR and entitled the document "To Kill a Nation."[16] While people were not necessarily the target of atomic strategic bombing, acceptance of massive casualties was now taken as a given in Air Force planning. Implicit in war plans of the era was the destruction of entire cities and their populations. Such operations were now an inherent part of modern warfare, and attempting to avoid such annihilation was no longer a planning constraint.

Reminiscent of the morale bombing issue from before the war and related to the large-scale effect from atomic weapons, the CROSSROADS board concluded:

> In the face of these negative findings, and of the bomb's demonstrated power to deliver death to tens of thousands, of primary military concern will be the bomb's potentiality to break the will of nations and of peoples by the stimulation of man's primordial fears, those of the unknown, the invisible, the mysterious. We may deduce from a wide variety of established facts that the effective exploitation of the bomb's psychological implications will take precedence over the application of its destructive and lethal effects in deciding the issue of war.[17]

Morale was again a major target despite the secondary importance placed on it at ACTS. However, Air Force leadership does not bear sole responsibility regarding the draconian application of nuclear bombardment. While these men did rely on their recent experiences for their targeting and planning methods, they received no real guidance from the Truman administration or civilian leadership regarding the ends expected from a bombing strategy.[18] LeMay recalled that "there wasn't anything that came out of Washington. As a matter of fact, I don't think we got anything out of Washington other than maybe a little guidance on targets that should be hit. We did the plan right up till the time I left [SAC] in 1957."[19] Lt. Gen. Jack Catton, an operations planner at SAC during LeMay's tenure, called SAC the "center of gravity for planning" during this time because only they had the expertise to design a bombing campaign.[20]

Conversely, an article written by the same General Anderson, who responded to the USSBS with the pro–USAF response rebuking the survey's tepid findings, argued for the morality of atomic weapons in light of self-preservation and the defense of democracy. Just after the "Revolt of the Admirals," he published in the winter 1949 issue of AUQR an assertion that in modern war the "soldier and the worker are complementary" and that the idea of strategic bombing as immoral is a "fallacious argument."[21] He further argued that "the informed viewpoint" knows that the western civilization is dependent upon nuclear weapons and military leaders would be "derelict in their duty to the people of the U.S. and the western democracies if they did not fully exploit the power of the air offensive."[22] In closing, General Anderson argues that the United States had a moral obligation "as the champion of the dignity of man and human rights" to defend itself within the means available.[23] In essence, Anderson and many others believed that America had a moral obligation to defend the free world with nuclear weapons.

NSC 20/4

During the budget battle for FY 50, Forrestal queried the State Department in July 1948 to articulate national security goals and objectives in order to establish a baseline for military expenditures. Not until five months later, on November 23, did the State Department publish a document outlining national goals and objectives. "US Objectives with Respect to the USSR to Counter Soviet Threats to US Security," known as NSC 20/4, clearly identified the Soviet Union as the primary threat to U.S. interests and stated that the Russian goal was domination of the world with accompanying expansion of communist ideology. NSC 20/4 specified that Western Europe was the immediate goal for Soviet expansion and that Russian capabilities to expand would continue to grow in the coming years. However, the State Department did not see decisive Soviet military reach extending to the continental United States at that time but did estimate that by 1955 the Red Army would be capable of sustained air attacks with atomic, biological, and chemical strikes.

Additionally, authors of NSC 20/4 did not see evidence that the Soviet Union was planning to conduct deliberate military action to advance its goals. State Department strategists estimated that if war broke out, it would be by miscalculation and blunder. Strategists believed that the Soviets would be too interested in rebuilding their own country and consolidating gains from the previous conflict. Furthermore, still remembering the Great Depression of the 1930s, Stalin believed that the same economic calamity in the West would happen again after the war. If the capitalist world was to suffer the same economic downturn again, communism and the Soviet Union would be the saviors of the world and civilization. Regardless of the capitalist fate, internal domestic actions were seen as the Russians' primary interests, rather than a global military offensive. However, the document speculated that a small insignificant incident might escalate into full-scale war, or that conflict could arise from a "failure of either side to estimate accurately how far the other can be pushed."[24] While the document did not validate the idea that Soviet military action was imminent, if war was to come, NSC 20/4 stated that prosecution of American war aims would reflect national objectives "without a predetermined requirement for unconditional surrender."[25] This statement refers to questions raised earlier. What does this statement mean regarding termination of hostilities? What were the national goals regarding military conflict? What were military planners supposed to use as a metric for victory?

While Forrestal was hoping to gain some traction in the FY 50 fight for defense appropriations, NSC 20/4 did little to help him. In fact the document warned against over-extending the federal budget and supported the argument Truman made regarding the re-establishment of national fiscal solvency. While the policy focused upon leveraging U.S. economic power as opposed to military power, it still provided very little useful information or guidance on military planning, goals, or objectives. For the most part, U.S. foreign policy goals were designed to reduce Soviet influence. In this vein, the U.S. was to encourage the "gradual retraction of undue Russian power and influence from the present perimeter areas around traditional Russian boundaries and the emergence of satellite countries as entities independent of the USSR."[26] The proposed "gradual retraction" was to be accomplished mostly by economic and political means. Toward this end, in addition to the Truman Doctrine, on April 3, 1948, Truman initiated the Marshall Plan in Europe as an effort to stem growing communist influence. As the Soviets exerted their influence in Poland, Romania, Hungary, Bulgaria, and Czechoslovakia, America sought to establish capitalist trading partners in Western Europe.[27] The Marshall Plan not only provided reconstruction opportunities to a worn-torn Europe for humanitarian purposes but also served as an economic bulwark against further communist gains. By encouraging capitalism and sowing the seeds for future markets, the Marshall Plan was a direct attempt to prevent further communist influence in Western European political arenas. The Marshall Plan served in concert with the Truman Doctrine, as the president claimed they were "two halves of the same walnut."[28]

5. National Security Objectives? 95

In the event of war with the USSR, NSC 20/4 directed that the U.S. should "eliminate Soviet Russian domination in areas outside the borders of any Russian state" and "destroy the structure of relationships by which leaders ... of the Communist Party have been able to exert moral and disciplinary authority over individual citizens, groups...."[29] Furthermore, after a potential war, NSC 20/4 intended to prevent the Bolshevik regime from having any military or industrial potential to conduct war with other regimes and expected that "it [the USSR did] not have sufficient military power to wage aggressive war."[30] Based upon these mandates, the USAF still had little definitive guidance from which to plan. As a result, it relied primarily upon its previous bombing experiences as the foundation for targeting methodologies.[31]

Due to the lack of strategic guidance from the national political leadership and with little real understanding of atomic effects, the wartime operational influences would dominate nuclear postwar planning efforts up into the 1950s. Postwar Soviet target sets would be of similar nature to those Axis areas bombed during the war. With the past war's effort clearly in mind, it could be expected that some of the same problems the CBO experienced during the war would have occurred again had an atomic air offensive actually been unleashed. War plans during this time showed very little imagination regarding target sets or Soviet critical vulnerabilities and were especially lacking in intelligence regarding Russian infrastructure, factories, power generation plants, military targets, and transportation nodes. These deficiencies suggest that the execution of the atomic air offensive planned in the late 1940s would have been just as (in)effective, or even less, as the CBO proved to be in the previous conflict.

6

War Plans

In any war plan against the Soviet Union, the first consideration must be an appreciation of the immense geographic size of the country. Physically the USSR was the world's largest country at over 8.5 million square miles. It covered about one-sixth of the earth's land surface, had a border of 37,000 miles, and spanned 11 time zones. While much of the Soviet Union was sparsely populated and a majority of the inhabitants and production capacities were located west of the Ural mountains, the gigantic state could easily house or hide factories, bases, production centers, airfields, and other significant assets. The USSR's vast geographic size dwarfed that of Germany's roughly 138,000 square miles. Even with the advent of atomic weapons, jet technology, and improved airframes, the conduct of an aerial offensive against the USSR was still fraught with strategic and operational obstacles directly related to the size of the Soviet land mass.

When the USAAF conducted the aerial offensive in Europe, it relied upon an air fleet of some 719,000 aircraft, dropping over two million tons of conventional bombs.[1] With the advent of the Cold War and the focus on the Soviet Union as the main threat to U.S. security, the Air Force inherited a postwar mission to conduct a strategic bombing campaign on a nation whose land mass was almost 63 times larger than the former Nazi state! Comparatively, SAC had approximately 1,000 aircraft in the late 1940s to cover this larger area. Additionally, Soviet production centers were dispersed thousands of miles apart and defended by a seemingly robust integrated air defense. While the Germans eventually dispersed their production centers throughout the Reich, the CBO had an appreciably smaller area to target when compared to Soviet land mass. Furthermore, American intelligence officers had very little definitive information about Soviet production centers, factories, infrastructure, and military bases. The closed and secretive nature of Soviet society made intelligence gathering all the more difficult.

During the CBO, the Allies built an Allied Central Interpretation Unit

(ACIU) of some 1,500 officers and men to work in concert with an additional 12,000 signals intelligence troops to provide data on air raids and assess damage inflicted on Axis targets.[2] Supporting this intelligence effort, the Allies eventually flew over 1,000 reconnaissance sorties per month just to obtain images of German targets for photographic analysis.[3] By the end of the war, the ACIU had produced over 30 million prints of Germany and her occupied territories.[4]

With these numbers in mind, obviously the scale and scope of an American strategic bombing campaign against the Soviet Union would require an intelligence effort whose dimension went far beyond any that had proceeded it. Even the Spaatz Board in late 1945 outlined the mandate for a robust postwar intelligence organization that would have current information on the strategic vulnerability, capability, and intention of potential enemies. The collection, interpretation, and dissemination of intelligence for planning and targeting of Soviet infrastructure and military installations would require a massive effort far beyond postwar capabilities. When faced with the very issue of intelligence gathering for planning purposes, General Earle Partridge, Chief of Air Force training, wrote, "The scope of the reconnaissance needed to carry out atomic bomb attacks in Russia staggers my imagination."[5]

Intelligence collection for targeting purposes during the postwar era was very poor and relied largely upon captured German documents, interviews, and U.S. bombing operations from the war.[6] Even basic, up-to-date maps depicting the interior of the Soviet Union were hard to come by. Before 1949, the United States had no agents in the USSR, and following the war, before the CIA was established, there was no concerted effort to collect, coordinate, and disseminate intelligence data. Even when the CIA was established, it merely superimposed itself over a disparate and disjointed community.[7] Despite the specific mention in the USSBS of the importance of shared, accurate, and correct targeting information, SAC had very little data regarding Soviet target sets. In 1950 SAC planners had a skeptical view of CIA collection efforts and believed that it had not fully embraced the enormity of their task. One SAC general considered the CIA's collection efforts as "somewhat of a country store basis with its sights set too low."[8] Most of what SAC obtained came from Project WRINGER, an Air Force initiative started in 1946 in the Far East Command.[9] WRINGER employed 1,800 trained civilians and military personnel in Germany, Austria, and Japan, questioning 300,000 former prisoners of war or soldiers who had served in areas of the Soviet Union.[10]

During the war, millions of Germans were forced to work in Soviet industries, kolkhozes (collective farms), mines, railways, and various work projects. These prisoners were also shuttled from location to location, gaining an appreciation of the areas in which they toiled.[11] While these interviews provided an abundance of information, the data collected was fragmentary and not necessarily current or accurate. Postwar intelligence gathering efforts also included captured German photographs for the areas south and west of the Leningrad-Kazan-Astrakhan-Baku line.[12] Taken during the war, these photos did not show the current state of these locations or if these areas were still legitimate military targets.

The Air Force leveraged the former German Wehrmacht Abwehr intelligence officer Reinhard Gehlen and a ring of associates to help create a clearer picture of Soviet targets. Outside the German photo collection and Abwehr help, the Air Force utilized the espionage services of the Swedes and Turks to help take photographs of select areas of the Russian frontier. However, the vast remainder of the interior Soviet land mass was left unphotographed, leaving a dearth of information for planners. While photos could be taken from oblique angles along the Soviet borders and electronic intelligence (ELINT) could be gathered by specially equipped aircraft flying outside Russian airspace, photographic imagery of the interior targets was sorely lacking. In a vain attempt to obtain such interior photos, as late as 1955 the Air Force released hundreds of high-attitude balloons equipped with cameras and sensors over the Soviet Union. Of the over 500 balloons launched during Project GENETRIX, only 41 were recovered with only 34 providing useful information. The majority of balloons crashed or were captured. The program was cancelled after the development of the U-2 spy plane and the initiation of secret overflights. Until the U-2 program started operational missions, followed by the advent of satellite technology, the United States was left with few intelligence resources regarding interior targets.

Adding to the dearth of information, most of America's photo-reconnaissance assets were focused upon postwar mapping requirements in the United States and occupied Europe and Asia.[13] Until mid–1948, photo-reconnaissance efforts were made for local requirements and tasking and not based upon larger strategic missions.[14] No deep overhead reconnaissance of potential targets was available to planners during the time. While the Air Force did conduct "Ferret" missions that used electromagnetic reconnaissance of Soviet radar systems and air defense, strategic air planners lacked the intelligence data required to develop proper threat assessments and build target sets and associated folders based upon current and accurate information.[15] Furthermore, the radar, electronic, or photographic technology at the time did not provide sufficient definition to assist in adequate target determination or help to establish priorities.[16] The lack of timely and highly reliable overhead reconnaissance was a significant shortfall in strategic threat assessment.

Despite the paucity of information regarding Soviet infrastructure, as early as 1946 the USAAF began compiling a listing of potential sites worthy of bombing.¹⁷ This listing eventually was named the "Bombing Encyclopedia of the World" and by 1947 contained more than 5,000 potential targets, with the ambitious objective of having a listing of every potential target in every country.¹⁸ Using early computing technology and IBM punch cards, in June 1947 the Encyclopedia listed some 4,000 industrial targets in the Soviet Union alone.¹⁹ Analysts developing potential targets sets took their jobs very seriously and proceeded in an academic manner.²⁰ According to one analyst, getting a nominated site into the approved listing was a significant professional achievement.²¹ However, given the paucity of information available to analysts during the immediate postwar era, the quality of the listing and the anticipated secondary and tertiary effects of bombing were of dubious value.

Assisting bomber crews in their duties, the Air Force developed "target folders." These folders contained pertinent information and photos to help crews identify and locate a specific target. The development of target folders was assigned to the Strategic Vulnerability Branch of the Air Staff. This organization had the responsibility of:

(1) Compilation of a world bombing encyclopedia that located potential targets.
(2) Analysis of data compiled in the encyclopedia to include target name, geographic coordinates, function, output and transportation routes.
(3) The creation of target folders for aircrews that contained the specific information for a given target.²²

While concerted efforts were made to obtain as much information as possible, the target folders were devoid of detailed and up-to-date information on potential targets. This calls into question the effectiveness of targeting methodologies. How could the Air Force strike vulnerable target areas if the crews were not sure where they were? This lack of sufficient information for target folders would remain a significant issue until overhead imagery became available.

Much in line with the NSC 20/4, the JCS too did not feel that war with the Soviets was imminent. They believed that the U.S. atomic monopoly, its existing strategic air fleet, capable navy, and strong economic footing would be deterrent enough to prevent the Soviets from trying a major military offensive. The Joint Intelligence Committee (JIC) of the JCS further surmised, much as the State Department did, that the Russians would be too preoccupied with rebuilding their own country after the devastation of the war and that it would take years for them to fully recover. Furthermore, the JIC estimated that the USSR would be too busy domestically and looking to create a security buffer between herself and the Allies in Western Europe. However, that did not mean that the Soviet Union was a toothless threat. In 1946 the

Joint War Plans Committee (JWPC) saw the possibility of accidental war breaking out and thought that it might arise from some minor event, possibly in the Middle East.[23] While there was no specific mention as to what this spark might be, planners speculated that this would come as a result of miscalculation from one or both sides.

The initial postwar plan entitled PINCHER, submitted in April 1946, was intended to serve as a base document for joint war planning for the next few years and was not intended to be a plan worthy of execution.[24] In the PINCHER scenario, a non-specific localized event mushroomed out of control and caused the Soviet Union go on the offensive with over 200 divisions and 14,000 aircraft, seizing the Suez Canal and parts of the Middle East oil reserves.[25] The plan surmised that the USSR would also conduct an accompanying penetration into Western Europe as a hedge against an Allied response to the Soviet Middle East thrust. The estimated time for the beginning of U.S. operations in this scenario was January 1, 1948. Conceding much of Western Europe to the Russians, U.S. planners rejected another OVERLORD amphibious assault operation in Europe and envisioned conducting offensive actions through the Caucus and Dardanelles regions, with subsequent operations driving into the Soviet heartland.[26] Later versions of PINCHER included modification of the Soviet offensives and Allied responses, to include Asia, but this series of plans focus mostly on the European and the Eurasian regions.

PINCHER addressed only the first few months of war and did not outline a fully comprehensive analysis of the conflict or establish criteria for its termination. While a definitive end state was not specified, the concept of operations for PINCHER saw the "liquidation of the Red Army as prohibitive," but believed an "early objective of [the] allied military effort will be the destruction of the war making capacity of the USSR."[27] The Red Army was too big to destroy; the United States had to focus on Soviet production facilities and capabilities.

While the Soviet Union downsized the Red Army after the war, it still had a superior ground combat component compared to Western militaries. American estimates assumed that the Red Army comprised 4.5 million men; 3.15 million in ground forces, 550,000 in the air forces, 300,000 in the navy, and the remaining 500,000 in the security forces.[28] In addition, the Soviet Union could also count on the support of some 84 divisions from satellite countries.[29] Along with its ample ground combat power, the Soviet Air Force could also draw from some 50,000 aircraft of all types.[30] PINCHER deliberately tried to avoid decisive ground combat with the Soviet ground divisions, leveraged U.S. superiority in strategic aircraft, and planned a month's bombing campaign similar to the CBO. Trading ground combat power for air power, the United States pinned its hopes on strategic bombing.

6. War Plans

The Air Force plan under the PINCHER series, entitled MAKEFAST, was submitted in October of 1946 and designed to crush Soviet war-making capacity by bombing "...definite areas which contain a substantial portion of vital resources, without which the Soviet war effort would be seriously curtailed."[31] Initially the Air Force saw the Soviet transportation system as a critical vulnerability and a worthy target. However, requirements for a sustained campaign against the Russian rail network would require an estimated one million tons of bombs.[32] Due to the excessive requirements of targeting Soviet rail lines and the vast distances involved, the Air Force looked at other industries like steel, aircraft, and electrical power. But planners decided that targeting these industries would not yield quick strategic results. As a consequence, air planners decided upon a known liability from the previous bombing campaign: oil production.[33] While it took the CBO almost two years to start targeting Germany's oil production in earnest, Air Force planners focused upon this perceived Soviet critical vulnerability from the very onset. It was thought that some 67 percent of Soviet oil production was located in 17 cities. These cities were designated for atomic attack.[34] About 80 percent of these refineries were within range of B-29s operating out of the United Kingdom or the Cairo-Suez region.[35]

Targets selected reflected the priority given to oil production and included, in order of importance:

(1) Moscow and industrial suburbs
(2) The Baku oil producing and refining area
(3) The Ural industrial centers and the second Baku oil producing area
(4) The Volga railway bridges
(5) The Kuzbass mining and industrial area
(6) The Donbass mining and industrial area
(7) The Ploesti oil producing area[36]

However, the lack of specific information regarding the actual location of factories and production capacities led planners to name 30 urban areas also as targets.[37] In a staff study of the PINCHER plan in April 1946, the lack of intelligence regarding potential Soviet targets was acknowledged as the study reported that "the scarcity of reliable and detail intelligence on the USSR precluded the determination at this time of specific target systems for air attack. Any strategic bombing program established at this time would be provisional...."[38]

Despite the paucity of good intelligence, MAKEFAST surmised that within four months the Air Force would have six B-29 groups operating from Egypt and England using conventional bombs and would destroy three-fourths of Soviet oil production in nine months and cause the Soviet war machine to grind to a halt within a year.[39] Mission profiles would be similar to those of LeMay's XXI Bomber Command in the Pacific during the war, as B-29s would fly at night in bomber streams without fighter escort. Nighttime operations would provide a level of protection, while bombardiers utilized airborne radars for targeting.[40] While it was understood that the Soviets would have a significant integrated air defense, American planners believed that the Russians would use old, American-provided, lend-lease equipment and radars that could be easily jammed by American electronic countermeasures.[41] However, an accurate assessment of Soviet Integrated Air Defense (IAD) was a glaring omission in the planning process.

When MAKEFAST was briefed to Spaatz in December 1946, he directed that an atomic annex be included when such information was available and that the plan be updated regularly.[42] In PINCHER, the use of atomic weapons was implied but without any real specificity. Nowhere in the original draft of PINCHER was explicit use of atomic weapons mentioned, nor was it postulated how they might be used in the offensive.[43] MAKEFAST planners did not have the information regarding the number of bombs in the atomic stockpile or the production rates in order to design a campaign leveraging the technology.

In the February 1947 version of MAKEFAST, entitled EARSHOT, the Air Force included atomic weapons, but it lacked a full definition of requirements to employ the capability. Having to utilize the capabilities of AFSWP and the sole atomic delivery organization, the 509th Bomb Group, EARSHOT postulated dropping one atomic weapon per day for eight days or conducting a one day blitz with eight drops.[44] Again, Air Force knowledge of atomic technology, requirements, and effects was still sorely lacking. The AEC's close-hold on atomic secrets precluded any efficient planning regarding the use of the bomb. But Spaatz hoped that the MAKEFAST plan would serve as a foil for discussion and further refinement of both atomic and conventional bombing requirements and applications.

The plan outlined the use of 50 atomic bombs to be dropped on 20 Soviet cities.[45] This methodology of course had a number of flaws. As discussed previously, the number of atomic bombs available during this time frame was insufficient based upon the targets identified. Also, the logistics of the bombs' assembly, maintenance, and loading requirements would preclude effective forward deployment of the few bomb components available and their associated assembly teams. Absent the logistical considerations and with no coordination with the other military services, in June 1947 the United States still had no detailed operational plan for the use of atomic weapons.[46]

However, MAKEFAST was designed more to highlight what a potential bombing campaign would look like and what it would require rather than an executable war plan. PINCHER was never officially approved by the JCS and served largely as a way to identify requirements and capabilities more than it was a standing operation order or a comprehensive war plan.

Months after the drafting of the PINCHER plans, the Compton Report regarding the CROSSROADS atomic tests was published, arguing that the AEC should reclassify the test results and that the data needed to be shared with the military for planning purposes.[47] Additionally, the report stated that the selection of targets for atomic weapons needed constant updating and reconsideration.[48] Suffering from a paucity of information regarding atomic weapons and their effects, as well as a lack of specific information on potential Soviet targets in late 1946 and early 1947, the framers of PINCHER and MAKEFAST would certainly have agreed with the Compton report findings.

Lastly, while PINCHER was being developed, the Baruch Plan for outlawing nuclear weapons was still being considered by the UN. CNO Admiral Chester Nimitz and military presidential advisor Admiral William Leahy took issue with the inclusion of atomic weaponry in PINCHER. They feared that a potential leak about U.S. efforts to plan for atomic war might be a public-relations disaster, especially with the Baruch Plan pending resolution.[49] However, Spaatz's insistence that it be included was based upon the stipulation that the weapon might not be outlawed altogether.[50] Furthermore, PINCHER/MAKEFAST was also written a year prior to the drafting of NSC 30 and 20/4 and did not incorporate what little national security guidance those documents provided from the president or the NSC. What potential surrender terms would entail and how atomic weapons would fulfill national security objectives and serve as expressions of national policy were questions left unanswered.

Broiler

In July 1947, the Joint Strategic Plans Division (JSPD) drafted a mobilization strategy that signified a substantial change in American war planning. The plan, entitled JWPC 486/7, included a scenario similar to PINCHER and assumed that Europe and parts of Eurasia would be invaded by the Soviets. Again, as with PINCHER, American counter-offensives would not take place in Western Europe but would be southern offensives staged possibly from Turkey and the Balkans and then moving into the Soviet Union. However, JWPC 486/7 leveraged for the first time the atomic monopoly and used that capability as the basis for military operations. JWPC 486/7 was eventually revised and served as the foundation for a war plan entitled BROILER. This deliberate inclusion of atomic weapons was a significant doctrinal break.

While the USAAF lay waste to Axis cities in area bombing raids during the war, it still claimed that precision bombing was its primary methodology. As the war unfolded, precision bombing increasingly gave way to area bombardment for the many reasons stated in the USSBS. While the USAAF

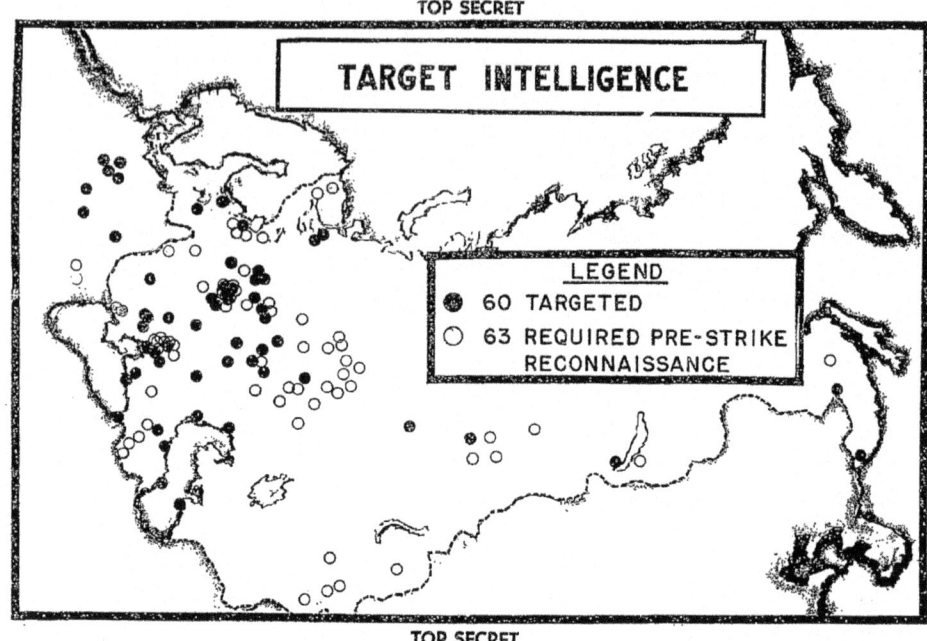

Briefing slide from the April 1950 SAC Commander's Conference depicting planned targets that still required overflight for reconnaissance purposes. Intelligence on many Soviet target locations was severely lacking. In the late 1940s, SAC relied mainly on interviews with POWs and soldiers who had fought the Soviets during the war (Special Collection: Some Key Documents on Nuclear Policy Issues, 1945–1990, edited by William Burr, posted June 15, 2007. http://www2.gwu.edu/~nsarchiv/nukevault/special/).

publically espoused its precision applications, it embraced widespread destruction but never included area bombing as part of its doctrinal foundation. In the BROILER plan, the Air Force, for the first time, tacitly at least, admitted that area bombardment was now acceptable and part of its mode of operation. This planned and deliberate use of atomic ordinance reflected this wholesale change in bombing doctrine as the BROILER plan listed cities themselves as targets.

BROILER recognized the Soviet advantage of superior ground forces and the threat it posed to Allied forces in the occupied areas and Western Europe. The plan updated Red Army strength and estimated it had some 173 divisions with an additional 68 coming from satellite countries along with the mobilization of more than three million reserves.[51] Much like in PINCHER, had the Soviets decided to go on the offensive, there was little Allied ground forces could do to stop the Red Army advance. The use of

6. War Plans 105

atomic weapons was thus less an act of strength and more an admission of U.S. conventional force weakness. The only way to counter Russian conventional strength was with the use of atomic munitions.

As in PINCHER, in the absence of political guidance, the plan did not lay out an envisioned American end state. Recalling the connection between Ends-Ways-Means, was it BROILER's goal to reduce the Soviet Union to its pre–1939 borders, or were planners hoping just to terminate its ability to conduct offensive war as opposed to completely destroying the communist state and its political institutions?[52] Drafting before NSC 20/4, military planners had to devise their own objective and end states. Since the plan reflected no established national goals, the sourcing of sufficient assets and their employment remained incomplete.

Despite the lack of political guidance, the atomic-based strategy in BROILER was founded on three major considerations:

(1) The United States is the only country now possessing atomic bombs.

(2) The United States will possess reasonable stockpiles of atomic bombs at the outset of an emergency, will be in production of atomic bombs during hostilities, and will have the capability of continued and increased production of atomic bombs during hostilities.

(3) No agreement exists for the international control of atomic weapons nor will such agreements be reached during this period.[53]

Still reflective of prewar doctrinal methodologies, BROILER target lists were aimed at key Soviet production capabilities and included both atomic and conventional bombing on:

—key government control facilities
—urban industrial areas
—petroleum industries
—submarine bases and facilities
—transportation system
—aircraft industries
—coke and iron industries
—electrical system[54]

However, in the process of targeting a production facility or capability, it was now understood that the associated city would be destroyed in an atomic attack. The lack of intelligence regarding the specific location of a given factory or refinery meant that the entire city area was now a viable target itself. Exacerbating the intelligence problem, in January 1947 SAC had some 55 reconnaissance aircraft, but by September that number was cut in half to a mere 24.[55] The paucity of intelligence and a reduction in reconnaissance platforms significantly precluded effective targeting.

With kilotons of blasting power available, atomic weapons could destroy multiple targets in a given area with one explosion. As a result, one bomb against a known target might also produce a "bonus effect" of hitting two factories for the "price" of one bomb. This was a significant transformation from previous thinking. When this shift in mindset occurred, a member of the Air Force Intelligence Directorate recognized the change and stated, "I think it was a sort of shock to a lot of people when a few began to talk about bonus effects and industrial capital and particularly when some began to ask what was a city besides a collection of industry."[56]

No longer was the Air Force subscribing to the perception that it bombed with humanitarian precision applications that avoided civilian casualties. Now the civilian populations became included as part of the target set. By targeting population centers, planners saw utility in the psychological shock effect of an atomic offensive. Attacking with atomic munitions would supposedly affect Russian morale, helping to lead to the capitulation of the Soviet Union or at least have an effect on its ability to prosecute war. This same line of reasoning espoused by Guilio Douhet in the interwar years was loosely adhered to by CBO planners. Air planners believed that bombing alone could break the will of the Russian people. However, much like other aspects of the CBO, claims of bombing's effectiveness on national morale are specious. Regardless of the validity of the claim, the air planners still thought morale a worthy target.

These ideas were not universally accepted, as George Kennan retorted that if you bomb Russian cities, "all you will do is convince them that you are barbarians trying to destroy their very way of life."[57] Others argued that targeting the masses would incite such animosity on the part of the Russian people that a guerrilla/partisan war would erupt, lasting years, and that reverberation over the atomic attack would taint any lasting peace.[58] While not deliberately attacking cities, Spaatz argued that the role of air power was not to attack cities per se but to attack the source of enemy strength—which of course happened to be in cities. Furthermore, he still subscribed to the idea that precision strikes might "fatally cripple Soviet industrial power."[59] By conducting these raids with atomic ordnance, planners thought that a devastating blow to Russian military power could bring about a decisive and quick victory. JWPC 486/7 also assumed that such destruction would disrupt Soviet society to such an extent that the physical damage would also manifest into psychological shock. This psychological shock and its effects on national morale might lead to the capitulation of the Soviets or at least prevent them from continuing the war.[60]

This idea of hitting a "collection of industry" eventually became the foundation of targeting strategies. In 1951, three years after LeMay assumed command of SAC, he already realized that pre-strike reconnaissance and attacks and varied and disparate target locations would be a difficult task, even for SAC's resources. Finding targets in hostile, unfamiliar terrain within the immense Soviet land mass was difficult enough. In an effort to maximize the striking power of his command and cause a more devastating blow to the enemy, LeMay believed that SAC should focus on industries in urban areas, so that if a bomb missed its primary target, other infrastructure might be damaged—thus the "bonus effect" might result.[61] This methodology would also make the most efficient use of the limited supply of materials available in the atomic stockpile.

BROILER was first briefed on November 8, 1947.[62] In the scenario, war was initiated by the Soviets in 1948 and was to last some three years.[63] It utilized existing forces as a base line for planning and envisioned the United States using atomic weapons from the very onset of hostilities. Bombers would launch strategic air strikes from bases in North America, the United Kingdom, and the Cairo-Suez area. The use of atomic weapons would not only retard the Soviet offensive in a few months but would then be used to help regain lost territory by reducing Soviet war production.[64] The target list was probably based upon the one established in 486/7 and called for 34 bombs on 24 cities.[65] Cities targeted in 486/7 included Moscow (seven bombs), Leningrad (three), Kharkov and Stalingrad (two each), and 20 other cities (one each).[66] Additionally, the plan assumed that after the initial strikes, the United States would have an available atomic bomb reserve of 100 percent follow-on attacks if required.[67]

However, the plan incorrectly assumed that the United States would have a stockpile of 100 to 200 bombs available.[68] In June 1948 the nation had only 50 implosion-design weapons on hand—or at least in pieces stored at Sandia—with components for only two gun-type bombs.[69] Planners admitted that they had scant knowledge of the number of bombs available and production capacities, and it can be assumed that they had very little knowledge of the AFSWP and its limitations at the time.[70] Logistical consideration for forward deployment and assembly of atomic weapons was also unknown by the planners, and the service's ability to stage such operations was questionable at best. Also unknown to the planners at this time were the woeful state of SAC and its lack of operational readiness for combat. Crews were largely undertrained to conduct such operations, and their ability to successfully complete their mission was doubtful. In fact in the beginning of 1948, only a few crews were fully trained to drop atomic ordnance.[71] While in the case of a national emergency it was estimated that another fourteen crews might be quickly trained, the number was still short of what the operation called for, especially in light of potential combat and operational losses.[72]

In addition to the operational and tactical problems, the limitations of the B-29 and B-50 aircraft in the atomic offensive were also inescapable. Even with the absence of Soviet interceptors and an IAD, many bombers might find themselves on a one-way mission based upon the target location.

B-50 in flight. While similar in look to the B-29, the B-50 had only a 25 percent commonality with the B-29. The B-50 was powered by the R-4360 engine that was also used in the B-36. It too was designated a "medium" bomber and, along with the B-29, carried a majority of the workload in published war plans (U.S. Air Force photograph).

BROILER was written in fall 1947 before the intercontinental B-36 bomber was fielded to operational units. Introduced into the bomber fleet in late 1948, the B-36 had a combat range of 4,000 miles as compared to the B-29's 3,000 miles. However, atomic-capable versions of the B-36 were not introduced into the fleet until mid–1949. The same could be said for the updated version of the B-29, designated the B-50. Until the B-36 was introduced into the operating forces, planners had to rely on the shorter-range B-29s for the atomic assault.

Another issue faced atomic planners: up to 20 percent of the BROILER targets were outside of the B-29's combat range. While the B-29 was designated as a "very heavy bomber" during the war and was built for long-range bombing missions from Asia Minor to Europe, the size of the Soviet Union and its disparate target sets proved a challenge. As a result, these targets might be hit by use of a single B-29 on a "one-way trip" to bomb its target. This idea was proposed in AUQR, with the author arguing that "our inadequate air bases, coupled with the relatively short range of our B-29s, makes one way combat a necessity for the immediate future if we are to employ our air power offensively in such a way as to be victorious."[73] Supportive of this idea was Major General Earl Partridge, who stated: "Expend the crew, expend the bomb, expend the airplane all at once. Kiss them goodbye and let them go. That is a pretty cold blooded point of view, but I believe that it is economically best for the country."[74] Obviously many within the command took umbrage with the issue of a one-way trip, as General Tommy Powers, Deputy Assistant Chief of Staff for Operations, commented, "[Crews] are not stupid ... they might change plans many times along the way."[75]

SAC only had thirty-two atomic-capable bombers in the inventory at the end of 1947.[76] These precious few bombers had logged many flight hours and were described as "quite weary."[77] Sending a single aircraft on one of these one-way missions would have serious implications for the bombing fleet, as the number of available atomic-capable aircraft would drop with each one-way sortie. The same could be said about the scarce number of atomic-qualified aircrew as well. This was especially important given the paucity of atomic-trained crews. Any one-way trip with these specially trained crews would have seriously degraded the command's pool of available manpower. Until the atomic bombing fleet was flush with both capable aircraft and trained aircrews, the aerial offensive required in BROILER was seriously deficient in equipment and capability.

Even if the American atomic bombing fleet was fairly robust in aircrews, aircraft, and atomic ordnance, the attacking bombers would be facing a formidable Soviet IAD. By 1948 it was estimated that the Soviet Air Defense Fighter Force, entitled ProtivoVozdushnaya Oborona Strany (PVO Strany), had a strength of some 1,600 fighters, including 1,200 jet aircraft of various airframes.[78] These fighters could also be augmented in the interception mission by aircraft from the Red Army and Soviet Navy. Planners estimated that attacking bombers could possibly experience interception three times: passing over the communist border, at the target area, and during withdrawal again at the border.[79] Furthermore, estimates stated that some Soviet aircraft were fully capable of operating at altitudes as high as 40,000 feet with speeds up to 465 knots, easily capable of catching the lumbering bombers.[80] While some Soviet aircraft were of dubious quality, by the end of 1949, the Soviet Union had produced and fielded up to 3,600 very capable MiG-15 fighters. This same fighter would eventually become the bane of existence of B-29 crews flying over North Korea.[81]

In support of the fighters, it was assumed that the Soviets had an extensive early warning radar system with sufficient coverage for the entire Soviet border plus redundant coverage for critical areas.[82] However, it was also surmised that the Russians had only limited Ground Control Intercept (GCI) coverage that SAC crews might be able to work around and evade.[83] But a full assessment of Soviet GCI capabilities as late as 1950 was still incomplete. Electronic reconnaissance of GCI operations found that the Soviets leveraged American-equipped lend-lease radars while also producing some capabilities of their own.[84] Even if the GCI radars and fighters were successfully avoided, crews were still faced with some of the same issues that the USAAF struggled with during the war—potentially bad weather, navigation error over a large area, high-speed winds aloft, and crew fatigue.

The Soviets also maintained a substantial Anti-Aircraft Artillery (AAA) force. While the West shifted its primary focus of air defense to Surface-to-Air Missiles (SAM), the Soviets maintained a robust program of AAA development. After the war the Soviets introduced new AAA designs (100mm, 57mm, and 130mm) with vertical ranges over 38,000 feet.[85] As late as 1950, planners were unable to predict how much AAA the Soviets had available but estimated some 10,000 to 15,000 guns. This is comparable to the 12,000 that the Germans had during the war.[86] Analysts estimated that the Soviets probably utilized captured German equipment, including some 3,500 88mm guns, 3,500 "Taifun" rocket launchers, and 8,000 conventional guns.[87] Threat assessments also stated that the readiness of the Soviet air defense system, like much of the strategic targeting information, was largely unknown. Training, manning, and competency of the Russian anti-air systems would have been a key component regarding IAD efficiency. While their wartime experience might result in a fully competent Soviet IAD, how often they exercised the capability could not be determined.[88] This was a glaring omission in the planning process.

In totality the BROILER plan clearly illustrated deficiencies in the planning for the atomic air offensive and highlighted resourcing problems both in numbers of bombs available and aircraft. Inadequate threat analysis combined with a lack of intelligence information regarding the targets compromised the effectiveness of the overall air campaign. While BROILER clearly represented the embrace of the atomic offensive as an acceptable military strategy, targeting both infrastructure and national morale, it also highlighted inherent problematic issues.

HALFMOON

While PINCHER and BROILER served as touchstones for the use of U.S. airpower in a confrontation with the Soviets, both plans largely eschewed the defense of Western Europe. In the plans Western Europe was at the mercy of Soviet forces while liberation was ancillary to U.S. offensives coming from the Middle East. In March 1948 with the crisis in Berlin starting to fester and with the February Czechoslovakia coup d'état freshly in mind, the United States was looking at the defense of Western Europe as a priority. With this concern in mind, the United States began considering its Allies, specifically Great Britain and Canada, as part of the war effort and included them in the planning process. In May 1948 a new war plan entitled HALFMOON had Allied nations working separate operations, but functioning together in a coordinated manner in defense of Europe. Drawn up as the Berlin Crisis was beginning to escalate, HALFMOON's execution would include the British and Canadians working a "unilateral but accordant" plan for a defense against Soviet aggression.[89]

HALFMOON was not a comprehensive war plan but was developed as an emergency, short-range measure based upon recent events unfolding in Europe.[90] Looking much like BROILER, the plan envisioned a Soviet attack starting in 1949 and beginning with a Soviet offensive into the Middle East. The Soviet assault south was again accompanied by a thrust into Western Europe. However, unlike previous scenarios, the HALFMOON plan did not forgo the defense of Europe entirely and tacitly leave the continent to Soviet forces. Still acknowledging the superiority of Soviet ground combat power, the plan specified that Allied forces conduct a fighting withdrawal in the European continent with U.S. forces pulling back to the Rhine River. If further withdrawal was required, these units would then conduct a delaying action in the face of the Soviet advance. Allied forces would conduct combined operations with their American partners while evacuating the continent as the tactical situation unfolded. Similarly, the plan also envisioned a Red Army advance into China, Manchuria, and Korea. Given that HALFMOON was an emergency war plan, it was based upon the maximum utilization of U.S. forces and estimated combat power initially available during the first year of the war.[91] The Cairo-Suez region again was prominent in the plan as it served as a strategic base for subsequent operations.[92] In the Far East it was estimated that U.S. forces would withdraw to Japan, but stand and defend the island nation while supporting nationalist forces in China and conducting strategic operations from Okinawa.

Planners assumed that the authority to use atomic weapons would be approved and planned SAC missions out of bases in England (or alternatively in Iceland), the Cairo-Suez area, and Okinawa.[93] Atomic bombing would again be conducted on selected, vital elements of Soviet war-making industry, of which urban industrial area concentrations were the highest-priority targets. HALFMOON planned to hit 210 objectives, 70 of which were major urban centers.[94] The plan specified Moscow and Leningrad as the targets for the first attacks because these cities held a concentration of Soviet production.[95] Much as in BROILER, these urban strikes were planned to have severe psychological effects on the Soviet citizenry and help lead toward the capitulation of the communist state. Morale again was a target. Additionally, petroleum production was also a significant objective, as planners surmised that ten refineries in Russia, and 72 percent of total Soviet petroleum production, would be neutralized by atomic attack in the first 70 objectives.[96] In addition to the use of atomic weapons, SAC would also conduct a conventional bombing campaign on the Soviet transportation networks and hydro-electric plants and a mining campaign on important waterways and port areas.[97] Given what the AEC had on hand for atomic components, the plan was already deficient in the amount of atomic ordnance required.

However, for the first time the plan included the use of U.S. naval forces in the strategic air-power mission, but carrier aviation's role was not clearly defined. Navy aircraft carriers were to "supplement and support the air offensive to the extent practical consistent with their primary task."[98] Obviously this vague, ill-defined wording was a result of the ongoing fight between the Air Force and Navy over roles and missions and their all-important fiscal implications. The inclusion of carrier aviation reflects the emerging FY 50 budget battles between the Air Force and Navy and echoes some of the points made at the Key West conference of March. This inclusion of the Navy also had implications at the Newport Conference in August when the Air Force assumed primary sponsorship of the AFSWP.

Whether or not Navy carriers were included, the use of atomic weapons played a key factor in the success of the operation. While a defense of Western Europe was intended, the Allies still had very little to work with given the number of ground forces in the region. Much like earlier plans, HALF-MOON was absent larger national security objectives or defined military goals. Military planners assumed that there was no mandate for unconditional surrender but that Soviet capitulation was a requirement.[99] Like BROILER, HALFMOON was drafted before the publishing of NSC 20/4. Assumptions on end state were tacitly made by the military and were presumed to be similar to earlier plans that intended to reduce Soviet gains to its 1939 border and destroy its ability to conduct aggressive military operations. Outside military applications, domestically HALFMOON also had its utility, as it assisted in the budget battle for FY 50 and served as a baseline for planned military expenditures. Forrestal's Budget Advisory Committee used the force structure listed in HALFMOON when it met in summer 1948 to determine military requirements for the upcoming fiscal fight.

When the Berlin Airlift began on 26 June 1948, Truman not only ordered (non-atomic-capable) B-29 deployment to the United Kingdom, but also sent C-54 transport planes from the Military Air Transport Service (MATS) to assist in the airlift effort.[100] The requirements of the airlift grew exponentially, and at a 22 July NSC meeting, Truman ordered an additional 75 C-54s to Europe to support the effort. This deployment of cargo aircraft was done over the objections of Air Force Chief Hoyt Vandenberg.[101] This tasking of

C-54s had serious implications for the HALFMOON plan. The commitment of the cargo planes to the Berlin Airlift threatened SAC's ability to deploy men and material to the Cairo-Suez, United Kingdom, and Okinawa air bases.[102] Vandenberg objected to the C-54 deployment based upon SAC's lift requirements. The Air Force Chief also expressed concern that if war did break out, many of the cargo aircraft in Europe would be lost to enemy action, creating an even bigger lift deficiency.[103] By September, another request had been forwarded that the airlift employ 248 C-54s, a figure that represented 52 percent of the fleet.[104]

Had the Berlin crisis escalated to full-scale war, the few atomic bombers SAC had on hand could flight-ferry to their designated forward airbases. However, SAC would have been hard-pressed to deploy associated maintenance equipment and personnel in support of bombing operations due to the lack of airlift. Atomic bombing operations at all three locations were to begin on D-15 with conventional bombing operations starting on Okinawa on D-Day.[105] The logistical effort of staging, loading, unloading, and organizing forward airfields to support atomic bombing operations would have been difficult from an airlift perspective alone. While atomic bombs were few, components for the weapons could be flown in the bombers, but the lack of lift support would have affected the movement of support equipment to the airfield locations. While Okinawa probably had sufficient stocks of conventional bombs and equipment on hand remaining from the war, it is doubtful that the same could be said for the UK and Cairo-Suez locations. This lack of logistical support also begs the question as to how bulk fuel support and other important airfield functions would have been established, especially at the Cairo-Suez location.

For atomic bomb transportation, it was too risky, and difficult, to load a completely assembled bomb into a B-29 and fly it over the United States to a forward base. An inadvertent drop of a weapon or the potential crashing of a B-29 was too big a hazard with a fully fused weapon in the plane's bomb bay. Only a partially assembled weapon would be loaded into a bomber for forward deployment. Throughout most of 1947, the AFSWP and Sandia's "Z Division" worked on procedures to assemble bombs at forward locations.[106] As mentioned previously, during Operation AJAX, the RAT-FAT method allowed the safe movement of the weapon but required a forward-deployed assembly team and associated equipment to fully arm the bomb. The AFSWP forward location assembly effort included a 20' × 100' expeditionary building that could be flown to a forward area and provide shelter for the assembly process.[107] This process was augmented by an airborne capability called CHICKENPOX that allowed assembly of the weapon in a specially configured C-97 aircraft. While CHICKENPOX seemed like an elegant solution, it had its limitations and was not necessarily a satisfactory solution to the issue of forward assembly. While some preliminary work and coordination had been done in the United Kingdom regarding the staging and storage of weapons components, very little was done at the proposed Cairo-Suez and Okinawa sites.

In addition to the deployment of assets and material to the forward locations, the number of assembly teams from the AFSWP would also be a problem. As discussed earlier, three SWU teams were established to support the assembly operations, but a paucity of equipment and support personnel plagued their operations. In order to field a single SWU team, the other two teams were required to hand over equipment and personnel to build a complete team to support MK III assembly operations.[108] With planned atomic bombing operations conducted from three disparate locations, fielding a complete SWU was difficult, if at all possible. Eventually the number of teams and weapons available would grow, but in 1948–49 the ability to support a deliberate and continuous bombing campaign in the near future made HALFMOON unfeasible.

Concurrently, the emergency nature of the HALFMOON war plan would have been difficult given the tense AEC and AFSWP relationship. While coordination for the transfer of mechanical components from the AEC to the AFSWP had started, transfer procedures of fissionable components were not yet fully established. The first test of such transfers was not done until December 14, 1948, in an exercise called Operation UNLIMITED. The process for the transfer was clumsy and complicated. General K. D. Nichols of the MLC had his doubts about the efficacy of the procedures. At the time he was unconvinced of the AEC's ability to conduct a handover of atomic components in certain emergency situations. Concerned about the recently established transfer procedures, he said, "There were too many possibilities for a SNAFU to contemplate making the plan a permanent part of our defense planning. For the present we had to live with it—I hoped not for long."[109] Concurrently, the Air Staff's Atomic Energy Office also realized that it had no procedure for the emergency transfer of atomic weapons.[110] Lt. General Jack Catton, one of SAC's air division commanders, commented that it was a "very complicated transfer procedure from the AEC to SAC ... there were so many hurdles ... it was ridiculous."[111] In the case of war, undoubtedly procedures would eventually have been developed to effect a transfer of fissionable materials. But HALFMOON was an emergency war plan, and had it been ordered to execute, the ability to deploy the bombers, acquire access to atomic ordnance, and support assembly operations abroad would have been problematic at the very start.

Aside from the airlift problems, other logistics considerations hamstrung HALFMOON execution. While the priority of lift support was an issue needing to be rectified given the current fleet of MATS at the time, a report by the Joint Logistics Plans Committee (JLPC) to the JSPC estimated that the U.S. forces had a lack of aircraft and spare parts and added that facilities at the air bases in the Cairo-Suez region were substandard given their intended use.[112] The lack of aircraft and spare parts did not necessarily make HALF-MOON unfeasible in the opinion of the JLPC. However, the deficiency in worldwide aviation engineering support units for airfield development and improvement rendered the plan impractical.[113] SAC staffers determined that bases in the Cairo-Suez region designated for use required extensive improvement and construction before they could support sustained air operations.[114] While the area had a number of airfields, it had only one regular airfield and one emergency field over 7,000 feet long and two other airfields 6,000–7,000 feet long.[115]

A 7,000 foot runway was certainly ample for most aircraft of the day, but a fully loaded B-29 carrying a MK III bomb on that length of runway was only marginally adequate. When the *Enola Gay* took off for its fateful mission on 6 August 1945, carrying the "Little Boy" gun-type design bomb, pilot Paul Tibbets reported using "every inch of runway" of the 8,000 feet for take-off.[116] When *Bocks Car* took off on August 9 for the attack on Nagasaki, with the heavier MK III weapon, pilot Charles Sweeney also used all of the available runway.[117] With these missions as a precedent, airfields in that Cairo-Suez region would need at a minimum a runway extension and improvement before they could be used as staging bases for both atomic and conventional bombing attacks. In a classified briefing in April 1950, the issue of runway length came to the fore at facilities in the United Kingdom. In the course of the discussion the 6,000 foot runways at select bases in England were described as "inadequate for the B-29 and marginal for the B-50."[118]

Furthermore, bombing operations required more than just runways. Engineers would be required to build adequate support facilities like maintenance spaces, bomb dumps, taxiways, and parking aprons. However, adequate engineering support was at a premium in the postwar defense establishment. In the plan, by D+6 months the Army and Air Force needed 73 construction battalions, but only 23 were available, and of those, only 15 were fully trained.[119] Prioritization of the few assets available would have been a requirement. To make the plan workable, these engineering assets would have had to be committed to the bombing effort at the very beginning and to the detriment of other taskings. If committed to the bombing effort, the engineers would need to move their assets and equipment into the theater as soon as possible. Given the requirement to improve these runways and associated facilities, combined with the lack adequate airlift, preparing airfields for bombing raids in accordance with the specified timeline would have been difficult.[120]

However, an Air Force evaluation on HALFMOON published in December

1948 recognized that the plan had issues associated with it but said that the overall strategic effort was feasible.[121] The evaluation acknowledged that both personnel and material shortfalls existed but stated that the strategic bombing effort would work if "accorded first priority ... even though the Berlin Airlift is continued at its contemplated level."[122] Painting a rather positive picture, the Air Force claimed it had sufficient intelligence and specific data on planned targets, downplayed the Soviet fighter interceptor threat and GCI capabilities, and estimated an initial loss rate of only 25 percent.[123] However, CNO Denfeld took issue with the Air Force report and called into question its impartiality. While accepting some tenets of the Air Force position, in his rebuttal Denfeld argued "that the national interests ... demand that this subject receive both joint intelligence evaluation and joint operational evaluation before any interim estimate of chances of success and the risk involved be made."[124] The effects of the Denfeld rebuttal had implications for later evaluations of strategic bombing plans and eventually led to the establishment of the Weapons System Evaluation Group (WSEG).

In total, the HALFMOON plan suffered from some of the same issues outlined in BROILER regarding the size of the U.S. stockpile, the nation's strategic bombing capabilities at the time, and the lack of comprehensive intelligence on potential targets. HALFMOON also had other equipment and personnel shortfalls that seriously affected its execution outside the strategic atomic attack. While the strategic bombing effort was the priority, the same problems inherited from earlier plans combined with the paucity of airlift, trained assembly teams, engineering support, and adequate airfield/facilities would seriously have hampered the strategic bombing execution as specified in the plan

OFFTACKLE

In January 1949, an updated emergency war plan was forwarded that provided better definition of the strategic bombing effort and included a few minor modifications regarding potential U.S. allies. Called TROJAN, the plan was similar to HALFMOON, but its biggest difference was its inclusion of a more detailed annex addressing specific targets sets and an increased list of cities designated for attack. TROJAN had the Air Force hit 70 cities with some 147 atomic bombs, again focusing largely upon Soviet petroleum and other war-related industries. Eight bombs were designated for Moscow and another seven were intended for Leningrad.[125] The first atomic attacks would occur on D+9 and would include some 20 strikes.[126] In the plan the JCS again assumed that the stockpile of atomic weapons would support such an offensive. But by this time the atomic stockpile may have been large enough to support the number of atomic strikes planned. While the stockpile of components was enough to build some 50 MK IIIs in June 1948, there is no accounting of what the total was a year later in 1949. However, by June 1950, the number of nuclear components was sufficient to make at least 292 weapons of either the implosion (MK III) or gun-type ("Little Boy") design.[127] As a result it is reasonable to assume that the stockpile by June 1949 might have been approximately 150 bombs, a sufficient number to service all the initial targets. Concurrently the number of trained assembly teams in 1949 was estimated at five to seven, again a sufficient number to assemble the atomic ordnance.[128]

TROJAN still inherited the same logistical issues of HALFMOON and did not rectify the existing unit and equipment shortfalls. Budgetary constraints precluded any improvement on the force structure issues, and given Truman's fiscal policies, execution of the plan was nearly impossible as a result of the logistical challenges. Similarly, Dwight Eisenhower in his role as acting chairman of the Joint Chiefs in early 1949 also thought the plan incomplete, not because of logistics issues, but largely because it did not sufficiently defend Western Europe. For Ike, the control of Europe was essential and required that a "substantial bridgehead" be maintained for the reintroduction of U.S. forces into the continent. Furthermore, he envisioned a possible assault through the western Mediterranean while only conducting a holding action in the Middle East.[129] With this in mind, Ike thought that this course of action might expedite an earlier return to Western Europe and invite "communization of that area with long term disastrous effects on U.S. national interest."[130] As a result, the JSPC was directed to develop a new emergency war plan based upon a number of considerations: Eisenhower's ideas and concerns, an envisioned force structure planned for FY 1950, a two-year commitment to war, and a 1 July 1949 start.[131]

A new plan was developed over the course of 1949 by the JSPC and submitted to the JCS on 8 November. Approved by the JCS on December 8, the new plan, entitled OFFTACKLE, officially replaced TROJAN. OFFTACKLE was something new, as it was the first plan to reflect political guidance regarding national security goals and objectives. With NSC 20/4 approved a year earlier in November 1948, military planners for the first time designed a war plan that included atomic weapons and had overarching political guidance. From NSC 20/4, JCS planners realized that war plans need not require unconditional surrender of the Soviet Union and only need mandate the reduction of her ability to prosecute war. However, NSC 20/4's input to planners was minimal, as it merely validated that national defense planning should focus on war against the Soviets, an obvious consideration. Furthermore, how the military was supposed to reach the goals outlined in NSC 20/4 was still unanswered. Lastly, guidance provided by NSC 20/4 was also only marginally useful, as OFFTACKLE dealt with opening phases of the war, not necessarily the entire conflict. But based upon tenets of 20/4, the military could safely assume that the war they planned against the Soviets would not be limited, but total and unrestricted. While NSC 20/4 did not necessarily provide a definitive military end state, and OFFTACKLE was not a comprehensive plan, at least some national political guidance was provided to the military for the first time. This was an important first step.

OFFTACKLE was similar to its predecessors regarding Soviet offensive thrusts in Europe, Asia, and the Middle East, with the war coming about because of miscalculation. However, as a result of the Marshall Plan, some planners thought that war might come about as the Soviets might wish to reduce the U.S. influence in the economic and political future of Europe.[132] With the U.S. trying to stem communist influence in Western Europe, the Marshall Plan had both humanitarian and political objectives at its core. By providing stimulus to capitalism in the European economies, the Soviets may have perceived the Marshall Plan as an economic and political threat.

As in previous plans, the Allies would try to hold a strategic defense in Asia while a delaying or denial action occurred in Europe. Again, the atomic air offensive would serve as a cornerstone of the U.S. response. However, the plan included some new additions, both detrimental for the United States. Chiang Kai-shek's Kuomintang would fall to Mao and his forces. As a result, Red China would aid the Russians in the goal of global communist expansion. Additionally, planners assumed, quite correctly, that the Soviets would have an atomic capability, but estimated further that they would have up to 30 atomic weapons at their disposal.[133] As a result of this development, planners assumed that both sides would use atomic weapons.

OFFTACKLE planned that the United States would again start its offensives based upon an atomic air campaign. However, what was markedly different from other plans was that the intent was now to "destroy" Soviet war-making capacity, not merely be directed "against" it.[134] This change in wording and intent was reflected in an early draft of Air Force Chief Spaatz's article for *Collier's* magazine when he claimed that future war "[will be] designed to destroy an enemy's home base and spare him nothing."[135] In addition, the plan also called for atomic weapons to be used against the Soviet Red Army in what was referred to as "retardation." While trying to defend Western Europe on the ground against a Soviet juggernaut, the Army would need the support of air power to hold a defensive line at the Rhine River, or, as later revised, to support a fighting retreat hoping to retain the "bridgehead" Ike envisioned.[136] Later it was thought that retaining even the "bridgehead" was unfeasible. However, with a paucity of tactical air, the Army looked to the strategic offensive as a way to help "retard" the Soviet ground advance. Using strategic bombers with atomic weapons, the Air Force would conduct deep interdiction strikes at certain Soviet lines of communication.[137] Unusual for the time, but the services came to agreement on the idea of retardation with planned targets including the enemy's transportation lines, arms factories, and oil industries.[138] While not intending to use atomic weapons directly against the Soviet forces in the field, the stated objectives of the air offensive not only required the "destruction of vital elements of enemy war-making capability" but now included the "retardation of enemy advances in western Eurasia."[139] However, once LeMay assumed command of SAC he found that the idea of retardation was a waste of scarce resources and that it detracted from his command's primary mission of strategic bombardment. For him, this looked more like interdiction than strategic bombing.

In OFFTACKLE, the scale and scope of the strategic air offensive was larger than previous plans. Air Force planners looked to target Soviet industry, eliminate political control over the USSR, undermine the will and morale of the Russian people, and disarm the Red Army.[140] The offensive's objective was to bring to a halt Soviet production capabilities and war-supporting capabilities while, as in previous plans, causing chaos in the Russian labor force and her people. To do this, targets sets reflected those listed in earlier plans. But with the atomic stockpile starting to grow appreciably, and with the introduction of the new longer range B-36 bomber into the fleet in 1948, the Air Force's capabilities were just beginning to match some of the planned objectives. B-36s would fly from bases in the continental United States and, during the summer months, from bases in Alaska. At the time Eielson Air Force Base did not have the facilities to support B-36 operations during the winter months, as the ambient temperature dropped as low as -30 degrees. The B-36 would fly over the Arctic to targets in the Soviet Union and then require an airfield somewhere in the Middle East.

In addition, by mid–1949, the Air Force had six bomb assembly teams with more in training to support atomic ordnance operations. OFFTACKLE was a four-phase campaign that targeted 26 Soviet war-making industries by dropping 220 atomic bombs in 104 urban centers.[141] Supporting the long-range mission, in addition to the B-36, the Air Force began looking at the idea of using aerial tanking for refueling operations to extend the range of the bombers. Reconfiguring existing airframes to pass fuel to bombers while airborne was a significant advancement and greatly increased the range of the fleet. In March 1948 SAC acquired a "looped-hose" system from the British and experimented with it at Wright-Patterson Air Force Base. While an awkward configuration, the system did work. As a result, the Air Force began converting B-29s into refueling platforms, with extra fuel pods added into the bomb bays and a hose and reel system. These modified Superfortresses, designated KB-29s, were just arriving at bases in late 1948, but they would not become fully operational until 1949. By April 1950, SAC had 77 KB-29s all equipped with the British system. However, refinement of aerial refueling was still required before this methodology could be used in combat conditions. While inflight refueling would eventually mature, SAC was only expected to have a limited capability by May 1950.[142]

Using force structure numbers planned for May 1, 1950, the Air Force would have some 570 medium bombers (B-29/B-50) and 54 heavy bombers (B-36) available.[143] For atomic delivery, a force of some 300 bombers would be employed. OFFTACKLE was an ambitious plan that utilized all three strategic bombing airframes in the SAC arsenal, with 6,000 sorties required in the first phase of the operation.[144] B-50s would strike just over half (51 percent) of the targets flying, from the United Kingdom, along with B-29s hitting 35 percent.[145] The newly operational B-36 would service the remaining 14 percent.[146] To maximize the psychological impact, the atomic strikes were to be made in a relatively short period of time with the majority of missions flown in the first 30 days.[147] Phase I of the plan, lasting some three months, included both conventional and atomic attacks with MK III– or MK IV–laden aircraft accompanied by similar escort planes providing electronic countermeasure (ECM) support. A cell of attacking aircraft would consist of three to five planes flying at about one-minute intervals between platforms.[148]

With Truman's fiscal mandate, OFFTACKLE still reflected problems of an inadequately equipped military. In December 1948, Air Force Chief of Staff Vandenberg submitted JCS 1952/1 that evaluated the existing HALFMOON/TROJAN plan. In the evaluation the Air Force argued that despite requirements of the Berlin airlift, a lack of solid target intelligence information, unknown status of Soviet IAD, and paucity of atomic weapons, "a powerful strategic air offensive against vital elements of the Soviet war-making capacity could be delivered as planned."[149] The report at least admitted that certain risks were involved regarding basing, personnel, and material, but these shortfalls could be overcome without "unduly jeopardizing the successful execution of the strategic air offensive."[150] In the continuing fight between the Navy and the Air Force over roles and missions, JCS 1952/1 was again called into question by CNO Denfeld. The Air Force's dubious conclusions in 1952/1 were challenged by a review conducted by the newly formed Weapons System Evaluation Group. The genesis of the WSEG started months earlier, when in October 1948 Forrestal began to call into question the chances of successful delivery of atomic bombs and their effect on the Soviet war effort. Officially established on 11 December, the same month 1952/1 was submitted, the WSEG was to "provide rigorous, unprejudiced, and independent analysis and evaluation of present and future weapon systems under probably future combat conditions ... prepared by the most advanced analytical methods that can be brought to bear."[151] The

WSEG continued in this role until 1976, and during its existence, it was tasked to provide "an impartial, supra-service perspective" regarding defense-related matters.[152] Initially headed by Lieutenant General John E. Hull of the Army, a 22-man military-civilian team evaluated OFFTACKLE and its operational tenets in January 1950 and submitted their findings in February.

In the WSEG's assessment, serious problems existed with the feasibility of the OFFTACKLE plan. OFFTACKLE required three times the number of sorties that SAC had the ability to execute during the plan's opening phase. With the current air fleet, SAC could only support roughly 2,000 sorties during Phase I of the operation, far short of the 6,000 planned.[153] The WSEG also estimated that SAC could conduct 1,500–2,000 sorties for about two months, but only if the command was given priority over the rest of the Department of Defense for airlift support.[154] Estimates by SAC claimed that it required 360 C-54 equivalent sorties to be completed in the first few weeks. However, MATS reported that only 260 sorties were available to SAC.[155] Given Ike's mandate regarding the defense of Western Europe, other elements of the military establishment would no doubt require significant airlift support. As a result, the prioritization of airlift solely for SAC use was highly unlikely.

A shortage of B-29s and B-50s was also seen as a problem, given mission requirements to support other SAC operations outside the strategic bombing effort. The WSEG noted that while the number of B-36s available was sufficient, a shortage of spare parts for B-50s, and possibly B-29s, would seriously affect medium bomber sortie generation.[156] In the OFFTACKLE Commander's Conference of April 1950, the shortage of medium bombers came to the fore. The war plan assumed that a fleet of 1,800 stored B-29s would be available for use, but at the time of the brief, the stored airframes were due to be reduced.[157] Furthermore, Phase I required an excessive amount of 100/130 aviation gasoline and jet fuel. Bulk fuel either in the current military supply or available in the emergency war reserve was insufficient to support planned Phase I operations. However, WSEG did find that sufficient amounts of fuel would eventually be available in subsequent phases.[158]

Additionally the WSEG found the number of available airbases in the United Kingdom to support medium bomber operations was inadequate, and some of those available were deficient in facilities.[159] Distribution of fuel and aviation gas at United Kingdom bases was also identified by SAC planners as a problem.[160] While bases in the United Kingdom were too few, in the WSEG's opinion, these bases were also not sufficiently defended from possible air attack. Airfields lacked an IAD and were equipped with only a few .50 caliber machine guns to repel an aerial assault. To this the WSEG warned that the vulnerability of these airfields "might nullify the Strategic Air Command's ability to launch an air offensive on a time and weight scale as contemplated in present planning."[161]

Intelligence for the strategic bombing effort also remained incomplete. At the same April 1950 commander's conference, a SAC briefing showed that of the 123 targets currently on the list, pre-strike reconnaissance was still required on 63.[162] Quality of the 60 "known" targets is speculative due to the nature of U.S. intelligence capabilities at the time given the lack of overflight and current information. To make up for this deficiency, reconnaissance planes would be dispatched to untargeted locations during the first strikes and gather intelligence for those facilities for later bombing sorties. At the April conference, SAC admitted that it needed at least four reconnaissance wings to support OFFTACKLE while it currently had only one available.[163] When discussing the OFFTACKLE plan with other SAC commanders, LeMay stated, "We cannot expect to get very much more target material prior to the opening of hostilities. Some type of aerial reconnaissance information is absolutely necessary to get the target folders together."[164] While lacking reconnaissance support for target folders, the lack of reconnaissance aircraft also had huge implications on post-strike damage assessment. Without having imagery for evaluation, how was SAC to know if another follow-up raid was required or if the initial attack was successful? This was identified as a "very critical shortage."

Additionally, SAC also identified its lack of ECM capability for the designated strike packages. At the same conference, it was reported that the command's ECM support was only 35 percent effective due to a shortage of jammers, chaff, chaff dispensers, and electronic maintenance personnel.[165] The manning issue was not expected to be rectified until late 1951, while many aircraft required significant modifications in order to be fully equipped with electronic equipment.[166] This issue was especially relevant given the lack of information on Soviet IAD and the importance of avoiding the defensive radar net.

An additional concern for SAC was the lack of long-range fighter escort.[167] In 1950 SAC had no ability to provide protection for the bombers as they lumbered toward their objectives. The F-84 aircraft that were planned to provide this kind of coverage were not yet fitted with long-range fuel tanks.[168] This problem was reminiscent of the issue plaguing the 8th Air Force during the opening phases of the CBO as B-17s and B-24s suffered horrible losses to the Luftwaffe's fighter attacks. Given what little the Air Force knew about PVO Strany, and the vulnerability of multi-engine bombers to swift defensive fighters, combat losses might have precluded successful delivery of both atomic and conventional bombs. This very issue would indeed manifest itself over the skies of Korea as B-29s became easy targets for Soviet-piloted North Korean MiG-15s.

The WSEG's assessment was not all doom and gloom for SAC and the OFFTACKLE plan. While the WSEG found that SAC could support only

1,500–2,000 sorties, it did conclude that these attacks could facilitate the entire atomic offensive for Phase I.[169] However, the atomic assault would only be if the atomic attacks were given the priority during this part of the campaign.[170] As a result, the conventional bombing effort, consisting of an estimated 3,522 sorties dropping some 17,000 tons of high explosives, was considered unfeasible if the atomic effort was given priority.[171] Given the overall importance of the atomic attack, this increase in priority may have occurred, but only at the expense of other targets and missions. The atomic assault alone constituted about a third of the weight required by the plan's first phase. Interestingly, at the same 1950 commander's conference, SAC reported that it had received a favorable report from the WSEG despite glaring deficiencies in the February evaluation.[172] In fact LeMay commented that "we have our troubles, however, we can carry out our mission. I think we can carry it out very well."[173] It seemed that SAC started to have an inflated opinion of its capabilities despite some rather significant limitations.

With the increase in the atomic weapons stockpiled and the new operational status of the B-36 intercontinental bomber, SAC would still have been hard-pressed to execute OFFTACKLE as drafted in late 1949. Even without considering operational losses due to accidents or combat, the plan was unfeasible given the size of SAC, the entire Department of Defense, and the military's budget allocations. Despite its obvious shortfalls, the plan was approved as an emergency measure on February 8, 1950. This approval was based upon the premise that "an undue amount of planning time has already been spent on the current emergency plan, to the detriment of mobilization planning, intermediate range planning, and next year's emergency planning."[174] Basically it was approved because the JSPC spent too much time on OFFTACKLE at the expense of everything else. The "sunk cost" of manpower time and resources into developing the plan were too much to just disregard. In the JCS's thinking, an unfeasible and ill-resourced plan was better than no plan at all. As a result, OFFTACKLE, and its subsequent variations, became the standing emergency war plan for the United States and its allies and remained so until mid–1951.

7

Assessments

Even before Vandenberg's submission of JCS 1952/1, elements within the U.S. military were beginning to doubt the efficacy of atomic strategic bombardment. While the war plans put America's defensive eggs largely into one atomic basket, would this atomic strategy really work? A critical analysis of the strategic atomic offensive was initiated by General Hubert Harmon of the Air Force at the behest of the JCS in December 1948. A six-member committee, which included two senior officers from each service, began its analysis in January 1949 to evaluate the potential effect of the strategic air offensive. Using the TROJAN war plan as a basis for evaluation, the committee considered the efficacy of the strategic air offensive.

On May 11, 1949, the Harmon committee submitted its unanimous findings to the JCS. Despite TROJAN's planning shortfalls as discussed previously, and disregarding the Soviet IAD threat to the attacking fleet, the committee assumed that all the planned targets were successfully struck in the aerial assault. The committee considered the aerial offensive occurring in two phases: the initial phase striking the planned 70 targets list with atomic weapons, and a second phase that included both atomic and conventional bombing. In its analysis, the committee found that as a result of the offensive, 30 to 40 percent of Soviet industry would be reduced. However, this effect would be temporary, the net result depending upon Russian recuperative capabilities and the effectiveness of follow-on strikes.[1] Especially effective were the attacks on the Soviet petroleum industry, as the committee believed that high-grade fuel, especially for aircraft, would become critical.[2]

As far as casualties, the aerial offensive might produce as many as 2.7 million deaths along with 4 million additional casualties. In addition, the 70 targeted cities would suffer enormous damage in terms of housing and infrastructure, making life appreciably difficult for another 28 million Soviet citizens.[3] In addition to the deaths and physical destruction, the committee also considered psychological damage done to Soviet citizens. While the shock of the attack would be significant, it was not thought that the psychological effects would destroy or critically weaken the communist influence on the masses. As a result the associated effect of the atomic assault would not "per se bring about capitulation."[4] In fact, the committee thought that the opposite effect might be produced by the bombing. The attack would merely reinforce Soviet propaganda messages regarding Western intentions and their nefarious nature. The atomic offensive might have the opposite effect and stiffen Russian resistance to the American onslaught and undermine the overall Allied objectives.[5] This thought regarding resistance was well founded, as Air Corps studies in the interwar years found that Chinese, Spanish, and Ethiopian populations became more resilient as a result of air attacks. This same phenomenon occurred in the United Kingdom during "the blitz" in 1940 as Luftwaffe bombers pounded British cities. During the CBO, the USSBS found much of the same evidence regarding German workers' motivations, with no appreciable change in performance.

However, the committee estimated that the Soviet Union's ability to conduct offensive operations would be impaired, but not enough to stop advances in the Middle East or into Western Europe. The committee felt that the supply of petroleum would affect military operations, reducing the mobility of the Red Army and the Soviet Navy, affect air operations, and curtail a myriad of logistical functions that would degrade overall military effectiveness.[6] As a result, the Soviet high command would need to reassess its overall strategic situation and adjust war plans accordingly. Additionally, with the use of atomic weapons on the USSR, a precedent would be established and the Soviets would be free to retaliate with like weapons on American cities once they had developed the capability—one that they were sure to develop in the next few years.

Much like the results of the USSBS published earlier, the overall findings of the Harmon Committee were equivocal and could be interpreted based upon the reader's individual inclinations. While there were military benefits from the use of atomic weapons, the committee felt that the use of such ordnance in the long run undermined overall allied war aims, as vague as they were in NSC 20/4. Committee members believed that the effects created by the atomic attack on Soviet infrastructure would be "transcending."[7] The report went on to advocate preparing for the prompt and effective delivery of atomic weapons on the appropriate targets. However, committee members also felt that the destruction caused by such attacks would only complicate the postwar reconstruction and recovery period. They warned that the atomic assault would produce "certain psychological and retaliatory reactions detrimental to the achievement of Allied war objectives."[8]

The WSEG report in February and the Harmon Report in May gave military planners plenty of food for thought. While the Harmon report did not reject the idea of atomic warfare, it did call into question its effectiveness in the larger strategic/political objectives. The Harmon Report merely reinforced the prevailing idea that American conventional strength was so weak that use of atomic weapons was the default military response. With this thought in mind, weeks later on June 14, 1949, the JCS requested a further expansion of the atomic inventory. However, with the WSEG assessment, the ability to actually execute the plan as specified had serious shortfalls. Until NSC-68 and the Korean War spurred military spending, the American atomic offensive was not only unfeasible but also did not appear to fully satisfy larger national political objectives.

While the USSBS focused upon the strategic bombing campaigns of the previous war, parts of that assessment were relevant to postwar atomic planning. Conceivably, atomic weapons changed the nature of strategic bombing, at least in theory. But a number of the USSBS, as well as the USAAF's experiences in World War II, had applicability to war plans built subsequent to the Axis defeat. Planned bombing strategies reflected many of the same target sets and methodologies used during the CBO and Pacific campaigns. Therefore, comparing USSBS findings and USAAF experiences of the war to the established plans is useful for identifying continued deficiencies. The PINCHER, BROILER, HALFMOON, and OFFTACKLE plans had their own limitation, as discussed previously. However, certain legacy problems and conditions experienced in the previous war were still prevalent. These legacy issues would have had significant implications for national military strategies and the accomplishment of overall goals and objectives in late 1940 war planning.

An important finding in the USSBS was that a strategic bombing campaign required careful analysis and selection of targets. Picking the right targets that were the key points of the enemy economic or military value was of paramount importance.[9] Targeting itself is its own strategy. However, determining key points of the Soviet economy and targeting those relevant areas required accurate and current intelligence support for a strategic bombing campaign. In order to obtain this information during the war, the Allies relied on a number of sources that included thousands of photo interpreters providing trained analysis, scores of reconnaissance aircraft conducting thousands of dangerous sorties over enemy territory, and a concerted electronic communication-gathering effort that included both ULTRA intercepts and other low-grade cypher and communication collections.[10] This effort also relied on a significant human intelligence (HUMINT) effort that included refugee interviews and other individual personal accounts.[11] This intelligence effort was required not only in the initial targeting process, but also played a key role in bomb damage assessments that helped determine parameters for subsequent strikes.

7. Assessments

In the years following the war, the United States was nowhere near having the same intelligence capability to support an atomic bombing offensive. The glaring deficiency for SAC and strategic bombing planning was a lack of high-quality, relevant, and current intelligence on the Soviet Union. Not only did the United States lack the latest information on Soviet industry and military bases, but also had little idea about the IAD threat facing the bombing force. Without benefit of aerial flyover and before the advent of satellite imagery, the primary means of obtaining information in most cases regarding potential targets was via Project WRINGER and captured German images and maps. These methods were a cornerstone of the U.S. intelligence effort and at best based upon information at least a few years old. Without having a full and comprehensive picture of Soviet industry or military infrastructure, how could SAC reasonably expect to hit known and relevant targets and then assess the results with a high degree of confidence? During the building of the HALFMOON plan, the head of SAC's 311th Air Division expressed his concerns in September 1948, arguing, "I think our reconnaissance techniques are antiquated, I think our equipment is inadequate and insufficient...."[12] SAC clearly recognized its intelligence-gathering deficiency during discussions regarding OFFTACKLE as commanders lamented having only a quarter of the reconnaissance effort required to support the operation. This lack of a clear picture on the latest status of factories, production centers, transportation networks, or refineries may have led SAC to target areas no longer used for war production or erroneously hit areas misidentified or improperly reported by WRINGER interviews.

The Soviet Union had much to rebuild following the biblical scale of destruction it experienced during the war. Relocation or reconversion of factories and production centers was a distinct possibility. Even if the interviewed Germans were correct regarding a particular production center, SAC still had no large-scale library or capability to gather photographic imagery of potential targets to aid in bomb placement. While atomic weapons had greatly increased explosive yields over conventional munitions, they still required proper placement to ensure target destruction. At best, SAC could use only oblique photography from aircraft flying along the Soviet border. That photographic field of view was limited to only a few dozen miles inland from the Soviet border at the most. Given the early paucity of atomic ordnance, expending even a few bombs on the wrong target or one that was no longer relevant would have a significant effect on the entire operation.

During this immediate postwar era, SAC referred to its targeting methodology as its "city busting phase."[13] It determined that rubble equaled victory and looked to level as many Soviet cities as possible with the few weapons it had available. SAC used what was described as a "horizontal target system ... we didn't care if we were shooting at churches, industry, government centers, we wanted to level the town."[14] Obviously this is reflective of the experiences of the CBO and Pacific efforts, but not necessarily the doctrine that underpinned them. While strategic targets were picked by the JCS, SAC planners determined the operational aspects of the attack such as ingress routes, drop points, tactics, and egress.

After the war, targeting was facilitated by a new organization called the Strategic Vulnerabilities Branch (SVB), its mission being to "ensure the right bombs may be delivered to the right targets concomitant with the decision to wage war."[15] Under this organization was a Physical Vulnerabilities (PV) branch, and it was their job to determine the susceptibility of a damage for a given target. However, how does one assess damage if you do not necessarily know the specific nature of a given target? For example, one analyst in the PV branch described how they estimated damage to light steel-framed structures:

> We didn't deal with any individual installations because we didn't have that information. The people who ran the study ascertained that X city had so many steel installations or other kinds of installations ... we know the outline of the area, we knew all the installations were inside that area. We did separate weapons requirements for each city, depending on the area they gave you. We assumed everything was in the urban area. We considered these cities as targets because, well, in the first place, we didn't have anything like the detailed intelligence to conduct a more detailed study, so we considered them as area targets and estimated the amount of damage there would be for ... industrial structures ... and I did this in a very crude fashion.[16]

As mentioned earlier, a "Bombing Encyclopedia" was established as early as 1946 that included a collection of information on individual targets that were part of a larger integrated system.[17] The first attempts to determine atomic effects on targets in the Soviet Union started in summer 1947. However, according to the same analyst, "[we] were requested to do a limited target study of the atomic damage to certain industrial cities in the USSR.... These cities had been selected because they contained installations considered important to the war effort ... we didn't have any idea of where these installations were located. And the idea was to put enough weapons on them to achieve sufficient damage."[18] While this method of targeting is far from what the United States had initially subscribed to in its prewar precision doctrine, it also would have been problematic given the few bombs that the United States actually had available in the postwar period. However, what is more interesting is the "close hold" nature of atomic weapons information. Because the AEC refused to share its atomic secrets, the individual analysts who were to make predictions on bomb damage assessments were not given access to atomic bomb data that would have assisted in their studies.[19] As mentioned previously, analysts were force to use the USSBS as their main

7. Assessments

source of information regarding atomic damage assessments. Concurrently, expected damage may also have been underestimated, as planners based their predictions on blast damage and did not include the results from fire or radiation. These secondary and tertiary effects would have caused much more damage and havoc at the designated targets but were not modeled in pre-strike planning.[20]

Additionally, post-strike reconnaissance would also be required, as planned follow-on sorties might be required, depending upon initial strike results. The USSBS clearly saw the need for follow-up raids on German targets and observed that "no indispensable industry was permanently put out of commission by a single attack. Persistent re-attack was necessary."[21] During the war this was part of the ACIU's responsibilities, with its thousands of analysts along with dedicated reconnaissance aircraft flying hundreds of sorties obtaining post-strike photographs. While atomic weapons certainly would have created larger areas of destruction, a single strike might not have created the knockout blow planners envisioned for a given target or even for a collection of them. An erroneous drop or mistake could very easily negate the effects desired from a given atomic attack. The same would hold true for the conventional bombing attacks as well. Follow-up attacks would be required based upon bomb damage assessments. Of course this bomb damage assessment assumed that SAC bombers hit the right targets in the first strikes and that no bombs were wasted on dummy or irrelevant targets. Furthermore, SAC commanders were concerned about the vulnerability of the reconnaissance versions of the B-29 (RB-29) during daylight missions and believed given PVO Strany capabilities. The RB-36 was fielded in December 1949 but suffered from the same problems as the RB-29 in terms of vulnerability to interception. Carrying a crew of 22, the RB-36 contained a host of cameras, radars, and ECM equipment in the bomb bays. But, for all its capability, the RB-39 did not become operational until June 1951.[22] The fast, long-range reconnaissance aircraft SAC was looking for was the RB-47 "Stratojet." However, the RB-47 was not scheduled for operational use until 1953.[23]

In addition to the lack of intelligence support regarding the target sets themselves, SAC also had very little detailed information regarding the IAD threat facing inbound aircraft. Even if crews had accurate maps and images of their intended targets, what they could expect during their combat sortie in terms of enemy defense was unknown. The WSEG report expressed concern over the lack of solid intelligence regarding Soviet PVO Strany capabilities, stating that the United States had "the most meager and vague details on the quantity, type, and performance of Russian equipment. That this condition exists, is a grave deficiency...."[24] Even if the threat was known, the lack of long-range fighter support from single-engine F-84s would make the bombers easy targets for the PVO Strany. SAC planned to use the law of averages in its opening strikes by saturation of the Soviet air defenses as much as possible. By having as many bombers in the air as possible, SAC hoped to dilute PVO Strany assets that would, hopefully, in turn see a number of bombers hit their primary targets.[25] The USAAF employed this same tactic against the Luftwaffe fighter defenses with varying degrees of success in the CBO. Much as 8th Air Force bombers experienced at the hands of the Luftwaffe, SAC may have experienced a loss rate equal to or greater than the 8 percent seen during the CBO's opening phases.

After the war, illustrating its growing importance in Soviet national defense, in 1948 PVO was removed from the Directorate of Artillery and became its own separate branch of the military.[26] Understanding that one bomber with an atomic weapon could cause considerable damage to military capability, the Soviets focused on trying to prevent the incoming aircraft from reaching its intended target. While air defense was initially a tactical application for the Red Army, the Soviets began to build a larger nationwide strategic air defense capability.[27] Immediately after the war, the Russians established an all-weather, 24-hour local air defense of their critical installations and facilities and grew the capability on a national scale.[28] Utilizing many late-model, Western-designed radars given to them by Allied lend-lease during the war, PVO Strany also began to build its own radars and incorporated them into a larger IAD structure.[29]

Concurrently as Western aircraft became more capable in terms of both speed and altitude, Soviet anti-air defenses countered. The Russians initially focused on improving ground-based AAA with increased ranges and improved firepower. By the end of the war, the existing Soviet 85mm cannons already in the Red Army inventory could range as high as 37,000 feet, easily reaching B-29s flying at altitudes up to 35,000 feet.[30] However, when the B-36 became operational in 1948–1949, it could operate at altitudes as high as 45,000 feet. As a result, the Soviets countered in 1950 with the introduction of the 100mm cannon that could range as high as 49,000 feet.[31] By the mid–1950s, with introduction of the more advanced B-47, B-52, and B-58 aircraft, PVO Strany included a 130mm gun that could range up to 70,000 feet![32] Furthermore, some 100mm AAA units were upgraded from four-gun battery sets to eight-gun sets, thus increasing fire densities.[33]

In addition to the increased ranges of AAA, the Soviets also introduced larger numbers of jet interceptor aircraft that were able to operate in the rarified air of higher altitudes. By the end of the Korean War, MiG-15s in regiment-size formations were highly effective against B-29s operating in daylight over the northern half of the small peninsula. Making slashing attacks against the slow-moving bombers and avoiding turning dogfights with the capable U.S. F-86 "Sabre" fighter, the MiG proved an effective point interceptor. The MiG-15 first took to the air in December 1947 and was powerfully armed with two 23mm cannons and a single 37mm. When introduced, the MiG-15 was one of the lightest but fastest fighters of the time.[34] While the Russian design had its limitations in stability and control, especially at high speeds, the nimble little fighter was capable of Mach .86 and was produced by the thousands. From 1948 to 1956 the Soviet Union manufactured between 15,000 and 16,000 MiG-15s.[35]

By the time the Korean War ended, the Soviets had established an effective and integrated command and control system that operated 24 hours per day. Soviet ground radar operators were capable of vectoring interceptor aircraft to within two to five miles of the incoming SAC bombers. Additionally, Soviet radars were capable of conducting this operation from ranges up to 70 miles.[36] Eventually, the radars could also direct an increasingly capable AAA inventory that had the ability to range incoming bombers at higher altitudes. Had SAC attempted a sustained bombing campaign deep into Soviet territory during daylight hours under constant exposure to both AAA and swift MiGs, the losses might have proven to be excessive.[37] Night bombing operations would have better overall defensive characteristics for SAC crews, but this application too had its drawbacks.

Despite the lack of solid intelligence on Soviet IAD, the WSEG did attempt to estimate potential losses. In its evaluations, it assumed a 17 percent overall average loss rate for SAC bombers when attacked by PVO Strany fighters in 1950 during a day attack in the execution of OFFTACKLE.[38] Figures for loss rates are generated from the below chart.

Probability of [a] Bomber Being Shot Down by Fighter in a Single Pass on the Bomber (Stern Attacks) After Contact Has Been Made (1950 Daytime)[39]

Fighter Type	Bomber	Altitude	Probability of Kill
LA-11	B-50	20,000 ft	0.2
LA-11	B-36	20,000 ft	0.15
MiG-9	B-50	35,000 ft	0.25
MiG-9	B-36	40,000 ft	0.25
MiG-15	B-50	35,000 ft	0.1
MiG-15	B-36	40,000 ft	0.1

The report went on to evaluate the success of a daylight bomb raid given Soviet fighters, AAA, and potential mechanical failures of attacking aircraft. For a day mission consisting of 223 B-29/B-50s carrying 32 atomic weapons, the WSEG estimated a loss of 35 aircraft to enemy fighters, two to AAA, five for operational causes, and another 14 aborting before reaching the target.[40] In all, 24 out of 32 atomic bombs would be delivered, with three lost, two returned by aborting aircraft, and three missing the target. This sample raid equated to a roughly 19 percent loss rate for the SAC aircraft and an atomic

Soviet AAA and SAC Bomber Capabilities

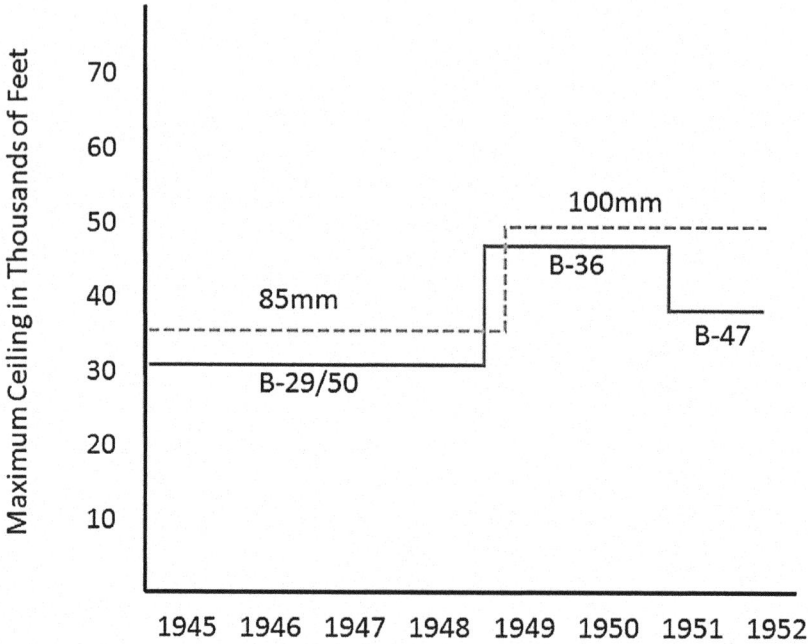

Source: Development of Soviet Air Defense Doctrine and Practice

Comparison of SAC bomber fleet maximum altitudes to Soviet Anti-Aircraft (AAA) capability in the postwar environment. PVO-Strany was able to field AAA that could easily range incoming bombers. This ground-based capability was augmented with the introduction of the MiG-15 jet fighter and provided for a formidable integrated air defense capability.

ordnance delivery rate of 75 percent.[41] The 19 percent loss rate is double the average rate of the 8th Air Force in the early days of the CBO and matches the figures experienced by many bomb groups during some of the bloodiest raids over Germany.

For a night raid evaluation, the WSEG used 96 B-29/B-50s carrying a total of 32 atomic bombs. Its analysis figured a loss of seven bombers to night fighters, two to AAA, with two operational losses.[42] Another eight aircraft would abort before reaching their targets, with 23 bombs hitting their intended targets.[43] Three bombs would be lost, four bomb-laden aircraft would abort for mechanical failure, with two bombs missing their intended targets.[44] Overall loss rate would have been much less, 12 percent, with 72 percent of atomic weapons hitting their marks. While the night raid losses were appreciably smaller, the sustained loss rate would have quickly decimated the bombing force, as experienced by the USAAF during the CBO.

However, upon reading the WSEG's report on bomber losses at the hands of PVO Strany, LeMay rebuffed the analysis. He did not think much of the Soviet air defense and believed the report inflated SAC bomber losses. He believed Soviet defenses during that time were too weak to create the kind of unacceptable losses that the Air Force initially experienced at the beginning of the CBO in Europe. In support of this assertion, he remarked "We didn't have to worry about winning the air power battle because the Russians had no threat against us ... we could ignore the rule book in winning the air power battle and go about destroying their resources."[45]

Lastly, all of the approved war plans developed over this period made a deliberate effort to affect the morale of the Soviet worker, undercut control of the communist regime, and use a psychological effect to bring about capitulation. As mentioned previously, the efficacy of this was debated by senior civilian and military leaders but became a staple of targeting methodologies. Hoping to smash Soviet resilience, especially after the pounding the USSR endured at the hands of the German Wehrmacht, is an idea that had little foundation. With over 20 million people killed during the war, their cities destroyed, and employing scorched-earth policies, the USSR continued to fight and defeat the German invasion. Additionally, the USSBS saw much of the same resiliency in the German population during the CBO. According to the survey, the cracking of German national morale as a result of strategic bombing never materialized. Living under the Nazi regime, the German citizens were resilient under both the terror of the bombing itself and the conditions under which they came to live.[46] While eventually losing confidence in their national leaders, their homes, and their friends and families, German workers continued to toil as long as the means of production allowed.[47] The idea that the Soviet regime would fall as a result of flagging morale and a reduction in national resiliency was not based on any substantial evidence. Given the Soviet Union's performance while engaged with Germany, this same resiliency would probably manifest itself as a result of an atomic offensive.

Perhaps the biggest shortfall of all postwar atomic air planning was a lack of coherent doctrine regarding strategic bombardment and its integration with the entire defense establishment. While most Air Force leaders understood the basic tenets of a strategic bombing campaign, there was little consensus regarding how this atomic campaign would integrate with other elements of national defense. All the services took a myopic view regarding future war without looking at an upcoming conflict from a larger joint perspective. While the inter-service rivalries of the time did not encourage such discussion and organizational preservation was the order of the day, the Air Force failed to develop its own internal doctrine regarding atomic warfare. With the advent of atomic weapons, there was no wholesale review of Air Force doctrine regarding strategic bombing and what the new weapons meant to the aerial offensive. Additionally, there was no real review of how this offensive fit it with other sea and land components. Planners were left to their own devices and designed bombing campaigns based upon prewar doctrine or their own experiences in the war. As a result, target sets and methodologies were based on doctrines written before the advent of atomic weaponry.

In summary, all of the war plans developed during this period were deficient in many ways. Materially the United States was nowhere near adequate in structure to carry out these various offensive plans. Forward bases, logistics, airframes, and capability were all sorely lacking in light of SAC's envisioned mission. Even if the United States had had what it required materially, it would still have suffered from a paucity of current, relevant, and accurate intelligence on which to base an effective and comprehensive bombing campaign. Furthermore, successful delivery rates of atomic ordnance to the intended target were expected to be 70 to 85 percent, and that was with the few bombs the nation had available at the time. War plans also lacked a definitive end state, and those NSC policies that did exist provided very little in the way of useful guidance to military planners. Aircrews flying into the USSR faced both an unknown enemy and a potentially high casualty rate with little chance of surviving the entire campaign. In all, the ways in which the United States sought to defeat the Soviets by an atomic aerial offensive were poorly funded, ill-conceived, speciously planned, badly organized, and yet relentlessly optimistic.

Part III. Strategic Air Command

8

Men

After having helped establish the Berlin Airlift in the summer of 1948, LeMay was relieved of command of U.S. Air Forces in Europe. He returned stateside and in October assumed command of SAC. LeMay would remain as the head of the command for the next nine years until relieved in 1957. During his unusually long tenure at SAC, he would mold his charge into the most powerful military organization ever built. When LeMay assumed command, SAC consisted of some 46,000 uniformed personnel and only 837 aircraft of various types.[1] By the time he left, SAC had grown to almost five times its size, to 200,000 airmen with almost four times as many aircraft, with 2,700 airframes in its inventory.[2] However, this overwhelming growth did not come about overnight, as it required time, money, and men. The professionalism and capability that SAC came to represent had to be built from the ground up. However, in the period immediately following the war, SAC was not only ill-equipped to conduct its assigned mission but also deficient in manpower, with many of those in the ranks poorly trained. As a result of this problem, along with many others, the command would have been hard-pressed to conduct the atomic offensive if required.

Shortly upon assuming command, LeMay wanted to evaluate SAC's ability to execute its wartime mission. In January 1949 he ordered practice "all-out" maximum bombing raids on the city of Dayton, Ohio. Aircrews were given an old aerial photograph of the city taken in 1938 and instructed to fly their new B-36s and older B-29/B-50 aircraft at night from their bases and "attack" the designated target using only radar bombing methods.[3] Up until that time SAC had sortied large numbers of aircraft, but mostly to support the cause of air power at public demonstrations and other events. These operations provided very little in terms of realistic combat training or enhanced readiness. SAC had tried this same kind of practice bombing event in May 1947 against the city of New York. In this earlier exercise, 101 B-29s took to the air in what was also supposed to be a "maximum effort." However,

30 Superfortresses, 23 percent of the bombing fleet, remained on the ground because of maintenance and supply problems.[4]

Up until the 1949 raid, postwar SAC aircrews habitually flew practice missions around 10–15,000 feet, where the air was warmer and more dense.[5] Even with pressurized cockpits, flying at lower altitudes allowed the crews to be more comfortable and did not require them to wear oxygen masks. The warmer, dense air did not affect aircraft equipment and systems as badly and also provided the added benefit of easier targeting. In the period prior to the 1949 raid, bombardiers often practiced targeting reflectors placed in rafts in the open waters in the Gulf of Mexico.[6] These reflectors were clearly visible and easy to distinguish among the ocean waves, and were distant from any ground clutter or distraction that would be reflected in their radar scopes. Therefore the reflector target stood out in clear view as opposed to being hidden in the clutter of an urban area.

However, for the January missions, crews were instructed to fly at 30,000 feet in order to simulate combat conditions. The higher altitude required the crews to fly with the cabins pressurized and with oxygen masks on. As expected, the colder temperatures took a toll on aircraft systems and their crews. Furthermore, targeting a city with APQ-13 or APQ-23 radar among the ground clutter made the task all the more difficult, especially since bombardiers were unfamiliar with what the target would look like on their radar scopes. While the APQ radars had their own issues regarding reliability, adding to the frustration of the crews, weather patterns affected both navigation and bombing equipment as thunderstorms surrounded the target area.[7]

As LeMay expected, the results were disastrous. According to the SAC commander, "Not one airplane finished that mission as briefed. Not one."[8] He went on later: "…aborts all over the place, equipment wouldn't work, the crews didn't work, nothing worked."[9] Of the 303 runs actually made over the target by the command, nearly two-thirds of the simulated drops were more than 7,000 feet off target.[10] Indicative of SACs performance, the 20th Bombardment Squadron from Davis-Monthan Air Force Base, Arizona, launched six B-29s on January 7. Two of the bombers had pressurization malfunctions and failed to make the bomb run.[11] The 46th Bombardment Squadron was scheduled for January 13, with two aircraft aborting on the ground, a third aborting en route, and a fourth failing to make the bomb run due to a microphone failure.[12] B-36s from the 7th Bombardment Group at Carswell Air Force Base were programmed for missions on January 7, 11, and 13. On January 7, two aircraft aborted on takeoff due to engine/propeller malfunctions. Days later on January 11, all eight scheduled B-36s cancelled to due to freezing rain. On January 13, one B-36 aborted on the parking ramp and three others aborted on takeoff. Of the six aircraft making it over the target, three failed to bomb because of bombing radar malfunctions.[13]

The average bombing error was over 10,000 feet from the intended target. It was estimated that had the "Little Boy" bomb, with its ~20KT-yield explosion, been dropped that far from the aim point over Hiroshima in August 1945, the designated target area would have been relatively unscathed.[14] Some crews even failed to locate the city of Dayton altogether. These results were similar to other units in the exercise and indicative of the command's state of combat preparedness. One of the participating units admitted that the gross errors came from the aircrews' "inability to observe proper procedure previous to, and during the bomb run, [and] that target identification and non-standard procedure were at the time extricably related."[15] The report went on to state, "Improper or inadequate target briefing, combined with inobservance of the radar bombing SOP [Standing Operating Procedure], played an important role...."[16] LeMay later admitted that weather and thunderstorms were an issue for the crews, but overall "our crews were not accustomed to flying at altitude. Neither were the airplanes, far as that goes. Most of the pressurization wouldn't work, the oxygen didn't work.... Nobody seemed to know what life was like upstairs."[17] LeMay recalled that this exercise was "just about the darkest night in American aviation history."[18] As one observer noted, "As a deterrent to aggression in its early years, SAC was far more a symbol than a reality."[19]

Following the war, men left the military in droves to pursue peacetime careers, and the USAAF, like the other services, suffered serious manpower shortages due to the postwar exodus. When asked about the demobilization process, Medal of Honor winner General Leon Johnson, first commander of the 15th Air Force, following the establishment of SAC stated, "We fell apart ... it was just a riot really."[20] In 1947 General Ira Eaker, standing in for Spaatz, addressed the National War College and lamented, "Our principle difficulty arose from the fact that concurrently with the tremendous wrecking job[of dismantling the military], we had to let out the most experienced personnel...."[21] This exit of sufficient numbers of trained personnel had immediate and severe operational effects for postwar operations. Leon Johnson remembered that the exodus was so quick after the conflict that his command's wartime records were left unsecured and abandoned on the floor.[22] The situation was so bad that when the USAAF looked to deploy five B-29 groups to Europe in a show of force called Project WONDERFUL, the service had to cancel the operation for a number of reasons, one of them being the lack of trained manpower. This shortage was not just of men in the aggregate, but the Air Force also suffered from a lack of properly trained and skilled airmen to fill highly technical and difficult jobs.

The structure for the postwar Air Force was not just an ancillary thought given the conduct of the war. Designs for the organization of peacetime air power began as early as 1943. An independent air force had been a goal of many air-power advocates as early as the 1920s and was Hap Arnold's ultimate objective while he was chief of the USAAF. While the independent air force was to come to fruition in 1947, many of the assumptions made during previous wartime planning proved erroneous, as Truman's austerity measures and the mass demobilization took their toll. One of the biggest problems facing the Air Force was the same issue it had with the various atomic attack plans: a lack of guidance from the national authority with regard to its mission and what was expected of the service.[23] What was the postwar Air Force supposed to accomplish? What were to be the service's goals and objectives in the postwar security environment? Ultimately, without any real political guidance or input, Air Force planners envisioned a postwar structure that included a 70-group force composed of some 400,000 men.[24]

While the 70-group structure was less than what air-power advocates had initially wanted, others argued that the size was too big. Many recognized the fact that the U.S. sphere of influence in the postwar environment was much larger than before the war. America had become the leader of the free world and would serve as the bulwark against Communist aggression. Additionally, most Air Force officers believed that war in the future would occur in a quick and accelerated manner and not allow for the slow, deliberate building of an air fleet once hostilities began. In a speech to the American Legion in Denver, Colorado, in 1947, USAAF General Frank Anderson argued, "The key factors which gained us victory in World War I and World War II were time and space. Our Allies gave us time. Our oceans gave us space. In any future planned aggressive war, we will be the first to be attacked.... Time will not be ours.... We will not have time to build an Air Force. We must have an Air Force in being."[25] Toward this end, the 70-group structure was looked upon by air-power advocates more as a minimum requirement rather than the full one.[26] Despite Air Force desires for a larger force, in 1947 SAC consisted of 16 very heavy bomber groups (B-29s), with 30 aircraft each, and one atomic group. Five of these heavy groups had no aircraft assigned, and SAC as an organization stood at a paltry 45,000 officers and men. Considering the primacy the Truman administration placed on atomic weapons, what was more telling of SAC's status was that in late 1948, only six crews were fully trained to drop atomic ordnance.[27]

Within the proposed postwar structure, a Very Heavy Bombardment (VHB) capability would serve as a key component of national security, especially with the advent of atomic weapons and belief in the efficacy of strategic airpower.[28] Organization of the postwar Air Force started with the creation of a temporary organization known as the Continental Air Force (CAF). Officially activated in June 1945, the CAF was responsible for redeployment planning and continental defense during the transition to peacetime. Subsequent postwar planning efforts developed the idea that a U.S.-based, global atomic strike force needed to be maintained for American national interests and to help secure global peace. Taking this idea one step further, newly appointed USAAF Chief of Staff Spaatz created three major combat commands, each with their own sphere of responsibility.[29] These were SAC and two other organizations: Tactical Air Command (TAC) and Air Defense Command (ADC). SAC was officially established on March 21, 1946. Its mission:

> Be prepared to conduct long range offensive operations in any part of the world either independently or in cooperation with land and naval forces; to conduct maximum range reconnaissance over land and sea either independently or in cooperation with land and naval forces; to provide combat units capable of intense and sustained combat operations employing the latest and most advanced weapons; to train units and personnel for the maintenance of strategic forces in all parts of the world; to perform such special missions as the Commanding General AAF may direct.[30]

On the same date, Headquarters CAF, located at Bolling Field, Washington, D.C., was redesigned as Headquarters SAC and eventually moved to Andrews Field, Maryland, in October. Concurrently, the combat resources of the CAF were also divided into the new TAC and ADC structures.[31]

General George Kenney was named the first commander of SAC and came to the job with an excellent wartime resume. During the global conflict, he served as the Commander of the USAAF in the Southwest Pacific and successfully supported Douglas MacArthur's offensive thrusts through the Bismarck Archipelago and subsequent operations into the Philippines. He made the most out of the few resources assigned. Improvisation and innovation become the hallmark of his command. During the war, the 5th Air Force continually developed new and effective tactics, techniques, and procedures. Furthermore, he employed and maintained an air fleet in harsh tropical jungles that provided their own difficulties in the wet

General George Kenney, first commanding general of SAC. Enamored with celebrity, he spent little time attending to his command and left day-to-day operations to his deputy, Clements McMullen. McMullen's manpower policies and Kenney's inattentiveness seriously eroded SAC's combat capability (U.S. Air Force photograph).

and humid environment of the southwest Pacific. Although he thought MacArthur had little understanding of air operations, Kenney enjoyed the trust of the Supreme Commander, and the two established an excellent working relationship. Upon arriving at South West Pacific Headquarters in July 1942, MacArthur had a list of grievances regarding the USAAF and its lack of support. After listening to MacArthur's complaints, Kenney recalled, he told him, "I know how to run an air force as well or better than anyone else ... [and] that I would be loyal to him. If at any time this [loyalty] could not be maintained ... I would be packed up and ready for the orders sending me back home."[32] To this MacArthur replied, "George, I think we are going to get along together all right."[33] While Kenney had little to do with the strategic bombing campaign over the Japanese islands, he was a proven commander and enjoyed an outstanding reputation both inside and outside his service.

However, during the war, Kenney's loyalty was largely toward MacArthur rather than the USAAF. This loyalty was not unnoticed by USAAF leadership and possibly led to his being passed over for the position as USAAF chief once Arnold retired.[34] Since Kenney served in the Pacific under MacArthur, he did not have the same relationship with Arnold that Spaatz had, especially with regard to Eisenhower, who was appointed as the incoming chief of staff for the Army. Given that SAC was the very embodiment of the Air Force vision, it would require an officer of four-star rank to lead the service's flagship command. At the end of the war, the USAAF had only four four-star officers: Arnold, Spaatz, Kenney, and Joseph McNarney. Given such a small field of officers available, the choice of Kenney for SAC was easy. Arnold was retiring and was being replaced by Spaatz. McNarney held mostly staff positions and served with distinction, but he did not have the excellent combat record Kenney had in the Pacific. As a result, Kenney became the default choice.

By mid–1947 the Air Force consisted of 70 groups with a mix of heavy bombers, fighters, light bombers, tactical reconnaissance, troop carriers, all-weather fighters, long-range photo reconnaissance, long-range mapping, and long-range weather reconnaissance. However, many of these organizations were on paper only. Due to the austerity measures of the Truman administration, only 55 groups were manned, and of those only 36 were operational, with only 300,000 airmen.[35] Looking to maintain a 70-group structure, which was supported by the JCS, the Air Force required a budget of $5.2 billion for FY 49.[36] Secretary Symington argued that the 55-group structure seriously impaired the Air Force's ability to fulfill its given mission, as vague as it was, but understood the nature of the fiscal environment and submitted a proposal for only $4.21 billion.[37] The fiscal situation for the Air Force was to become even worse. When the budget for 1949 was finally approved, the Air Force received only $2.9 billion.[38] This figure was approved despite the 1948 pro–air power findings of the Finletter and Brewster Commission reports that endorsed the 70-group structure. Symington voiced his displeasure, stating, "We are more shocked at the decision of the Bureau [of the Budget] than anything that has happened since we came into the government."[39] With these fiscal constraints, the Air Force was stuck trying to make the most out of what little money it had.

In addition to a lack of funds, both SAC and the USAAF were suffering from a lack of skilled manpower. In May 1946, SAC was authorized at 43,729 men, but with the postwar exodus, that number began to drop significantly.[40] By June, the number of personnel dropped to 37,000, and including civilians leaving SAC, by the end of the year personnel strength dropped another 12,478.[41] This shortage of manpower was not just a SAC problem, but one that affected the USAAF as an organization. By the end of 1946, the service overall was lacking some 7,000 men.[42] By mid–1947, the number of men began to increase but not enough to fill the number of positions required for the 55-group structure. Still short of men, SAC resorted to a number of solutions.

In order to classify men to meet the needs of the war effort, the Army developed a General Classification Test (AGCT) that measured a recruit's potential for mechanical/technical training. During the war, the Army Air Forces received most of the higher-scoring (Class I and II) enlisted personnel and concurrently had the smallest number of the lower-scoring (Class IV–V) recruits. Because of the technical nature of the USAAF mission, during the war it received a sort of special status in the accession of higher-scoring enlisted personnel. In 1943, 41 percent of the USAAF was of the highest classes of enlisted personnel while the Army Service Force and Ground Forces were staffed with only 35 percent and 29 percent respectively.[43] Conversely, for the lower-scoring men, the USAAF had only 27 percent of the Class IV and Vs while the other two elements of the Army had 35 and 37 percent respectively.[44] Generally men with an AGCT score over 100 were given technical skills and training while those with less than 85 were generally placed in unskilled assignments. With the war over, a majority of the technically trained and higher-scoring men left the USAAF, while a disproportionate number of the unskilled men remained in the service.[45] One bomb group had 30 aircraft, but only four qualified crew chiefs, only nine men in the entire 15th Air Force were qualified to maintain B-29 radars, and nearly half of the enlisted men lacked a specific skill set.[46] With the peacetime exodus, and still needing skilled airmen, the service lowered the AGCT score required for technical training to 85. In some cases, men with a score of 85 were so scarce that the Air Force lowered it to 60.[47] As the higher-scoring veterans exited the service, remaining units were lacking skilled personnel, which had huge operational effects.

This same problem existed when garnering new recruits for the Air Force. The quality of manpower the Air Force was receiving in the postwar years was less than stellar. While the Air Force raised the minimum AGCT score from 60 to 70, recruits often still scored poorly. In a group of 33 men sent to a 15th Air Force unit in 1946, 32 of the new airmen had scores between 42 and 69.[48] Additionally, by the end of the year, SAC was still short of trained personnel, with 25 percent of those on the rolls having less than six months' experience in the military.[49] When LeMay took over command of SAC, he observed that "the whole force was ill manned. We didn't have the people we needed, and there were a lot of people we didn't need and couldn't use."[50]

With dwindling material and personnel resources, SAC needed to maximize the assets assigned to the command. This was an issue needing the direct and full attention of the SAC commander. However, in addition to lacking enlisted men and officers, for a period of time SAC was also lacking an effective and engaged commanding general. While appointed commander of SAC at its establishment, Kenney had also been tasked to serve as the senior American officer on the Military Staff Committee of the newly established United Nations (UN). He began serving in this capacity in January 1946 and thought the UN assignment a promising one, recalling that "if [the] United Nations [had] a force big enough to impose peace on the world, why boy, that air force commander would be the most powerful military commander in the world."[51] Hoping for something potentially greater from the new international body, much of Kenney's time up until January 1947 was focused on his responsibilities at the UN and not on his command and the assigned mission.

With the potential of greater opportunity in the international arena, Kenney made frequent speeches in support of the UN and pressed for a larger U.S. involvement in the new organization. Sometimes his words overstepped his bounds and at times fell into the realm of national policy, an issue he had to be warned about by Spaatz.[52] In addition to his UN duties, Kenney was also tasked by Secretary Symington to make speeches and public appearances advocating air power and an independent air force. A vain, gregarious personality, Kenney eagerly took to this with great vigor, having to go "all over the damned country yelling for a separate air department" while basking in the limelight and public adulation.[53] As a result he left much of the day-to-day operations to his deputy commander, Major General St. Clair Streett, with SAC as the commander's lesser priority.

On June 5, 1946, Kenney received a letter from Lieutenant General Ennis Whitehead, a longtime friend and onetime subordinate, warning him that "rumors which I hear indicate the UNO [United Nations Organization] is taking an ever increasing amount of your time and energy."[54] In the letter,

Whitehead suggested that SAC should be Kenney's focus and predicted that the UN assignment eventually would become a dead end.[55] The next month Whitehead again wrote Kenney regarding his concerns about SAC:

> While you have had all your energies absorbed by your duties at UNO, you are nevertheless completely responsible for the success of Strategic Air Command. If anything should happen and units of the Strategic Air Command be called upon for combat operations, the only thing which people would remember would be that George Kenney was the commander.[56]

During the summer of 1946, Kenney realized that his friend was correct with regard to the UN assignment. The idea of an international military air force keeping world peace was indeed a chimera, and the desire to build such an air fleet eventually died quietly. Seeing that the UN job amounted to nothing, days later he called Spaatz and tried to have himself replaced. However, the USAAF chief replied that no other four-star officers were available to backfill the position. As a result Kenney was stuck in the posting until October 15, 1946, when he was able to finally rid himself of the international obligation. After his UN experience, in January 1947, Kenney submitted his after-action report to Secretary of War Robert Patterson and cynically reported, "I see little hope that the Military Staff Committee will accomplish anything worthwhile during 1947."[57] Like the Baruch plan regarding atomic technology, the idea of an international air force securing world peace proved too ambitious and wildly optimistic.

In the same July 1946 letter addressing Kenney's responsibilities and his concerns over SAC, Whitehead offered to transfer himself and/or Major General Clements C. McMullen and Brigadier General K.B. Wolfe to assist the command overcome its many challenges.[58] All three of these officers had proven records and volunteered to be assigned to SAC headquarters to ameliorate the command's problems. In January 1947, SAC's deputy, St. Clair Streett, was reassigned as chief of military personnel procurement and departed the command. At the same time, McMullen was transferred to SAC and replaced Streett as the deputy commander. McMullen was an able aviator during the interwar years and, like Kenney, had an excellent wartime record. Serving under Kenney during the war, McMullen proved a tough, capable logistician who ran maintenance and depot-level support operations for the 5th and 13th Air Forces in the Southwest Pacific. As a known quantity to the SAC commander, McMullen enjoyed Kenney's full confidence. This trust in his deputy commander was especially convenient, as Kenney continued his many public-relations engagements and frequently traveled, leaving McMullen to run the day-to-day operations. However, McMullen's influence on the command through ill-conceived personnel policies and organizational initiatives became a detriment to a command that clearly had enough challenges.

Looking to make the most out of the meager manpower assets SAC had, McMullen implemented a policy that tasked rated officers to be crosstrained in all functions relating to their aircraft. Pilots were expected not only to be trained to fly the plane, but were also required to function as navigators, bombardiers, flight engineers, and/or radar operators. With this vision in mind, aircrew could be assigned different stations in the aircraft depending upon the mission. This initiative provided flexibility in the scheduling process as it made assigning crews to sorties much easier. Not a bad idea in theory, the practice was common in the interwar years and one that McMullen and pilots of his generation were very familiar with.[59] During the interwar years, Curtis LeMay made his professional reputation as a navigator finding the Italian luxury liner "Rex" at sea in horrendous weather and also as the lead navigator for a group of B-17s on a South American goodwill mission in 1938. In 1929, future USAAF Chief of Staff Carl Spaatz, along with future General Elwood Quesada, were the crewmen executing one of the first air-to-air refueling operations. Given the nature of aviation technology during the interwar years, this kind of multifunctional tasking was reasonable and well within the capability of most airmen. However, along with the war came an exponential growth in technology and complexity in aircraft engineering and function. As a result, the ability of one crewman to master all the required skills to operate a bomber was unrealistic if not altogether unsafe. Major technological advances in radar, aircraft systems, and power plants required specific expertise and experience. These newer aircraft and supporting systems required skill sets not always easily mastered. In conjunction with the new technology and the skill sets they required, proficiency also became increasingly important. Maintaining a given skill set required an individual crewman to exercise proficiency in selected tasks that was perishable over time.

Kenney and McMullen both also thought that if the command had more rated aircrews that were crosstrained in a number of duties, the subordinate units could also be staffed with fewer overall personnel. Not only would the rated personnel be capable of doing multiple tasks when airborne, but McMullen also wanted these same officers to have more responsibilities doing administrative and support jobs when not flying.[60] As a result, the rated officer doing administrative functions when on the ground could replace a number of non-rated personnel assigned to the command. A unit not only would have more flexible aircrews, but would not need as many support personnel as previously required. As an example, a bomber squadron that had a normal table of organization requiring 81 officers could, theoretically, function effectively with only 34 on hand if many of them were multifunctional and assigned additional duties within the squadron or group.[61] If this idea was implemented in all units in SAC, the command might have experienced an overall savings of 2,300 officers.[62]

8. Men

Despite the problem inherent with the idea, it became standard manpower policy in SAC. However, this was also a policy that was in concert with larger Air Force actions, as Spaatz mandated that the service be composed of 70 percent of rated personnel, also requiring flying personnel to do more than one assigned function.[63] SAC took this idea one step further and wanted to staff its units with 80 percent rated personnel with the same intent.[64] This idea had merit, as the service had to make the most out of what it had available. However, this multifunction requirement and the additional tasking for administrative duties on SAC aircrews would have a detrimental effect on the command's overall performance. Leon Johnson recalled, "At SAC we couldn't do our job very well.... I think some of the other [commanders] agreed."[65] One pilot's evaluation of the command in 1948 was that under McMullen, SAC "wasn't pointed toward the goal of getting airplanes and crews that could take bombs across the seas and bomb targets in Russia."[66] Streamlined internal organization and efficiency became the goal, not combat effectiveness.

This also put a premium on flying personnel and relegated those who were not wearing wings to second-class status in their service of choice. Obviously this kind of policy had severe morale implications for both rated and non-rated personnel.[67] Pilots wished to fly planes and not become jack-of-all-trades crewmen, while non-rated personnel who had specific skill sets and proficiencies in their assigned fields were increasingly marginalized. Group and squadron commanders at SAC also disliked this practice because it reduced overall aircrew proficiency and unit function. Instead of working on his piloting skills, an aviator would now have to develop a host of other abilities. This was done at the expense of his capacity to operate and employ an airframe in a combat environment. This skill set is difficult enough to fully develop and maintain, but under the McMullen plan, the officer was required to obtain a whole host of other abilities in addition to his primary skill. Even SAC's own Operations Analysis Branch held the McMullen plan in low regard and reported that it would take months before any results would be seen.[68] As a result, proficiency in primary flying skills began to suffer. Lt. General Jack Catton, a commander of one of the atomic strike units, remembered that McMullen's plan "was destructive in terms of the flying proficiency of the organization."[69] With regard to the crosstraining initiative, even SAC's official history stated that it "added to confusion ... [and] It almost destroyed all proficiency in the combat units of SAC."[70]

Evidence of a lack of bombing proficiency is found in SAC's own training standards. In 1948, the Air Force claimed that a 3,000 foot circular error probable (CEP) was the consistent standard for bombing accuracy.[71] CEP is defined as the radius in which 50 percent of bombs dropped will fall when released from over 25,000 feet.[72] In training exercises during 1947, SAC crews had CEPs that varied from 2,600 feet to 4,400 feet[73]—not quite up to the standard expected. Recognizing the need to develop bombing proficiency, in June 1948, SAC held its first bombing competition at Castle Air Force Base, California. Crews from ten bomb groups in the 8th and 15th Air Forces, including the 509th Bomb Group, which was assigned the atomic mission, participated. Three crews from each of the bomb groups were tasked with three visual drops and three radar drops, both from an altitude of 25,000 feet. The 8th Air Force won the competition, dropping bombs within 2,000 feet of the target. The atomic-missioned 509th Group performance resulted in a CEP of some 4,000 feet.[74] While the 8th Air Force result was within the service's standard, it must be remembered that these were the best crews the bombardment groups had to offer. The 509th, supposedly the premier atomic strike force for the service, did not even meet the Air Force standard of 3,000 feet at the competition. While the 8th Air Force could claim a victory at the competition, CEP was certainly an issue command-wide, based upon the overall results. However, given the policies implemented within SAC at the time, with McMullen's crosstraining programs and other policies, decreasing the bombing errors was not going to happen any time soon.[75]

Six months later, as part of a briefing for OFFTACKLE in April 1949, SAC reported that standard bombing CEPs had grown and were between 8,000 and 10,000 feet, almost three times the Air Force standard! This bombing error was blamed largely upon "faulty techniques, poor mission preparation, and lack of experience at high altitudes...."[76] This combination of problems was similar to those experienced during the earlier Dayton raid. When the USSBS evaluated the atomic effects at Hiroshima, most of the blast and fire damage occurred within 5,000 to 7,000 feet from the "zero point" of the explosion.[77] If the "Little Boy" weapon had detonated 8,000 to 10,000 feet (SACs CEP in 1949) from the intended aim point, much of the targeted industrial center of the city would have been spared blast damage and the subsequent fire. Obviously a gross targeting error of this magnitude, even with atomic weapons with kilotons' worth of blasting power, would have serious detrimental effects on target destruction.

In addition to the importance of CEP, the quality of the crews also played a significant role, especially in the ability of a bomber to reach an intended target. In the WSEG analysis of OFFTACKLE, it was estimated that at an altitude of 35,000 feet, 95 percent of B-50s sortied could reach 71 percent of the targets in the plan. But the best crews could reach 88 percent of the targets in a "no-wind" situation, penetrating at 20,000 feet, but then bombing at 35,000 feet.[78] This ability of the best crews to hit longer-range targets meant that SAC would have to shuffle crews and missions based upon the various assigned targets. In a letter to the JCS, the WSEG endorsed a program that LeMay had already begun to establish that leveraged these more capable

8. Men

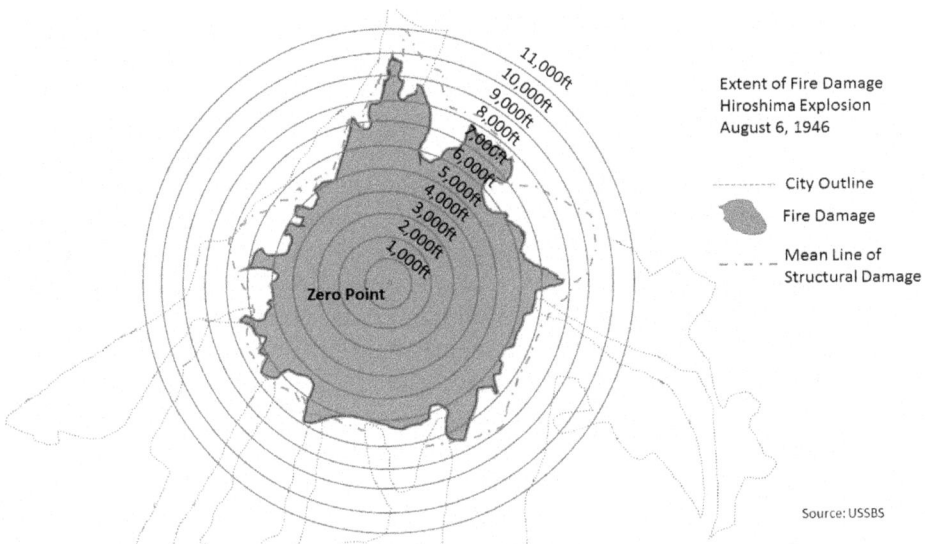

U.S. Strategic Bombing Survey map showing the range of "Little Boy" bomb damage to Hiroshima. Note how most of the damage for the 20 kiloton blast is contained in a 7,000 foot radius from the zero point of detonation.

crews. The idea first began in the war, when LeMay established what became known as "lead crews." In this concept, the most capable teams were chosen to take the bomb group to selected targets that the lead crews had studied. Lead crews were to be familiar with the nature of the target, its defenses, and peculiarities. LeMay instituted a similar training program for lead crews within SAC at Walker Air Force Base, New Mexico, in June 1949. The course included some 160 hours of instruction designed to improve the skill set of the best crews available.[79] In the first class, half of the crews failed to pass, with only two of the 19 B-29 crews attending passing in the second class.[80] This lack of success in the first class was because some commanders did not understand the importance of the new school and failed to send their top performers.[81] The idea was that these graduates would return to their parent units and instruct fellow aviators on tactics, techniques, and procedures. Eventually this course of instruction paid off, and by 1950, SAC had trained 80 crews and the reputation of the school as a useful institution rose appreciably, with accuracy improving some 50 percent.[82] With this kind of training, SAC expected accuracy to improve to below the 2,000 foot CEP level, provided the APQ-24 radar bombsight worked.[83] In the case of SAC in the late 1940s, the idea of a lead crew was a distinct break from the kind of training that McMullen was instilling with his crosstraining program.

McMullen's policies had other implications that went above the individual level. Organizationally, the training requirement McMullen imposed on units within SAC truly belonged to Air Training Command (ATC) as part of an individual initial Military Operating Skills (MOS) syllabus. It was ATC's job to conduct initial skills training for navigators, bombardiers, and radar operators. SAC was not manned, trained, or equipped to support such training and the exacting skills these positions required. McMullen attempted to get help from ATC in the form of mobile training teams, but the request was denied.[84] As a result, SAC was on its own to develop the cross-level skills McMullen wanted. Units would now have to establish their own programs and schedule aircrews and planes out of their own organic assets to provide the training needed. These added training requirements created burdens in addition to the normal operating commitments on a command that was already short of men, material, planes, and money. Shortly after LeMay took command of SAC, one of his commanders told him, "We are so busy fighting our headquarters and trying to get the training [required], that we didn't have time to do anything else."[85]

While many in SAC decried the crosstraining policy, McMullen was given a free hand by the ineffectual Kenney. Despite its detractors, the plan was implemented in late 1947, and SAC Headquarters mandated that each group was to have ten pilots fully crosstrained by July 1, 1948.[86] There was another rationale underpinning McMullen's manpower policy and the emphasis he placed on rated personnel. In McMullen's opinion, the most efficient USAAF units had a higher percentage of rated personnel than non-rated. During the war, the number of non-rated personnel mushroomed, with these officers accomplishing many of the administrative and support tasks that had once been done by rated personnel.[87] In McMullen's opinion, rated personnel were more understanding of flight operations and could better conceptualize the requirements of employing an air fleet. Leon Johnson observed, "McMullen had an obsession that only pilots were any good."[88] No doubt this was a misguided and erroneous belief. In the effort to maximize manpower resources and streamline personnel staffing, McMullen accepted lesser numbers of non-flying airmen into the command. In his opinion the USAAF during the war had acquired, "a large percentage of non-flying officers who will take away the dash and glamour of the Air Forces."[89] This policy manifested itself in a confrontation between Spaatz and Kenney regarding the assignment of three Colonels from the Quartermaster Corps to SAC. The three colonels, who had excellent qualifications, were denied assignment to the command. In McMullen's opinion, "supply officers that I see in this command are long-faced, non-flying officers who try to make an aurora [sic] over their head out of the mystery of supply. There is no mystery in the business of supply."[90] Spaatz sent a pointed letter to Kenney in May 1947 regarding McMullen's

8. Men

ideas on USAAF manpower policies, writing, "I expect that you and your staff will become familiar with the Air Force policies and plans and will carry them out promptly and loyally."[91]

The policies of crosstraining, primacy placed on rated personnel, and the desire to staff units with fewer than authorized numbers, created what became known as "McMullen ceilings."[92] These artificial "ceilings" placed limits on the number of people assigned to various SAC organizations, keeping units staffed below their authorized table of organization. The deputy commander went so far as to state, "Give them half of what they ask for, work them twice as hard, they will get twice as much done."[93] In addition to these practices, the deputy commander also looked to streamline headquarters organization, downsizing headquarter staff offices. In this effort, McMullen assumed the position of chief of staff, removed executive officer positions, and then had special staff functions report directly to him.[94] As a result, fewer people were required to do more work. McMullen's insistence and uncompromising nature regarding his policies and plans, despite the loud arguments against such efforts, earned him the nickname "cement head" or "concrete."[95] His insistence on following his misguided organizational efforts is ironic considering his excellent wartime reputation as a skillful administrator and manager. The various policies regarding the primacy of rated personnel, establishing lower staffing goals, and mandate for crosstraining aircrews had disastrous effects on the combat capabilities of the command. These issues, compounded with the lack of budgetary support and the poor quality of enlisted airmen, made SAC a paper tiger when America considered it as the first line of national defense.

Even before McMullen implemented his plan, Kenney had an overly optimistic opinion of SAC and its capabilities. More interested in concerns outside SAC and oblivious to the state of his command, when queried by a *Los Angeles Times* reporter in April 1947 about the state of American strategic bombing capability, Kenney reported, "We're not in too bad shape...."[96] In the article, Kenney addresses how the Air Force was developing newer and better airplanes and that this was a key element to maintaining national security.

However, his bluster was hiding significant problems within the command. A key indicator of an aviation unit's competency and capabilities lies in its safety record. In 1948, SAC had a miserable safety record, with 65 major accidents per 100,000 flying hours.[97] In addition to safety issues, at one time some 408 airmen were absent without leave, approximately 1 percent of the command, with about one-third of the B-29 fleet grounded for one reason or another.[98] Suspicious of the state of SAC, in spring of 1948, USAF Deputy Chief of Staff for Operations General Lauris Norstad asked famed aviator Charles Lindbergh and the first atomic strike mission commander,

Brigadier General Paul Tibbets, to evaluate the command. What these men found, in concert with other performance indicators, would eventually lead to Kenney's removal from command.

By September 1948, Lindbergh had finished his inspection of SAC and reported his findings to Vandenberg, who had replaced Spaatz as the new Air Force Chief of Staff in June. Having accepted the prevailing idea that future war would be short and atomic-centric, the famed aviator made the assumption that SAC needed to be prepared to deliver "maximum striking power" at the very onset of conflict.[99] Because of the nature of SAC's assigned mission, Lindbergh believed that aircrews designated for atomic delivery need to be "the best in experience, character, and skill that the United States can furnish."[100] Lindbergh toured the command for several months, flew approximately 100 hours in SAC aircraft, took part in mock raids, and visited six different bases. He focused his inspection efforts primarily on units with atomic attack missions. What he saw fell well short of expectations.

When comparing SAC crews to that of a contemporary civilian airline, Lindbergh expected SAC's standard to be higher. In his letter to the Air Force Chief, he reported that the command's proficiency standards were "considerably low."[101] According to him, the crews in the atomic units were not carefully selected, average pilot proficiency was unsatisfactory, teamwork was poor, and the maintenance of both planes and equipment was inadequate.[102] When accompanying a B-29 squadron landing at an airfield in the United Kingdom, he observed, "[It] turned back to its home base rather than land under instrument conditions, which were above normal minimums in the first instance and bordering on VFR [Visual Flight Rules] below 3,000 feet in the second instance. [Additionally] the GCA [Ground Controlled Approach] radar was operating."[103] He went on to report, "In general, personnel are not sufficiently experienced in their primary mission."[104] In these findings, Lindbergh reported that the policies of crosstraining and extracurricular flying duties hampered the abilities of crews to execute their primary responsibilities.[105] He found both air and ground crew morale poor, men overworked, and families severely disrupted. In the letter he echoed what other SAC officers and the command's Operations Analysis Branch had been complaining about for months. In one document he completely repudiated McMullen's instituted policies and ideas that had become the bane of the command.

While he painted a very grim picture of the command, he did make a number of suggestions so that SAC could fix itself, provided the Air Force had the means. In his opinion, SAC needed to make the atomic mission its own career path within the Air Force and that tours with the command needed to last several years. Aircrews needed to maintain their integrity and continually train together without mixing men from other crews. Furthermore, individual replacements within an aircrew team should be made only after the new member had been apprenticed and adequately trained. Much to the relief of many in the command, Lindbergh also recommended that the crosstraining effort be eliminated or severely curtailed until proficiency in the primary mission was attained.[106] He took this idea one step further and argued that atomic crews should be removed from all taskings not associated with their primary mission and that these men should be carefully selected.[107] Lastly he recommended that the Air Force needed to create conditions in pay and housing that would attract the highest quality of people.

In closing his report, Lindbergh recognized the problems that demobilization made for the Air Force and that SAC was doing the best it could with what resources it had. But in understanding what future war might look like, Lindbergh believed that the Air Force needed to make a significant shift in its operating principles and management if it were to conduct missions as envisioned. Tibbets reported much of the same to Norstad. Tibbets's observations were much more pointed, as he reportedly told Norstad, "There isn't anybody out there that knows what they hell they are doing ... the crews don't know how to fly the airplane."[108] Despite the primacy atomic warfare had in the American defensive plans, SAC, and the Air Force at large, had significant issues to resolve before an atomic offensive could be executed.

Coincidentally, Lindbergh's letter arrived a day after the Air Force Chief had just briefed the president on the need to prepare for war.[109] Fully cognizant of the problems facing SAC, Norstad reported his findings to Vandenberg. It was clear that a new commander would be required to effect the change needed. In response to Norstad's grim news, the Air Force Chief asked who should replace Kenney at SAC. In the course of the conversation, Norstad asked, "Who would you put in there in time—in case—of war?"[110] To this Vandenberg had a simple reply: "LeMay."

A month later, Kenney was reassigned to a more benign command as head of Air University at Maxwell Air Force Base, Alabama, and from there he would eventually retire in 1951. Concurrently, LeMay was placed as the new commander of SAC on October 19. A few weeks later, the command moved from Andrews Air Force Base, Maryland, to its permanent location at Offutt Air Force Base, Nebraska. The movement of the command from the Washington area to Nebraska was ordered by Vandenberg months earlier, much to the chagrin of Kenney. When LeMay assumed command, he also sought to bring in those officers with whom he was familiar and trusted. He appointed Brigadier General Tommy Powers as his deputy effective 26 October, with McMullen reassigned to the San Antonio Air Material Area at Kelly Air Force Base, Texas. In addition to bringing in some of his trusted subordinates, he assessed the staff at SAC and made replacements as he saw fit. According to one officer, "it was bloody."[111] In addition to Powers, LeMay brought in other proven air commanders whom he had known from the war to serve in key posts throughout the command. Many of these men had been with LeMay during the firebombing campaign and were like-minded in ideas regarding air power. In addition, he conducted a wholesale review of SAC's mission in a possible aerial offensive. In December 1948 at Maxwell Air Force Base, Alabama, he conducted the DUALISM conference that reviewed unit missions and roles in the given plan. From that point on, LeMay had his commanders examine their units' responsibilities in the aerial offensive and made sure that they clearly understood their specific goals and objectives.[112]

After assuming command, LeMay immediately started to determine SAC's combat readiness and ability to go to war. What he found echoed what Lindbergh and Tibbets observed earlier. Many aircrews failed to follow standard operating procedures, including failing to use checklists when operating aircraft.[113] A lack of discipline and failure to adhere to proven methods permeated the command. This included the leadership, as he found instances of group commanders who were not qualified in the planes they were supposed to be flying.[114] In his opinion, "We didn't have one crew, *not one crew* in the entire command who could do a professional job. No one of the outfits was up to strength—neither the airplanes nor the people nor anything else."[115] He found attitudes lax and was determined to install a frame of mind with one simple message: "We are at war now."[116] The first thing he had to do was to convince the bomber crews that were indeed substandard, poorly trained and ill-disciplined.[117]

When accidents occurred with SAC aircraft, LeMay surmised that it had more to do with the aircrews' cocky and careless attitudes than anything else. As he described sardonically:

> [Many perceived that] the stupid pilot followed procedures which had been outlined for him. The *best* pilot ... that was beneath him, of course. He didn't have to follow these checklists. That was for the neophytes. So he went out and busted his butt someplace along the line.[118]

LeMay was addressing all of SAC's units, both conventional and atomic units, and he did not differentiate the incompetence. Both types of units needed attention. However, given the primacy of atomic weapons in American plans, units with that specific mission were given priority. In the 8th Air Force, that included the 509th, 43rd, and the 7th bomb groups, as they were the only units designated for atomic delivery. Realistic and continuous training became the norm at SAC. Indicative of SAC's change in attitude regarding training, in 1946 the command flew 888 radar bombing runs in training. However, under LeMay leadership in 1950, SAC aircrews flew 43,733 bomb runs.[119] While LeMay quickly identified shortfalls within the command and instituted required changes, the results would not be immediate and would take months to fully manifest. While additional money and equipment would have to come from outside sources, LeMay made the most out of the assets available.

To counteract the command's overall lethargy, LeMay instituted a number of policies and programs that turned SAC into a powerful military organization. LeMay's goal upon assuming command was "to build a force so professional, so strong, so powerful that we would not have to fight."[120] Training became a hallmark at SAC. As one wing commander put it, "Training at SAC was harder [than war], It might have been a relief to go to a war."[121] For LeMay the goal was for SAC to be capable of dropping 80 percent of the atomic stockpile in a single massive strike.[122] LeMay said, "I never discussed it with President Truman or President Eisenhower. I never discussed it with General Vandenberg when he was chief of staff. I stuck to my job at Offutt and in the command. I never discussed what we were going to do with it.... All I did was to keep them abreast of the development of SAC. I told them what strength we had as fast as that strength grew."[123]

However, the turnaround for SAC would still take time. While LeMay did what he could in 1949, the atomic air offensive was to remain in a degraded state for months to come. Instilling discipline, enforcing regulations, and rebuilding effective leadership was within LeMay's capability. However, he was still dealing with a defense budget that precluded full development of a force capable of executing the envisioned war plan. In the April 1950 SAC commanders' conference, he recognized the fiscal shortfall's impact on SAC's ability to perform its given mission telling his subordinates, "I don't see how we can do it with the funds presently programmed. Furthermore if we proceed at the rate we have in the past year, it is out of the question."[124] LeMay prognosticated that "under the business as usual methods, it will take years before we can get a striking force in position to go."[125] He would have to wait until other global events provided the catalyst for full-scale change within the command. Not until the acceptance of NSC-68 and its budgetary implications would SAC truly be able to start accomplishing the atomic mission assigned.

9

Machines

The strategic bombing of Japan was conducted almost exclusively by a single weapon system, the Boeing B-29 Superfortress. Given the unique circumstances and distances governing military operations in the Pacific War, the Superfortress was the only weapon system capable of striking the Japanese home islands from bases in China and the Mariana Islands.[1] Known as the "3-Billion Dollar Gamble," because it was ordered into production while still just a design on paper, the aircraft could carry ten tons of bombs and had a range of over 3,000 miles.[2] The B-29 became one of the war's greatest military weapons, and its image as the first atomic bomber is permanently fixed in military history. As a result of the firebombing campaign and the subsequent atomic attacks, the B-29 came to symbolize American military might and its technological prowess.

After the war, the B-29 would remain the primary atomic bombing aircraft for SAC and was then augmented with the B-50 in February 1948. Adding to the atomic bombing fleet was the first atomic-capable version of the B-36 (starting with the last 47 airframes in the B-36B version) in 1949. While the B-50 was a highly modified version of the B-29's basic design, the B-36 was a wholly new aircraft that would take time to make fully combat ready. These three airframes served as the trifecta for America's air offensive and for a time provided a capability that no other nation could match. In April 1950, the SAC inventory of these three airframes included 27 B-36s, 148 B-50s, and 337 B-29s, for a total bomber figure of 512.[3] The 485 B-50s and B-29s constituted the medium bomber fleet, with the B-36s composing the entire heavy bomber inventory. Eventually all three airframes would be replaced by the B-47 when it became operational in 1951 or by the B-52 in 1955. However, much like the plans and men associated with the atomic offensive, these airframes had their limitations.

For most of the postwar period, the B-29 was considered "the big stick" in strategic bombardment. The B-29 enjoyed an excellent reputation in the public eye, and the USAAF was keen to display its capabilities whenever possible. The Pacific bombing campaign in the spring and summer of 1945 razed over 180 square miles of the Japanese urban landscape, destroyed over 600 factories and 2.3 million homes, injured one-half to one million, and killed 330,000 to 990,000 civilians.[4] These strikes were so destructive and deadly that they caused LeMay, who was at that time the head of XXI Bomber Command, to quip, "If we lost the war we would have been prosecuted as war criminals."[5] This damage was done well before the atomic attacks of August and is often overshadowed by the strikes on Nagasaki and Hiroshima. After the war the B-29 was used to showcase airpower to the American people by conducting well-publicized long-distance flights and flyovers for large public gatherings. However, as the possibility of atomic war grew, the B-29 increasingly became a legacy system that was becoming ill-suited for the new expanding global mission. With the lack of defense funds, slow development, and controversial nature of the B-36 program, the B-29s and B-50s were the only atomic-capable aircraft available for SAC.

However, for all the accolades and praise attributed to the B-29, the development of the long-range bomber was a painful process. The aircraft's initial operations suffered from numerous design problems and engine malfunctions. These early difficulties precluded the airframe from achieving its initial performance parameters. An old Air Force axiom states, "Never fly the 'A model' [first production series] of anything," and certainly in the case of the B-29 this statement rang true. As with most new airframes, the first model of the B-29 required the modification, redesign, and reengineering of many systems, subsystems, and components. However, the technical problems of the first production models of B-29s had consequences that went far beyond the engineer's T-square and the drafting table.

At the time, the B-29 was the most sophisticated and complex airplane ever designed. Built in the wake of the B-17 and B-24, the Superfortress included many technological innovations that substantially improved the bomber's capabilities and flying qualities. While pursuit aviation claimed priority of effort in the 1930s, the outbreak of World War II renewed interest in large bomber design. As a result of the war and the possibility of America's participation, in February 1940 the U.S. Army Air Corps announced a new requirement for a "Hemispheric Defense Weapon."[6] Boeing Aircraft Company answered the call, and its first prototype, the XB-29, made its maiden flight in September 1942. The airframe was powered by four R-3350 turbocharged engines designed to produce 2,200 horsepower each at takeoff. The aircraft featured self-sealing fuel tanks, heavy defensive armament, and the ability to carry eight tons of bombs.[7] The bomber also included a pressurization system for crew comfort, remote fire control defensive systems, specially designed four-bladed Hamilton propellers, and hundreds of other impressive engineering advances.[8]

The idea behind the B-29 came from a requirement for a "Very Heavy Bomber" (VHB) (also referred to the as the Very Long Ranger (VLR) bomber) in the Air War Planning Document (AWPDs) of the early 1940s. The concept of the VHB was built upon existing bomber designs while leveraging engineering advances to produce an aircraft that was considerably heavier, faster, and more capable.[9] According to the Aircraft Commander's Manual for the B-29: "It [the B-29] was built to do one particular job well, fly a long way with a big load of bombs."[10] General Arnold strongly endorsed the tenets of AWPD-1 and enthusiastically supported the VHB program. As a proponent of the VHB, he meticulously tracked its development.[11] Arnold, more than anyone else in the Air Force, took the chances on the enormously expensive and unproven B-29 project.[12] During the early phases of B-29 development, Arnold countered critics in the War Department who objected to the huge allocation of funds and resources dedicated to the project.[13] Given that the B-29 was an unproven design and was rushed into production to meet wartime requirements, Arnold's gamble had serious implications for the USAAF.[14] B-29s rolled off the production lines in late 1943 and early 1944. However, these early airframes were built before a number of technical problems with the B-29 became apparent. The biggest problem affecting the performance of the B-29 was her newly designed R-3350 engines made by the Curtiss-Wright Corporation. These powerful engines often overheated, had cylinder heads blow out during startup, were equipped with faulty ignition systems, leaked oil excessively, and were plagued with fuel system problems.[15] These problems as well as other design flaws led to the fielding of aircraft before important engineering corrections and changes were incorporated.[16] According to LeMay:

> [The] B-29 had as many bugs as the entomological department of the Smithsonian Institution. Fast as they got the bugs licked, new ones crawled out from underneath the cowling.[17] ... If you ever saw a buggy airplane, this was it.[18]

While many airframe changes were required, the R-3350 engine alone required over two thousand engineering modifications.[19] When the first B-29s flew to the China-Burma-India theater in April 1944, each bomber deployed with a spare engine loaded into one of the plane's bomb bays. After a number of operational losses, engineers discovered that the R-3350's thermo-couplers were often out of calibration, cowl flaps were improperly set for takeoff and taxi, cylinders in the rear rows were susceptible to exhaust valve seat erosion, and a leak in the exhaust port in the front cylinders would allow white-hot exhaust to blow over adjacent cylinder heads.[20] After the war in November

A regular occurrence, an R-3350 engine on a B-29 being changed. These engines required changing after only 270 flight hours and were troublesome from the very start. Mechanical limitations of the engine were one of the reasons LeMay started his low-level firebombing of Japanese cities in 1945 (U.S. Air Force photograph).

1945, in an address to the Ohio Society of New York and the Alumni of Ohio State University, LeMay explained:

> You do not draw a complicated, precision airplane like the B-29 out of a silk hat. The Air Forces had blueprints for [t]he B-29—but no blueprint ever dropped a bomb. So the B-29 was tested in combat. It is a tribute to the men who planned and built it that this great airplane lived up to what was expected of it after a few modifications.[21]

These design flaws had operational implications that eventually convinced LeMay to conduct low-level incendiary bombardment of Japanese cities. While this tactic was effective in the war, the number of problems that the B-29 experienced took years to correct, and the Air Force was still modifying the plane when it was withdrawn from service in the late 1950s.[22]

While the B-29 was designed for conventional bombing operations, in order to deliver atomic ordnance, a specially modified version of the plane was needed. These atomic-capable versions of the B-29 were first built in 1944 and given the code name SILVERPLATE. These atomic-capable B-29s had a number of upgrades that were phased into the design based upon when each SILVERPLATE aircraft was built. The biggest modification to these aircraft was the reconfiguration of the bomb bay to accommodate the atomic ordnance of "Little Boy" and the MK III and MK IV weapons.[23] The first phase of SILVERPLATE aircraft included the installation of upgraded R-3350-41 engines that included fuel injection, better cooling, and an improved manifold system.[24] In addition to the more powerful and cooler-running engine, the plane also included reversible-pitch propellers to improve aircraft braking on landing.[25] These designs also saved aircraft weight by removing the defensive armament provided by the remotely controlled gun turrets. Removal of the turrets was sometimes done at the operating base as opposed to the factory. However, the SILVERPLATE aircraft still retained the tail-gun armament.

Some of the first-phase aircraft also included pneumatic bomb bay doors that opened and closed faster than the standard electrically driven ones. It was considered especially important that the doors open and close quickly, as the bomber was required to make a 155-degree diving turn, at a 60 degree angle of bank, while losing 1,700 feet of altitude after release of the weapon. This rather dramatic maneuver for a plane as large as the B-29 was designed to avoid the weapon's blast and to exit the target area as fast as possible.[26] The evasive maneuver, practiced many times by pilots of the 509th Bombardment Group, was designed to put the crew and plane approximately ten miles away from the impact point when the atomic detonation occurred. Scientists with the Ballistics Group at Los Alamos determined that the ten miles distance would provide an adequate level of protection for the airplane and crew from the ensuing shock wave by a factor of two.[27]

By phase 3 of the SILVERPLATE modifications, the structure of the bomb bays was standardized by use of an "H-frame" harness and an improved sway brace arrangement that accommodated both the "Fat Man" and "Little Boy" designs.[28] In addition to the bomb bay modification, a number of electrical improvements were made that allowed the bomb to be monitored from a location in the pressurized forward cabin. By the time the war ended, 46 SILVERPLATES had been built. Of these, 26 aircraft were placed in operational units or at test facilities at Sandia or Wendover Field, Utah, and 17 were placed into storage.[29]

However, after the establishment of SAC, Air Material Command issued orders on July 26, 1946, for an additional 19 B-29s to be modified to SILVERPLATE versions.[30] While the order went out for more atomic-capable B-29s, by October 1, 1947, SAC had only 18 SILVERPLATE aircraft, and those in the active inventory were well worn and beginning to show their age. Additionally, while this modification process was under way, the program name for the conversion of atomic airframes was suddenly changed from SILVERPLATE to SADDLETREE for security purposes. While the name changed, the modification process did not and the program grew. Additionally, the SADDLETREE program was not just applicable to the B-29, but encompassed a larger modification process that included the newer B-50 and B-36 aircraft and configured them to carry atomic ordnance as well.[31] Later in April 1948, the modification process also included a Global Electronics Modification (GEM) that provided for a worldwide navigation capability. With the idea of flying attack routes from Alaska over the higher latitudes, many airframes were fitted with an Arctic cold-weather modification. In all some 65 SILVERPLATES and 80 SADDLETREES were modified to carry atomic ordnance.[32] In addition, 95 B-50s and 18 B-36s were also modified with both SADDLETREE and GEM capabilities. As for the B-29 fleet, of the 145 aircraft available, 28 were assigned to test and training organizations and 117 place in operational squadrons.[33] While an additional $25 million from the FY 1948 supplement was allotted to the modification process, making the changes and fielding all the allocated aircraft would take time. Additionally, these modifications would also fall behind schedule, as Boeing experienced a machinist labor strike in April 1948 lasting until mid–September.

Another of the workhorses for the early war plans was the B-50. Designated a medium bomber, the B-50 was the next evolution of the B-29. While similar in shape to the B-29, the design of the B-50 was some 75 percent new. Made from a lighter grade of aluminum, the plane was 650 pounds lighter, yet determined to be 16 percent stronger. Besides having a higher vertical stabilizer than the B-29 and a redesigned nose canopy, the biggest external change was that the troublesome R-3350 engines of the B-29 were replaced with R-4360 engines and had oil coolers located in a large fairing under each cowl. The newer engines, along with other design features, provided 59 percent more power than the standard B-29. SAC took its first B-50A in February 1948, but maintenance and technical issues precluded this first unit from becoming operational until 1949. Therefore, the B-29s continued to be the only airframe capable of dropping atomic ordnance almost four years after the end of the war. While the military was suffering from a lack of available bombs to drop, it was also facing a problem with the number of atomic bombers available. When the upgraded B-50D version was fielded in mid–1949, it too had a number of technical maladies that included problems with the fuel cells, inverters, and turbo superchargers.[34] As a result of these and many others technical issues, for a period, SAC refused delivery. Boeing also failed to design the aircraft to handle atomic ordnance, and retrofit kits had to be sent to operational units for field modification.[35]

Like the B-29, the B-36 was a legacy design that initially came about during the war. The Air War Planning Documents written during the conflict feared that England might fall to Germany, thus requiring the strategic bombing of Germany from the continental United States. As a result, an aircraft designed to execute such a mission profile would require extensive range and a worthwhile payload. USAAF specifications for such an airframe required that it have a cruising speed of 240–300 mph, a 40,000 foot service ceiling, an effective combat radius of 4,000 miles with a range of 10,000 miles, and a payload of 10,000 pounds.[36] The mock-up for the XB-36 was inspected in July 1942, and the first aircraft rolled out of Convair's Fort

Size comparison between the B-29 "medium" bomber and the B-36 "heavy" bomber. When first fielded, the B-29 was designated a heavy bomber. However, with the advent of the B-36, B-29s were downgraded to a medium status (U.S. Air Force photograph).

Worth hanger on 8 September 1945.[37] The first production model flew in December 1947, and the B-36A was delivered to the first operational unit in March 1948. With the introduction of the B-36, the B-29/50s were then designated "medium" bombers, while the larger airframe was given the title "heavy." Conversions of B-36B models to the SADDLETREE capability began in May 1947 and continued through June 1948. At the end of 1950, SAC had some 52 atomic capable B-36 versions.[38]

However, during the first full year of the B-36's operational life, SAC usually had no more than 40 aircraft on hand, and of those, only half a dozen were expected to be combat-ready.[39] Because the airframe was a new design, unforeseen maintenance problems surfaced, accompanied by a shortage of repair parts. Cannibalization of parts from one B-36 was often required to keep other bombers airworthy.[40] During the first half of 1949, the number of B-36s not out of commission as a result of repair parts or for maintenance was 16 percent of SAC's fleet. This rose to 20 percent for the remaining half of the year.[41] With the fielding of the fleet and more experience with the airframe, the WSEG expected that the number would again rise to 30 percent.[42] The low readiness rate was not an unusual circumstance given the nature of the technology and is a common phenomenon in new aircraft development. In spring 1950 the B-36 design was still suffering from major problems in her engine, fuel system, radar, and defensive armament.[43]

There was yet another limitation to the B-36 mission profile. Envisioned as flying polar routes to targets in the Soviet Union, B-36s would operate out of Alaska. However, the severe cold weather proved a significant obstacle when servicing an aircraft as large as the B-36, and the existing design issues were only exacerbated by the harsh Arctic environment. The conditions at forward bases in Alaska were difficult not just because of the cold, wind, and ice, but also because of a lack of suitable maintenance, billeting, and operations facilities in the remote location.[44] Additionally, getting spare parts and other materials to Alaska proved difficult given its distance from the lower 48 states.[45] SAC recognized this limitation early on but was not able to remedy the facilities issues until later.

Additionally, while these first aircraft were assigned to the 7th Bomb Wing at Carswell Air Force Base, Texas, this unit was largely a service test unit that was putting the B-36 through operational evaluation and not really a front-line combat unit anticipating combat operations.[46] Pilots reported good handling of the aircraft, but the aircraft's main drawback was its low speed, at 319 mph. The 7th Bomb Wing was developing standardization procedures, training aircrew and maintenance personnel, and identifying potential design flaws. As a result, during the late 1940s the legacy B-29s and newer B-50s would bear the brunt of responsibility in the aerial offensive. The OFFTACKLE plan assigned B-29s and B-50s to strike 86

162 Part III. Strategic Air Command

percent of the entire bombing target list, with the B-36 hitting the remaining 14 percent.[47]

The first strike in the OFFTACKLE plan would employ all three airframes striking 26 target areas. As such, 201 B-29/50s would launch from bases in the United Kingdom and penetrate Soviet airspace from both the north and south simultaneously.[48] In addition, 10 B-36s would launch from bases in the continental United States. Planners believed that the simultaneous raids would saturate PVO-Strany defensive capabilities and give the incoming bomber force better chances of success. This was the same tactic often used

One of the six R-4360 engines of a B-36 bomber undergoing repair—a common sight. Early operations of the aircraft highlighted many design deficiencies with its fuel system, radar, and defensive armament. A lack of spare parts also plagued the fleet (U.S. Air Force photograph).

by the USAAF during the CBO. Bombers hitting northern targets would return to the United Kingdom while the planes hitting southern locations would continue on to staging bases in the Middle East. (Where these staging bases were is not available. Given the lack of definition in the war plans, it is questionable whether they existed at all.)

While the B-29 and B-50s were the primary bombers envisioned in the atomic offensive, maintenance of the atomic and conventional bombing fleet was lacking. In May 1947, SAC planned a large simulated raid on New York City with some 181 B-29s taking part. In execution, 80 of the B-29s were unable to sortie because of maintenance or supply issues. Those 80 planes that failed to launch represented 44 percent of SAC's B-29 fleet.[49] As late as 1950, the B-50s were still suffering from major problems with the newly designed turbo superchargers and electrical systems.[50] While SAC did conduct record endurance flights in 1949 by flying nonstop from Texas to Hawaii, navigating the globe with aerial refuelers, and having one airplane stay aloft for over 43 hours, these public-relations events were not indicative of the overall state of the command.[51] During the same year, 56 percent of SAC's aircraft were out of commission for one reason or another. Meanwhile, the command's own standard required 60 percent of heavy bombers to be flightworthy, along with 70 percent of its medium bombing fleet.[52] With this kind of readiness, the command would have been hard-pressed to execute its assigned global offensive. In the February 1950 WSEG analysis for OFFTACKLE, abort rates for the planned airframes were estimated based upon expected aircraft operating altitudes:

WSEG Estimated Abort Rates for OFFTACKLE[53]

Altitude	B-29	B-50	B-36
20,000 ft	4.50%	5%	11%
25,000 ft	6%	x	x
30,000 ft	11%	6%	14%
35,000 ft	x	11%	x
40,000 ft	x	x	20%

The abort rates listed above do not differentiate between atomic and conventional versions, but the overall rates are disturbing regardless of the mission assigned.

Other issues affected the B-29 as an effective bomber. Engine life span was only 272 hours, thus making frequent engine repair a requirement.[54] Since aircraft had increased in complexity over the years, it was impossible for one crew chief to service all the airplane's systems as he had done in previous eras. With a significant problem in operational readiness, a review of SAC maintenance organization and procedure was required. Air Force officers studied maintenance organization and procedures with the RAF and at civilian air carriers such as United Airlines. Learning from these organizations, the Air Force started a production line process in its maintenance operations. In August 1949, a specialized maintenance program that was similar to those of commercial airlines was established that made better use of maintenance facilities and mechanics.

But for the majority of the period, B-29 maintenance and readiness rates remained an issue. SAC determined that cannibalization of the mothballed B-29s in storage was required to support the Superfortress fleet in the operational commands.[55] Exacerbating the maintenance problem was a lack of spare parts for the medium bomber fleet, especially for the B-50s. While the B-50 looked similar to the B-29, only 25 percent of their parts were interchangeable, and most of these were minor items like nuts, bolts, and gaskets.[56] As a result, maintenance personnel in units equipped with newly fielded B-50s were struggling to keep the airframe airworthy. Spare parts shortages affected not only SAC but the entire service, because in November 1947 some 15 percent of the entire air force fleet was grounded due to a lack of spare parts alone.[57] While parts could be sourced from mothballed airframes, the sustained OFFTACKLE plan also required 325 additional bombers from the stored fleet to augment the already deployed seven bomb groups directly involved in combat operations.[58] Adding to the maintenance burden, SAC was also going to deploy one reconnaissance group and one fighter group.[59] Additionally, the lack of spare parts was an issue discussed at the SAC commander's conference in April 1950 as the director of SAC operations, General J. B. Montgomery, reported, "We are still plagued with an excessive number of B-50 and B-36 critical spares, [and] a serious lack of current supply and maintenance publications...."[60] While spare parts would be an issue, the analysis does not address the quality and quality of mechanics in SAC at the time given the low AGCT scores of enlisted personnel. However, at the same conference, General Montgomery did at least make a passing reference to the shortage of personnel.

As mentioned above, organization of the maintenance effort was also an issue for the command. With the increased complexity of airplanes and crew chiefs' inability to repair everything on their assigned aircraft, more technical skills were required to repair the various systems and subsystems inherent in the newer designs. Reorganization and new management techniques were required to avoid the poor readiness rates the Air Force experienced during this time. It was not until late 1949 that LeMay initiated changes in SAC maintenance organizations to address these challenges. Years earlier, in November 1947, the Air Force reorganized each base's organizational structure under what was known as the "Hobson Plan." Under this plan, all airfield support agencies at a given base fell under control of the operational wing commander. The wing commander now had four subordinate groups under his authority: the combat group, the supply and maintenance group, airdrome group, and medical group.[61] As a result, units supporting combat operations had to answer to the combat wing commander for their performance. Under the maintenance structure in the Hobson Plan, the individual squadron and groups would have responsibility for first- and second-echelon maintenance, with a maintenance squadron having responsibility for third echelon.[62] This streamlined command and control and allowed for better logistical support to combat air operations. While modifications were made to the original Hobson Plan structure depending upon the particular base and command, in SAC, LeMay leveraged the existing organizational structure and molded it to fit the command's requirements.

To address this issue in SAC, LeMay pooled all the maintenance resources at the various bases in order to maximize the technical assets available to his operational commanders. According to Regulation 66–12, published in August 1949, a wing maintenance control office was established and was responsible to the operational commander. The centralized control office set maintenance priorities and managed all resources, personnel, and scheduling.[63] The central wing maintenance office also controlled supply functions by keeping spare part demands in concert with the repair efforts. The office also oversaw the training effort of mechanics, standardization of procedures, and identification of trends and conducted quality control efforts.[64] Under the new system, maintenance response times were cut appreciably as B-29 and B-36 maintenance turnaround times went from months or weeks to a matter of days for both airframes.[65]

During his tenure as SAC commander, LeMay made maintenance a priority and held subordinate commanders accountable for related efforts. On a 1950 *Time* front cover was a picture of LeMay and the B-36. The accompanying article supposedly quoted LeMay chastising a subordinate commander for a lower readiness rate than a contemporary. In the account, LeMay chides a commander who unfortunately experienced a bird strike on one of this bombers, thus affecting his readiness. LeMay supposedly replies, "I'm not interested in distinguishing between the unfortunate and the inefficient; the result is the same."[66] While LeMay was able to improve operational readiness rates for the strategic bomber force starting in late 1949, for the first few years of the command's existence, maintenance problems were a significant issue precluding effective employment of the force. The number of aircraft required to conduct the strategic air offensive would have been difficult to employ given maintenance efforts prior to late 1949.

In addition to the maintenance issues and readiness rates for the bombing fleet, performance of the B-29's APQ-13, the B-50's APQ-23, and B-36's APQ-24 radar bombsights also come into question. Depending upon the quality of the crew, the CEP with the APQ-13 radar bombsight was estimated at 3,000 feet while the APQ-23 and APQ-24 error was estimated to be relatively less. These capabilities were certainly within the standard required by SAC, if employed by a well-trained crew. However, these early radar bombsights were susceptible to jamming by high-powered noise-modulated jammers in Soviet air defense networks.[67] If the Soviet defenders engaged these electronic counter measures (ECM), the CEPs for the radar sights deteriorated significantly. All three bombing platforms during this time had essentially the same ECM packages and were susceptible to a jamming attack. If Soviet jamming efforts were employed, they could preclude the bomber's radar from homing on the target miles from the intended drop point. Furthermore, inclusive of average CEP errors, and then compounded with a small navigation error, the estimates on bombing accuracy are listed below:

WSEG Estimated CEPs Based Upon Soviet Jamming[68]

Distance to Target When Contact Is Lost	300 ft Initial Error and a 2 percent Navigation Error	500 ft Initial Error and a 5 percent Navigation Error	500 ft Initial Error and a 10 percent Navigation Error
10 Miles	3400 ft CEP	5600 ft CEP	7500 ft CEP
20 Miles	3600 ft CEP	7100 ft CEP	12000 ft CEP
30 Miles	4350 ft CEP	9300 ft CEP	16700 ft CEP
40 Miles	5100 ft CEP	1100 ft CEP	21000 ft CEP

If jamming were employed, even in the best cases, CEPs were outside the SAC standard for the time. While a later modification of the APQ-13 radar could mitigate some of the Soviet defensive measures, this specific fix was not available until 1950.[69] Additionally, it was estimated that 85 percent of bomb crews would experience navigation errors equal to or less than 3 percent. The remaining 15 percent of aircrews would have navigation errors up as high as 5 percent.[70] Regardless, the above findings certainly allude to a huge bombing error and an overall lack of accuracy if the Soviets employed an effective jamming capability and depending upon given conditions. As discussed previously, even with kilotons worth of explosive power inherent in atomic weapons, accuracy was still a factor, as bombs needed to be placed relatively close to the intended targets. However, due to the lack of intelligence available to U.S. analysts, the WSEG could not fully anticipate how much of a threat radar jamming was to the inbound crews. While the WSEG estimated that the known Soviet state of the art in electronics was inferior to that of the United States, it could not accurately determine how much of a threat jamming really was. During the Berlin Airlift, the Soviets did jam certain radio frequencies and unquestionably had such capabilities. We know now that the Soviet Union had developed a rather intricate and sophisticated

IAD during the period. While SAC crews may not have understood the extent of the threat at the time, the possibility was real and one that eventually grabbed LeMay's attention.

Along with the ECM issues, SAC was also suffering from a lack of qualified aircrews familiar with this area of expertise. Radio operators during this time served in a dual capacity as ECM operators. In order to develop these capabilities, the Air Force table of organization assigned three officers (Service Skill #7888) in each bomb group to supervise and train crewmen in the area of ECM.[71] However, based upon the existing force structure and staffing, SAC was unable to have the ECM officers train sufficient numbers of aircrew radio operators on ECM tactics and how to successfully conduct spot-jamming operations.[72] Most enlisted men did not have the requisite background to become fully competent ECM operators, and it was further determined that the daily time demands on these men often precluded effective training in this field.[73] As a result, most units were deficient in ECM operators in all squadrons. As a fallback, bomb groups could resort to relying on the resident 7888 officers on hand to serve as aircrew if operations required. The paucity of trained crewmen in ECM procedures was endemic throughout the command, and what training that did occur was not often representative of strike mission profiles.[74]

In conjunction, the specialized ECM equipment aboard the bombers was maintained by organic unit electronic repair shops. These unit maintenance shops already had a very high work load with other electronic equipment assigned to the organization and had difficulty keeping up with the special ECM maintenance demands.[75] The burden of both kinds of electronic repair demands caused problems with ECM equipment availability. As mentioned previously, electronic maintenance personnel were at a premium during the time, and it was forecasted that the number of trained repairmen would not be sufficient until late 1951.[76] Like the 7888s, the electronic shops could probably keep up if it surged repair capacities on ECM equipment during the high demand first phase of OFFTACKLE.[77] However, in a surge capacity it was expected that a high failure rate would occur with this sensitive and complex equipment.

Additionally, much of the ECM equipment was also outdated or altogether missing from the bombing fleet. During the war the Germans leveraged radar to assist in the defense of the Reich from the Allied aerial onslaught. Luftwaffe use of radar helped vector defenders to the oncoming Allied bombers and efficiently manage the airborne fighter force. In order to counter the German radar system, the Allies developed small strips of aluminum called "chaff" or "window" to jam the German system. The chaff strips were cut to half of the expected target radar wavelength and then dropped from bombers in hand-sized bundles. Used for the first time during the 1943 Hamburg fire raid, these strips reflected or scattered the German radar signals and reduced the effectiveness of the return on the operator's display. As a result the radar operator had a difficult time distinguishing between the chaff and the actual bombing aircraft. This tactic was especially useful for the Royal Air Force's nighttime bombing campaign, as German radar was a crucial element in locating the bombers in the dark.

Leveraging the CBO experience, SAC planned to use chaff as an ECM during the bombing offensive. However, in the late 1940s, SAC suffered from a lack of ECM equipment, chaff that could counter various types of radar frequencies, and a dearth of automated chaff dispensers. In employing chaff, most SAC bombers did not have dispensers installed on the airframe and crews would have to manually distribute the strips into the bomber's slipstream. This meant that crewmen would have to throw the strips from unpressurized parts of the plane into the slipstream at designated points along the route. Obviously this action detracted from the crewman's primary mission and required access to the non-pressurized part of the planes. While some B-29s were equipped with automatic chaff dispensers, these units held only three to five cartons of chaff. This amount of chaff was only enough to hide the bomber for approximately 20 minutes against a single frequency band radar.[78] In addition, a shortage of suitable chaff was also a concern for SAC planners. Depending on the kind of radar employed by PVO-Strany, the wavelength used by the specific system would respond only to certain types of chaff. This issue was also addressed by SAC commanders, and they realized the vulnerability of the bombing fleet and estimated that the command's ECM efforts were only 35 percent effective.[79]

In addition to the jamming issue, the B-36's newly developed bombsight had its own problems during the peacetime training environment. As the 7th Bomb Wing was putting the B-36 through its paces, it found that the APQ-24 sight was causing a 25-percent abort rate for training missions compared to just a 2 percent abort rate for the older APQ-13 and APQ-23 found in B-29/50s.[80] The APQ-24 was an accurate system if maintained correctly, and over 300 sets were made and installed in both the B-36 and in some B-50s.[81] The system was easy to operate from an operator's point of view, but the design included a morass of vacuum tubes and interconnected black boxes that posed significant maintenance problems. While the crew of a B-36 included a flight engineer who might be able to fix the APQ-24 malfunction, the components for the system were inaccessible to the aircrew during flight.[82] As late as 1951, LeMay was still complaining about the reliability of the radar and demanded a fix to the radar system, arguing that the Air Force's Armament Laboratory "had fallen completely on its face [in the attempt to produce a reliable bombing system]."[83]

Eventually, the APQ-24 problems were traced to faulty vacuum tubes that were prematurely burning out and to inadequate crew training.[84] However, the problems with the APQ-24 became so prevalent that the Air Force established PROJECT RELIABLE, a modification program designed to reposition APQ-24 system components within the B-36 so they could be calibrated and adjusted in flight.[85] While the sight was eventually modified, during the initial fielding of the B-36, the radar bombsights' problems had serious implications for the aerial offensive. Obviously losing a quarter of the B-36 bombing force to a radar malfunction had implications for any potential combat operations. Once the problem was addressed, by 1950 the APQ-24's CEP in the B-50s went from 2,348 to 1,094.

With the Revolt of the Admirals and the lighting rod that was the B-36, a debate ensued regarding the survivability of the B-36 in a combat environment given the advent of jet fighters and new aviation technologies. Looking to usurp the Air Force's claimed mission, and given its desires for a larger share of the defense budget, the Navy argued that the new bomber was too slow and vulnerable to perform its wartime missions. Even the Air Force's own Aircraft and Weapons Board determined in 1947 that the B-36 was an "obsolete weapon" and wanted to pursue jet bombers even if they had limited range and would not be available for some years.[86] Eventually the board compromised and decided to procure 100 B-36s, which was considered an adequate number given the inventory of atomic weapons at the time.[87] Despite the B-36's planned mission profile that would leverage its high-altitude capability and relatively high speed at bombing altitude, the Navy argued that modern fighters would easily obliterate a B-36 as it flew toward its intended target. The Air Force countered that at the 45,000 foot altitude at which the B-36 was expected to fly, a contemporary fighter could not keep up with the six-engined bomber, and with its larger wing area in the rarified air, the larger aircraft was more maneuverable. Furthermore, the Air Force argued that the bomber was well suited to defend itself with its considerable armament, radar-guided guns, and ability to lose as many as three of its engines and still survive. However, as the MiG-15 matured and entered PVO-Strany service in 1949, this formidable aircraft used in slashing attacks could easily cause problems for inbound bombers.

In support of the Air Force's argument, in 1947 the service conducted tests using P-80 "Shooting Star" jets from the 1st Fighter Group against SAC B-29s.[88] In the exercise, the P-80s had a difficult time intercepting a single bomber given the speed and altitudes of both aircraft. Kenney, who was the SAC commander at the time, surmised that interceptor fighters in a new air war would be able to make only a single head-on pass against an attacking bomber.[89] He envisioned that the classic dogfight and swirling combat seen over Europe was now a thing of the past given the increased performance of new aircraft. This gave more hope to the bomber-centric Air Force looking to win decisively and unilaterally.

In a 1949 *Collier's* article, former war correspondent Richard Tregaskis argued against the bomber based upon his observations from flying with U.S. aircrews during the CBO and in the Pacific. While Tregaskis lauded the B-36's capability, he wrote that the crews would be "sitting ducks" without some kind of long-range fighter escort.[90] In the article he counters Kenney's claim about fighter aircraft's inability to intercept the high-flying bomber. In the article the author mentions that famed test pilot Chuck Yeager flew an F-86 Saber jet fighter against B-36s at 40,000 feet over the Muroc Dry Lake Bed. According to Yeager, he was able to "shoot" gun camera film of a B-36 as he made passes at the bomber, simulating an attack. Supposedly Yeager scored "50 hits in 50 passes."[91] Tregaskis' claims ran directly counter to what Kenney and the Air Force supposedly argued. However, it should be noted that the article too was advocating naval aviation and the building of the USS *United States*.

Each side attempted to prove its point in this chapter of the interservice rivalry between the Air Force and Navy. In 1949, a test pitting Navy fighters against the B-36 was proposed, but never conducted, as each side felt that the rules of engagement and test parameters would favor the other side.[92] For either side, the stakes were just too high as each service was vying for defense dollars and trying to prove its relevance. The test was never conducted; the argument remained unsettled. When LeMay was asked to testify as to the bomber's vulnerability, he replied,

> I think that in certain circumstances it can be shot down. But I don't think whether it can be shot down enters into this controversy at all ... the thing that I am concerned about is whether the proper number of B-36s in the proper tactical disposition can penetrate enemy air defenses and destroy a target with acceptable losses to ourselves.... I believe the B-36 can do this job.... I expect that if I am called upon to fight I will order my crews out in those planes, and I expect to be in the first one myself.[93]

While the argument was more reflective of Washington politics and interservice rivalry, the question still remained about the bomber's ability to penetrate Soviet defenses and reach the intended target set.

While much of the emphasis in SAC was on bombers, there was still a requirement for fighter support for the long-range bombing mission. Keen from their experiences over Germany and from the pounding the 8th and 15th Air Forces took over the skies of Europe from Luftwaffe interceptors, SAC still saw the need for long-range fighter escort along the principal bombing routes. However, during this period, SAC was suffering in both numbers of fighters available and the limited ranges of available airframes. Operating from bases in the United Kingdom, B-29/50s would be required to fly in the daylight at some time during a given mission. Planners believed that fighter escort was required, as the bombers passed at medium altitudes from the United Kingdom to the USSR along two primary routes. A northern route took the bombers over southern Scandinavia; the second route stretched across central France and over the Balkans.[94] In addition to the fighter escort along the bombing route, SAC also required fighters to provide cover during the preflight period and when launching sorties from the forward bases. Fear of enemy attack at these vulnerable times required defensive fighter cover overhead.

To fully accomplish the mission as envisioned, SAC required four fighter groups for the escort and top cover missions. However, as late as 1950, SAC had only one group available for these missions, and it was equipped with the F-84 Thunderstreak.[95] The F-84 was a first-generation jet aircraft and a single-engine design, carrying four .50 caliber machine guns. At the time, SAC's one group consisted of only 27 aircraft. These F-84s were limited in range and had an internal fuel capacity of 452 gallons, giving them a basic combat range of some 850 miles.[96] F-84s could be fitted with long-range fuel tanks, but much like 8th Air Force's long-range fuel tanks during the CBO, these new tanks for the jets were not yet readily available in 1950. When fitted with four external fuel tanks, the F-84 could extend its range to more than 1,000 miles: roughly the same distance from the United Kingdom to Moscow.[97] With this range, the fighter could provide coverage to the two areas SAC was concerned with, but the lack of three other fighter groups for overhead protection at the United Kingdom locations remained problematic.

Maintenance upkeep of the F-84 was also problematic as late as 1950, as half of the operational inventory was out of commission.[98] This low operational readiness rate for the fighter was similar to that of the bombers due to a lack of spare parts and supporting equipment.[99] In addition to the lingering maintenance issues, the limited number of fighters precluded coverage of all the bomber bases and along the intended routes simultaneously. Furthermore, if fighter escort was required to and from a given target location, the F-84 was only able to travel as far as those targets located east of Moscow. As a result, long-range, penetration missions with fighter escort were out of the question. General Montgomery at SAC Operations highlighted the deficiency in fighter support and reported to LeMay and the other commanders, "SAC [has] no long-range fighter capability—none at all. We are going to need those fighters for about 30 to 45 days ... but we feel that this present plan [OFFTACKLE] is jeopardized now because of that daylight passage at medium altitude without fighter escort."[100] He closed the discussion regarding lack of fighter support by stating, "We look on that as one of the most serious soft spots."[101]

F-84 Thunderjet fighter. The escort fighter was planned to provide cover for bombers flying from bases in the United Kingdom to targets in the Soviet Union. Only one fighter group was available, while SAC required as many as four to execute war plan OFFTACKLE (U.S. Air Force photograph).

Interestingly, when called to testify in support of the B-36 program during the Revolt of the Admirals, Vandenberg argued that in places where air superiority was not attained, the bombers would "have new tactics, new techniques, new speeds, new altitudes, and an entirely different kind of explosive. Where at one time the losses might be unacceptable in another war, in order to destroy a target, they might be very acceptable."[102] Ironically, in this line of reasoning the Air Force Chief was undermining the whole argument in which the service claimed it needed to obtain air superiority in future conflict.[103] He argued further that none of the bombing missions set forth during the war was ever stopped short of its target.[104] While the statement may be true, it certainly does not address the accuracy of any given raid or its overall effectiveness.

In order to deal with this deficiency in escort aircraft the Air Force developed a number of radical approaches to the long-range fighter issue. They included the possible use of "parasite fighters" that would ride along in the bomb bay of a larger aircraft and deploy when required to defend the "mother" ship. A variation on this theme included a diminutive fighter called the XF-85 "Goblin" that proved to be difficult to reattach to the larger ship and also paled in performance when compared to PVO-Strany aircraft. Other ideas included attaching fighters on the wingtips of multi-engine bombers in order to extend the range of the single-engine jets. Like the idea of parasite fighters, "PROJECT TIP TOW," as it was aptly named, was discarded with the eventual development and refinement of inflight refueling.

While SAC was equipped with some formidable aircraft and machines, it was plagued with a number of technical issues during the postwar period that would have precluded it from effectively employing an atomic aerial offensive. In the new atomic warfare realm, the command was largely equipped with legacy aircraft that were built to counter a threat that has since been defeated. While SAC upgraded existing airframes and experienced overall better performance, the bombers were still hard-pressed to execute the kind of missions expected. Maintenance issues, ineffective management practices, a lack of spare parts, and shortage of qualified operators and maintenance personnel were significant obstacles. Additionally, the command had equipment deficiencies, namely in long-range fighter support, that would have been difficult to overcome in the event of war. Eventually the risk associated with the lack of long-range fighter escort would be mitigated with the advent of effective ECM, new low-level mission profiles, and of course the introduction of Intercontinental Ballistic Missiles (ICBMs) years later. However, during the late 1940s, SAC bombers would have been vulnerable targets for the Soviet defensive fighters. While Soviet air defense capabilities during this time were largely unknown to the aircrews at the time, we know now that the PVO-Strany threat was very real.

Between the legacy airframes, maintenance issues, lack of adequate ECM capability, scarcity of fighter support, and dearth of trained personnel, it is hard to imagine SAC fully conducting the planned aerial offensive. The command had significant operation and tactical hurdles during the late 1940s. While LeMay did his very best to fix much of what ailed SAC once he took command, these corrections would take time to be fully implemented and required sourcing from areas outside his control to come to fruition. In the next few years, LeMay would remold SAC wholesale, but until these changes could be effected, the command continued to languish.

Conclusion:
Turning the Corner

In the fall of 1949, the geo-political situation changed significantly. On October 1, 1949, Mao and the Red Army established a communist China, and a few days earlier, on 23 September, Truman announced the discovery of a Soviet atomic explosion. These two events in addition to others heightened the concern over American national security and military posture. Concurrently with the B-36 hearings in October, the NSC, in coordination with the AEC, recommended to Truman the acceleration of the atomic energy program.[1] These two organizations were fully committed to the idea of deterrence and stated in a report to the president,

> [W]e should develop a level of military readiness which can be maintained as long as necessary as a deterrent to Soviet aggression, as indispensable support to our political attitude toward the USSR, as a source of encouragement to nation's resisting Soviet political aggression, and as an adequate basis for immediate military commitments and for rapid mobilization should war prove unavoidable.[2]

The result was a presidential call for an increase in the production of fissionable materials. These world events, combined with the discussion on military strategy, provided fertile ground for an increase in America's atomic strategic bombing capability.

As events unfolded, Americans increasingly saw a need for an atomic Air Force. Even before Mao succeeded in China and the Soviet atomic explosion, in January 1949, 70 percent of polled Americans thought that the U.S. needed to increase the size of the Air Force.[3] The same poll suggested that the other services also needed to grow in size, but positive responses to Army and Navy increases were only 56 and 57 percent respectively.[4] In August, Americans were asked if they believed the United States should swear off the first use of atomic weapons.[5] Again, an overwhelming 70 percent disagreed with this idea, only 20 percent agreeing to the statement.[6] Regarding the actual use of the bomb, in an August 1950 poll, 77 percent of those asked answered in the affirmative that we should use it.[7]

As America entered the 1950s, the Truman administration's priority of effort was still the economy and a balanced federal budget. During his 1950 State of the Union address, the president chided Congress over tax cuts, called for a reduction in federal expenditures, and argued that his fiscal policy was "the quickest and safest way of achieving a balanced budget."[8] He boasted that American's GNP was over $225 billion per year and that continued economic prosperity needed businessmen to maintain initiative and enterprise, working men and unions to be more productive, and that America needed to conserve its natural resources.[9] Domestic programs and the development of economic prosperity were still the major themes in his address. While Truman emphasized the economy and internal stability, he expressed concern over foreign relations, stating, "People everywhere ... [were] being corrupted and betrayed by the false promises of communism."[10] However, as the year unfolded, the president found his priority of effort shift from one of domestic economic prosperity to national defense and fears over global communist threats.

Given the successful Soviet atomic test and fear of losing the lead on nuclear technology, at the end of January 1950, Truman directed that work begin on the development of the "super bomb" or what became known as the hydrogen bomb. However, months earlier when the Soviet atomic detonation was discovered, Truman also directed Secretary of Defense Louis Johnson and Sectary of State Dean Acheson to re-examine national security policy given the Soviet atomic explosion. This re-examination of U.S. policy eventually led to the drafting of NSC 68, a document that redefined the parameters of U.S. foreign policy for a generation and, along with the Korean War, set the stage for American rearmament.[11] NSC 68 paved the way for the increase in defense appropriations and what Allen Millet and Peter Maslowski have described as a "holiday on defense spending."[12] The Director of Policy Planning at the State Department headed this review of policy. The office had been led by George Kennan, originator of the "long telegram," but Policy Planning was now run by Paul Nitze. While Kennan framed the initial American foreign policy regarding the Soviets after the war, he was less inclined to use military power and emphasized diplomacy over force.[13] Acheson, while no great proponent of atomic weapons, believed that Kennan's emphasis on diplomacy in light of the nuclear age was impractical and simplistic.[14] As a result, Acheson sent Kennan to South America in a less influential and significant position.

Kennan's replacement, Nitze, was a member of the USSBS and a Wall Street investment banker. Acheson saw Nitze as a pragmatist who understood

Conclusion: Turning the Corner 177

the contemporary environment and as someone who could formulate effective and practical strategies.[15] Largely with Nitze's influence and ideas, NSC 68 was drafted and the policy sent to Truman on April 7. NSC 68 continued in much the same fashion as Kennan's long telegram regarding Soviet intention and stated that the goal of the Kremlin was "domination of the Eurasian land mass" and "to solidify their absolute power."[16] The draft offered four courses of action for American foreign policy: "Continuation of Current Policies, Isolationism, War, and a Rapid Buildup of Political, Economic and Military Strength in a Free World."[17] In the conclusion of the document, Nitze reiterated the continuation of certain elements of NSC 20/4 and recommended that the President choose option four as the best course of action.

NSC 68 speculated that the Soviets, by 1954 or 1955, would have a "military capability of delivering a surprise atomic attack of such weight that the U.S. must have a substantial increase in general air, ground, and sea strength, atomic capabilities, and air and civilian defenses to deter war and to provide reasonable assurance, in the event of war, that it could survive the initial blow and go on to the eventual attainment of its objectives."[18] As a result, 1954 was referred to as "the year of maximum danger," although the phrase itself does not appear in the document.[19] Nitze's conclusions also recommended a "rapid and sustained build-up of political, economic, and military strength of the free world."[20] This suggestion was in stark contrast to the fiscal conservatism of the Truman administration policies and recalled American defense spending during the war. However, this theme was consistent with the Finletter, Brewster, and Harmon commissions addressing similar topics.

The document was submitted in April. The White House forwarded the draft to the JCS for consideration, and it was still under review when on June 25, the North Korean Army attacked south across the 38th parallel, initiating the Korean War. This offensive effort on the part of a communist country had propitious timing for NSC 68's approval. Given the actions in other parts of Asia and on the Korean Peninsula, Truman could not refute much of NSC 68's speculation regarding communist intention and overall goals. Four months after it was submitted to the president, on September 28, Truman formally approved the document, and it became the basis for an explosive growth in the armed services and especially SAC.

NSC 68 was specifically designed to counter Truman's fiscal policies and to make a statement to senior officials that America had to make a change if it was to counter communist aggression throughout the world.[21] While the document included no actual cost figures, its tone and intent made it clear that option four would not be cheap and that the restraint on defense spending needed to be removed. The price tag in support of option four was around

$50 billion annually, a far cry from Truman's cap of $14 billion.[22] Many claim NSC 68 over-hyped the communist threat, and even Acheson said that the real purpose of the document was "to so bludgeon the mass mind of 'top government' that not only could the President make a decision, but that the decision could be carried out."[23] Regardless of the hyperbole, Acheson hoped that execution of option four, the rapid buildup of military strength, would create for America a position of strength if expected to be effective in foreign policy endeavors.[24] From FY 1950 to FY 1952 defense spending increased from Truman's cap of $14 billion and grew to over $44 billion along with a significant increase in the size of the armed services.[25]

At the end of 1950, SAC was a force of 85,000 and had less than 1,000 aircraft. But a year later, by the end of 1951, the small, underfunded command had grown to about 145,000 airmen with roughly 1,200 aircraft with plans to continue increasing its size.[26] By 1954 SAC had more than doubled in size with over 2,600 planes, of which 1,082 were bombers (B-36, B-50 and B-47), 410 were the badly needed reconnaissance platforms (RB-36, RB-50, and RB-47s), 683 tankers, and 411 F-84 fighters along with other support airframes.[27] Flight personnel in SAC alone by 1954 grew to over 1,000 crew with 490 fighter pilots and weapons operators.[28] Under LeMay's direction aircrews were under constant training and continued simulated bomb runs on a number of U.S. cities.[29] This training began to pay off as crew accuracy began to rise appreciably from the debacle of the January 1949 Dayton exercise. By 1954 when conducting a training exercise of 150 bombers, 133 aircraft successfully "hit" their targets, 24 having to abort prior to dropping their ordnance because the navigation system failed due to no fault of the aircrew.[30]

The result of SAC's growth and the approval of NSC 68 went hand in hand with contemporary American concerns of the early 1950s. Not only did NSC 68 see communist threats abroad, but the American public was alarmed by events at home that appeared to threaten American democracy. In February in Wheeling, West Virginia, Joseph McCarthy began his infamous run on communist infiltrators in the federal government. At a speech at a local Republican Club lunch, he made his dubious claim of having a list of 205 State Department employees who were members of the Communist Party. While the number of names on the list changed frequently, and many, if not all, of his charges were specious, debate over communist infiltration was a popular topic. A month earlier, in January, Alger Hiss was convicted of two counts of perjury in a trial on an original charge of espionage. This conviction came after years of proceedings where Hiss testified in 1948 to the House UnAmerican Activities Committee. Similarly, in 1951 Julius and Ethel Rosenberg were convicted of espionage and spying for the Russians by passing nuclear secrets. They were both executed at Sing Sing Prison in New York in June 1953.

Even before the Korean War started, in March 1950 when Americans were asked "Do you think the United States is winning or losing the Cold War with Russia?" 40 percent believed America was losing. Only 28 percent thought we were winning.[31] Regarding defense expenditures, Americans also expressed opinions that were in line with precepts in NSC 68. In May, when asked what the U.S. Government should do regarding national defense expenditures, 63 percent of those polled answered that the United States should increase spending. Only 7 percent believed it should be reduced, and 24 percent thought it should stay the same.[32] By the time America was fully engaged in the Korean War, in October 1950, 49 percent of those polled believed that American should "produce planes, tanks, guns and other war equipment on a full war time basis and cut out making autos, refrigerators, television sets, and other items which people may want and need."[33]

By the end of the 1940s, any arguments or concerns over development of the atomic bomb were largely silenced.[34] Americans largely accepted the bomb's existence as the best bet for national security given the international situation at the time.[35] In this vein, according to historian Gerard DeGroot, the American "fear of fallout [was] much less dangerous than the fear of falling behind" and the defense of the nation took priority over other considerations.[36] In July, a month after the North Korean invasion, in a special message to Congress, Truman called for an "increase in military strength and preparedness not only to deal with Korea but also to increase our common defense."[37] In the same speech he authorized the Secretary of Defense to go beyond the budget allocations of all the services and called for a study to increase the size of the armed forces.[38] By the end of the year, Truman called a state of national emergency "which required that the military ... [and] defenses of this country be strengthened as speedily as possible."[39]

In light of the TROJAN and OFFTACKLE war plans, the Air Force developed authoritative requirements regarding the atomic bomb stockpile. In support of these requirements, in January 1949 the JCS wrote to the AEC requesting an increase in the production of atomic materials.[40] Despite Truman's parsimonious fiscal policies, the request for the increase in fissionable materials on the part of the JCS did not apply to the civilian-controlled AEC. Coinciding with this request was the May publishing of the Harmon Committee Report that articulated the limited effects of a U.S. atomic attack. In June the JCS again recommended to the AEC an acceleration of the atomic energy program.[41]

In addressing the need for more bombs, on July 14, Senator Brien McMahon, chairman of Congress's Joint Committee on Atomic Energy, wrote newly appointed Secretary of Defense Louis Johnson and AEC Chairman David E. Lilienthal in support of an increase in the atomic weapons stockpile. In the letter, the senator argued that it was both the AEC's and the

Joint Committee's responsibility to ensure that in case of war, enough bombs were available for use on an enemy and "assuming enough bombs were not available, we [the AEC and the Joint Committee] would be derelict in the discharge of our responsibilities."[42] He wrote that he was "fearful that we may have not set our sights high enough so far as quantity of output is concerned."[43] Days later, on July 26, Truman appointed a special committee of the NSC to review the "adequacy of the then current program of production of fissionable material."[44] Correspondingly, Air Force leadership also reported that they were dissatisfied with the size of the current nuclear stockpile and production rate. However, Air Force Secretary Symington and Chief of Staff Vandenberg admitted that it was not the responsibility of the Air Force to determine an increase in the production of fissionable materials, but that it was "a matter which must be left to higher authorities."[45]

On October 10, the special committee of the NSC reported back to Truman about accelerating atomic production. The report specified that in light of the SANDSTONE series of atomic tests, "it is probable that atomic bombs may be employed economically in lieu of conventional bombs against relatively small targets."[46] The NSC argued further that such weapons "provide a swift and tremendous striking power for certain operations at a smaller over-all cost than other means."[47] Since the SANDSTONE series of test proved that more advanced atomic weapons could be built and stored, the report concluded that the proposed acceleration was "necessary in the interests of national security" and would yield a "net improvement in our military posture ... [that]was feasible ... and not untimely from the viewpoint of possible international repercussions, particularly in view of the recent atomic explosion in the USSR."[48] The NSC Report argued further that the acceleration of atomic energy production was "consonant with paragraph 21a of NSC 20/4 which states that as a requirement toward the attainment of our national aims vis-à-vis the USSR, we should develop a level of military readiness which can be maintained in the long run...."[49]

After reviewing the report, Truman concurred with the proposed expansion on October 17, 1949.[50] This would not be the last time Truman ordered an increase, as he ordered two more expansions in his remaining time as president, setting the stage for what became an arsenal of over 18,000 weapons by the end of 1959.[51] These additional increases in atomic weapons were also supported by the State Department, which responded in one instance that "the planned expansion program is essential to national security."[52]

Discussion about the increase in atomic material, as it turned out, preceded an even more contentious debate over the development of the hydrogen bomb. The genesis of the hydrogen bomb went back to the war, when scientists at LASL discussed the idea of a fusion reaction that could yield even more explosive power than fission. While fission bombs, as used in "Fat

Conclusion: Turning the Corner

Man" and "Little Boy," were theoretically limited to a yield of one megaton, the concept of fusion promised an unrestricted explosive yield assuming the reaction had sufficient access to thermal energy.[53] Early estimates placed the lower end of a thermonuclear bomb's explosive yield between one thousand to 10,000 kilotons.[54] A 1000-KT weapon, scientists estimated, would destroy an area of 65 square miles, while a 10,000-KT bomb could devastate an area of 300 square miles.[55] These numbers dwarfed the paltry four square miles of devastation wrought by the 20-KT "Little Boy" explosion at Hiroshima.

Discussions about building a fusion bomb began as early as 1942, and by summer 1943 a group of physicist at Los Alamos, including Edward Teller, began theoretical calculations.[56] At that time physicists had yet to develop a method to create the sufficient thermal heat to trigger a fusion device, and as a result the work on this concept was a lesser priority.[57] However, following the war, in an April 1946 conference, Teller reported that a fusion reaction was possible and recommended that this theoretical prospect be explored further.[58] Debate about creating such a powerful new weapon was a hot topic of discussion within the scientific community. Nevertheless, in the years following the war, and with the lethargy of American atomic efforts, work on the "super" languished. However, in light of the unexpected Soviet atomic explosion and the request to expand the atomic energy program, the timing for the "super" was propitious.

Prior to October 6, 1949, Truman never heard about the hydrogen bomb.[59] However, after the Soviet explosion, some within the U.S. government were pushing for a renewed effort in thermonuclear research. AEC Commissioners Lewis Strauss and Gordon Dean, along with JCAE Chair Senator McMahon, were proponents of a renewed "super" bomb effort.[60] On the same day the president authorized the expansion of the atomic energy program, McMahon urged AEC Chairman Lilienthal to be "as bold and urgent [with the development of hydrogen weapons] as the original [Manhattan] atomic program."[61] While many technical issues still existed, and the feasibility of such a weapon was still in doubt, the concern over falling behind in nuclear technology prompted many to favor a renewed research effort. A 1949 JCS report concluded that a "super" weapon might be developed in as little as three years.[62]

Not all elements of the Federal government were in agreement regarding the development of the "super." On October 5, AEC Commissioner Louis Strauss recommended to his fellow members that an intensive effort to develop the "super" be initiated in the same high-priority manner as the Manhattan Project.[63] In order to review the request, the AEC's General Advisory Committee (GAC) met at the end of October to deliberate on the matter.[64] This committee consisted of various prominent veteran members of the atomic scientific community including J. Robert Oppenheimer, Enrico Fermi, James Conant, and Isidor Rabi.[65] At the end of their deliberations, the GAC unanimously recommended against the development of the weapon for many reasons. First, the GAC believed that many technological issues still needed to be solved.[66] Furthermore, the GAC argued that researching the hydrogen bomb might squander precious nuclear resources, but more importantly, these men opposed the "super" largely upon moral grounds.[67] According to a history of the JCS, these scientists argued,

> There was no theoretical limit to its size. Clearly such a weapon could not be restricted to use against strictly military targets and would make possible a policy of exterminating civilian populations. Nor was it needed for national security. By the time the Soviets attained an atomic attack capability, the U.S. stockpile of fission weapons would be sufficient to permit an adequate reprisal.[68]

While the GAC unanimously opposed the "super," the commissioners of the parent AEC were split on the matter, two to three. Commission members Gordon Dean and Strauss were for the development of the "super" and the other three members, Chairman Lilienthal, Sumner Pike, and Henry Smyth, against.[69] As a result of this split in AEC membership, each commissioner communicated his respective position to the president via separate correspondence. Barely a month later, on December 3, 1949, the GAC filed a subsequent report that again unanimously protested the development of the "super" based upon moral grounds[70]

In response to the AEC's and the GAC's positions on the "super," on 21 November Senator McMahon submitted a seven-page letter to Truman outlining the positive aspects of the bomb and arguing for its quick development. McMahon emphasized the "super's" economy of mass and stated that "23 current-type fission bombs would be needed to duplicate the effect of one super which destroyed 150 square miles; about 143 fission bombs would be needed to equal the effect of one super bomb that destroyed 1,000 square miles."[71] He claimed that development of the bomb "is estimated at only $200 or $300 million—less than a sixth of what we spent on the Manhattan project and unit costs ... may be expected to decline markedly when production and design improvements are achieved."[72]

Senator McMahon also argued the case for the "super" by referring the issue of bombing accuracy, or lack thereof. "A fission bomb must usually detonate a mile or half-mile or even less distance from the target to be effective," he observed, "whereas a super might miss its target by ten miles or more and still serve the purpose intended."[73] With the higher yield of thermonuclear weapons, accuracy was no longer as important. This kind of reasoning reflected SAC targeting methodologies during this period. The bottom line: area targeting once again became acceptable.

Conclusion: Turning the Corner   183

Both advocates and proponents subscribed to the same argument used when developing the atomic bomb during the war. McMahon saw no difference between attacking an enemy with thermonuclear weapons or with conventional or fission-type bombs. This was the same argument made by J. Robert Oppenheimer regarding the use of the atomic weapons on Japan when compared to LeMay's firebombing efforts. In support of this argument, McMahon wrote,

> There is no moral dividing line that I can see between a big explosion which causes heavy damage and many smaller explosions causing equal or still greater damage.... What then is the distinction between 1,000 square miles which one super might scorch and the 1,000 square miles which 143 fission bombs might equally destroy? Is a given weapon to be adjudged moral or immoral depending upon whether it requires hours, days or weeks to take its toll?[74]

On November 23, the JCS submitted its report to Secretary Johnson. The overriding justification for the development of the "super" was that "possession of a thermonuclear weapon by the USSR without such possession by the United States would be intolerable."[75] If thermonuclear weapons were feasible,

> the possession of such a weapon by the United States may act as a possible deterrent ... provide an offensive weapon of the greatest known power possibilities thereby adding flexibility to our planning ... [and that] the cost in money, materials, and industrial effort of developing a thermonuclear weapon appears to be within the capabilities of the United States.[76]

The report speculated that the larger weapon might serve as a "substitute for a greater number of fission bombs ... [and] more efficient in utilization of available ore and production capacity per unit of destruction."[77]

The JCS elaborated their position in supplementary correspondence submitted on January 13, 1950. The JCS reported that "they did not intend to destroy large cities per se; rather only to attack such targets as are necessary in war to impose the national objectives of the United States upon an enemy."[78] Furthermore, in the same correspondence, the JCS saw the development of the "super" as a continuation of current strategic initiatives. Chairman of the Joint Chiefs of Staff (CJCS) General Omar Bradley argued that the "super" might have a great value against massed enemy formations.[79] Despite the position of the JCS, Lilienthal still clung to the moral arguments and continued to oppose development of the weapon.[80]

On 27 January, members of the AEC met again with the Joint Committee. The logjam between the two organizations could not be broken.[81] Now public opinion exerted influence. Once the press found out about the argument over the "super," various public figures rallied support behind the development of the weapon.⁸² Finally, on January 31, 1950, Truman directed the AEC "to proceed to determine the technical feasibility of a thermonuclear weapon, the scale and rate of effort to be determined jointly by the [AEC] and the Department of Defense."⁸³ One account states that when objections continued to be raised, Truman supposedly barked, "What the hell are we waiting for? Get on with it."⁸⁴ The president declared, "It is part of my responsibility as Commander-In-Chief of the Armed Forces to see to it that our country is able to defend itself against any possible aggressor.... Like other work in the field of atomic weapons, it is being and will be carried forward on a basis consistent with the overall objectives of our program of peace and security."⁸⁵

The decision to explore the possibility of the "super" was overwhelmingly supported by the American public. Polls taken shortly after Truman's announcement showed that 77 percent of those questioned supported the development of a hydrogen bomb with only 17 percent against.⁸⁶ Correspondingly, concerns over Soviet weapons also persisted, as months later 68 percent of those polled thought that Russia would use a hydrogen bomb on the United States if it had it.⁸⁷ While there was much objection to the development of the technology, months after Truman's initial decision, 78 percent of polled Americans still supported U.S. development of the weapon.⁸⁸

Truman's statement called for the development of thermonuclear technology and not necessarily the approval to build a weapon. However, once Truman made his announcement, the momentum behind the development of the "super" built appreciably. On February 3, the Joint Committee was informed of Klaus Fuchs's spying efforts for the Soviets during the Manhattan Project. On February 16, a memo authored by Brigadier General Herbert Loper, member of the MLC, speculated that because of Fuchs's espionage, the Soviets might have embarked upon an atomic program as early as 1943.⁸⁹ If this was the case, the memo argued, the Soviets might already have developed a larger weapons program and production capability that might yield more plentiful and powerful bombs.⁹⁰ Furthermore, Loper speculated that the Soviets might already have established thermonuclear weapons production.⁹¹

Given Fuchs's spying and the suspicions over Soviet intent during this era, U.S. leaders saw merit in Loper's speculation.⁹² In March, the JCS forwarded a request to Secretary Johnson asking him to give the thermonuclear effort the highest priority. Forwarded to the president, the request was reviewed by Truman and approved on 10 March.⁹³ When the North Koreans crossed the border into the South in June, any lingering arguments against the development of the "super" had been muted.⁹⁴ The push by civilian members of the government for the "super," along with popular U.S. sentiments, clearly made a difference in Truman's decision to develop the weapon. When

Conclusion: Turning the Corner 185

Ed Teller was asked who deserved credit for overriding the GAC's argument regarding the H-bomb, Teller replied, "Senator Brien McMahon, Lewis Strauss, and Klaus Fuchs."[95]

On November 1, 1952, two days before the presidential election, the small island of Elugelab was vaporized by the world's first truly thermonuclear explosion. The U.S. effort to develop the technology paid off, as the test-bed device, two stories high and weighing some eighty tons, yielded an explosion of ten MTs. The explosion proved the feasibility of a thermonuclear device but was not yet a deliverable weapon. That advance came afterward with the CASTLE series of tests. The only thing needed now was an Air Force capable of delivering such a weapon, and by the time of CASTLE BRAVO in March 1954, the United States was already on its way to building that instrumentality.

On February 2, 1950, the *Fort Worth Star Telegram* ran an op-ed article lauding Truman's decision to pursue thermonuclear technology. The author claimed that the president had faced "a Hobson's choice. He could not, for the security of the nation, have decided otherwise than he did. He nevertheless has assumed an enormous responsibility. It required great courage."[96] While the paper praised the president, it also argued that the decision required further action. According to the newspaper, what Truman needed to do now was provide the capability to deliver the "super." The article specified: "The hydrogen bomb is worthless unless the means exist to deliver it to its target. Russia is at work to establish a far-flung warning and interception system and is pressing research in jet aircraft and guided missiles. Sure evasion of interception is as important as the bomb itself."[97] These words argued the case for an increase in Air Force capability to leverage the destructive potential of thermonuclear technology. Considering that Convair Aircraft Corporation, builder of the B-36, was located in Fort Worth, the op-ed's argument had a distinctively partisan tone. Regardless of the paper's local interests, the actions of both the Truman and Eisenhower administrations reflected this idea and provided sufficient resources for the growth of America's strategic air arm.

While the AEC and the Joint Committee were initiating debate regarding the "super," on 8 November 1949, Air Force Secretary Symington wrote to Louis Johnson regarding the size of the Air Force and the role it was expected to play in the future. The letter stated that, given the unexpected Soviet atomic explosion, "we must conclude that the question of the survival of the United States may be involved."[98] The Air Force Secretary argued that the Russian achievement meant that they would have "a militarily significant number of atomic bombs ... two or three years earlier than was expected."[99] As a result, to deter a Soviet attack or to conduct a strike against the Russians, the Air Force needed to accelerate the planned modernization program.[100]

Symington observed that the current expansion plan was actually "decelerating instead of accelerating" the size and capability of the Air Force.[101] Based upon the planned budget allocation of $1.1 billion per year, the Air Force would have only 29 groups equipped with modern aircraft by 1955. While the Finletter Commission and the Brewster Board both advocated a 70-group air force as a minimum requirement, the trend analysis done by Symington predicted that the 1955 Air Force would fall far short of this requirement in terms of modern aircraft.[102] Additionally, he argued that the 70-group Air Force was the minimum peacetime requirement, and in light of the recent Soviet activity, this structure was now outdated and needed revision.

Air Force planners adjusted their perceived requirements, and in August 1950, Vandenberg forwarded to the JCS a request to increase the number of air groups to 130.[103] By September the JCS gave the Air Force approval to grow to 95 wings, and after the Chinese entered the Korean War, the NSC directed the Air Force to grow to 87 wings by mid–1951 and then to 95 by 1952.[104] While the Air Force did not initially get the approval to grow to 130 wings, Vandenberg and Finletter accepted the 95-wing figure and still hoped to achieve their goal in the future.[105] Although Truman still concerned himself with economic solvency and a balanced budget, the North Korean invasion, followed by the Chinese entry into the conflict, changed the political climate in Washington.[106] By 1953, Truman's defense budget included $48 billion with just under half, $21 billion, allocated for the Air Force.[107] Indicative of air power's newfound importance was that an additional $2 billion of the Air Force budget came from trimming the Army's allocation.[108]

In support of the importance of air power, in 1951 Robert Lovett, Assistant Secretary of Defense and the designated successor to George Marshall, argued, "We must put first things first and not everything at once."[109] Lovett assigned priority to strategic bombing as America's number one defensive priority. Seeing the growth of Soviet air power and capability, the JCS agreed that the USAF needed to continue its expansion.[110] CJCS Bradley, while still holding to the idea that air power itself cannot win a war, understood that air power was critical.[111] By 1953 the JCS supported the idea of increasing the USAF to an unprecedented 143 wings while holding the size of the Army and Navy at existing levels.[112]

Because NSC 68 stipulated 1954 as the year in which the growing Soviet capability could credibly threaten the United States, the JCS recommended that the 143-wing air force be accomplished by January 1954.[113] Truman concurred with the assessment but asked Lovett to adjust the timeline so that defense expenditures would still be less than $60 billion annually.[114] However, by allocating this much to defense, the nation faced a budget deficient by almost $10 billion for 1954, and if this spending trend continued, the deficit could climb to $15 billion by 1955.[115] Despite Truman's guidance to extend the funding timeline, nuclear deterrence and the role of the USAF ensured the primacy of the service for the rest of the decade. Apart from President Dwight Eisenhower's 1954 budget, for the remainder of the decade, the Air Force alone consumed the lion's share of the defense budget at the expense of the other services.[116]

As the Air Force grew in size, it took steps to remediate its precision bombing capability. LeMay's efforts to whip SAC into shape were paying off. In May 1950, radar bombing accuracy improved as the average error dropped from 10,000 feet, from the 1949 Dayton mission, to 4,500 feet.[117] By 1951 bomb scores and accuracy continued to improve, with average error now only 3,000 feet.[118] Some crews were able to place their loads within 2,500 feet and by late 1951, CEP was approximately 1,800 feet.[119] Eventually, by 1954, SAC reported that its CEP for all crews using radar bombing from an altitude of 25,000 feet was 1,400 feet.[120] Utilizing visual methods, the figure dropped to 600 feet. For lead crews only, those crews specifically designated to initiate the atomic assault due to their superior airmanship, SAC reported that dropping from the same altitude the CEP was 1,390 feet using radar and 352 feet using visual methods.[121]

Throughout the Korean War period, SAC grew in both men and machines. The new B-36 began to mature and come into operational service in increasing numbers, replacing the older B-50s and B-29s. Not only were pilots and planes important, but trained personnel were key to arming and handling atomic ordnance. The command doubled in size from 85,000 personnel in 1950 to 170,000 by December 1953.[122] In 1950, Boeing received its first contract to build SAC's new all-jet bomber, the B-47, and after the outbreak of the Korean War, the company received production orders for what became the mainstay of the strategic bombing fleet: the now venerable B-52 Stratofortress.[123] By 1952, Convair won the contract to build the first supersonic bomber, what eventually became the sleek-looking B-58 Hustler.

In September 1952, Truman concurred with a request to have the AEC transfer atomic weapons custody to the Department of Defense despite his initial rejection of such a request years earlier.[124] In addition to increases in capability and in aircraft, SAC continued to grow in prestige and importance. Along with this meteoric rise came unmatched authority in the nuclear targeting process, as war planners agreed to run all nuclear target nominations through SAC before submitting them to the JCS.[125]

During the first part of the 1950s, SAC planners picked aiming points that were important population and industrial areas that if attacked, would represent damage not only to infrastructure, but also upon Soviet morale.[126] However, by 1954, LeMay thought that SAC needed to shift targeting priorities to Soviet air forces in an attempt to cripple Russian military capabilities, but the explicit targeting of urban areas with nuclear weapons during this time certainly subscribed to a Douhetian methodology.[127] Regarding this dichotomy between targeting people or equipment, Air Force Chief of Staff Nathan Twinning, who replaced Vandenberg in June 1953, stated, "Machines and weapons, not people, are the principal targets to be destroyed.... It would be a moral blunder and a military blunder to concentrate our hopes for victory on the piling up of casualties when the opportunity now exists to concentrate with great effect on the enemy's weapons and weapons factories."[128] While the Air Force Chief of Staff recognized the dilemma posed by SAC's "bonus damage" targeting methodology, the net effect of a nuclear attack would still yield much of the same effect by generating massive numbers of Russian casualties.

Ironically, with the potential of hydrogen bombs yielding five, ten, or twenty MTs, the issue regarding targeting would eventually come down not to what to target, but to what not to destroy.[129] RAND strategist Bernard Brodie concluded that war was controlled chaos and violence and, as argued by 19th-century military philosopher Carl von Clausewitz, was merely "policy by other means."[130] In this regard war was a rational act, meaning it was a calculated event based upon deliberate actions with definitive ends. However, Brodie argued, with the advent of hydrogen bombs and their mass effects, the use of the weapons was no longer rational and use of such a weapon would equate to national, if not global, suicide.[131] Despite this conundrum, Brodie too supported development of the "super."

Much of the Air Force concurred with the growth of the strategic bombing fleet and argued in support of the rearmament efforts. While moral and legal implications were debated, a spring 1951 article in AUQR argued,

> To say that it [strategic bombing] violates international law is technically correct if the law is taken in light of the times in which the law was created—times when war was treated as combat primarily between easily identifiable military forces.... But with the advent of total war these distinctions [between combatant and noncombatant] have now faded. Without an established court of final resort with power to bring violators before it and to enforce its judgments, the application of international law to war has faded in the face of nationalism.[132]

While disregarding international legal interpretations and moral underpinnings, the same author stated that "the United States should not feel that strategic bombardment violates the humane principles to which international law would compel adherence" and argued, "Few can doubt that the moral intentions of our country are of the best as regards for mankind, even though history may record some failures."[133] While this article is indicative of American ethnocentric thought and reiterated General Anderson's argument in his 1949 AUQR article, other commentaries in this periodical during the early

1950s repeated this same sentiment by proffering a moral foundation for the Air Force and defended America's strategic bombing capability.

Indicative of this idea was the American sentiment regarding the first use of an atomic bomb. In February 1951, a poll asked Americans, "If the U.S. gets into an all-out war with Russia, do you think we should drop the atom bomb on Russia first—or do you think we should use the atomic bomb only if it was used on us?"[134] About 66 percent of respondents thought that we should drop the atomic bomb first with 19 percent answering that we should drop it only if it was used on the United States.[135] Use of the weapon was generally accepted as likely, but more interesting is that "first use" was a policy many Americans subscribed to regarding nuclear confrontation with the Russians.

Two days after the thermonuclear explosion on Elugelab in November 1952, Dwight Eisenhower easily defeated his Democratic opponent, Adlai Stevenson, for the presidency. With a change in administration and political parties in the White House, American defensive policy took a different direction. While the United States conducted rearmament in light of the Soviet atomic explosion and the Korean War and enacted a policy of containment regarding communist incursion under NSC 68, the Eisenhower administration developed a policy to take the initiative away from the Soviet Union and place emphasis on general war while avoiding smaller regional conflicts.[136] Truman's rearmament plan was based upon a balanced, equal-share approach to defense, but Ike brought nuclear weapons to center stage in U.S. military planning.[137] After assuming office in January 1953, the Eisenhower administration eventually embraced policies called the "New Look" that had their foundation in nuclear bombing and were a complete reversal from what ACTS taught only a few years earlier. At this point, Air Force bombing theory had changed appreciably and accepted wholesale destruction.

Much as had his predecessor, Ike too concerned himself with the nation's economic solvency, especially in light of the cost of America's rearmament under NSC 68. During his election bid, he promised to balance the federal budget and campaigned against the "Democrats' profligacy" regarding national defense.[138] Supporting this contention, during his presidential campaign, Ike claimed "A bankrupt America is more the Soviet goal than an America conquered on the field of battle."[139] While still acknowledging the requirement to maintain a strong defense given communist expansion, Ike wanted to review American defensive policy in accordance with his campaign platform in hopes of a balanced budget. Similarly, many Americans during the campaign season were of a similar mindset, as 53 percent of polled Americans supported the idea of having a small armed force equipped with special weapons that might be as effective as a large military based upon manpower.[140] In keeping with his campaign promises, upon assuming office, the new administration called a halt to all new defensive spending pending a review of each program.[141]

Under the Truman administration's policy embodied in NSC 68, American planners identified 1954 as a target year for the full development of U.S. military capability. However, by placing emphasis on 1954 and estimating that during this year the Soviets would have a sufficient stockpile of nuclear weapons and sufficient ability to deliver them, the Truman administration allocated funds to meet a specific timeline. This method of planning essentially front-loaded costs for national defense and, in Ike's opinion, set the stage for a possible economic disaster. To mitigate the fiscal danger and reduce the rapid expenditure of funds for defense, Ike thought the nation should not prepare for some fixed date, but needed to establish a military posture that would suit the nation's needs for the long term.[142] In order to strike a balance between fiscal solvency and the emerging nature of nuclear war, at a Legislative Leadership meeting in May 1953, Ike queried, "The real question ... was how fast can you translate a peace time economy to a wartime economy, having enough force in being to meet the immediate situation."[143]

While the Eisenhower administration reviewed the nation's overall defensive policy, it also proposed to reduce military expenditures for the upcoming fiscal year. Continuing his effort to conduct a review of national policy, in May 1954 Eisenhower initiated "OPERATION SOLARIUM." Aptly named because it started in the White House's solarium room, this effort analyzed existing national strategy, established new defense priorities, and set the stage for Ike's new military polices with regard to the Soviet power bloc.[144] The review included input from some of Ike's closest advisors and included former Army General Bedell Smith as the new Undersecretary of State, Director of the CIA Allen Dulles, Special Assistant for National Security Affairs Robert Cutler, and Chairman of the Psychological Strategy Board C. D. Jackson.[145]

The SOLARIUM effort came to fruition. On October 30, 1953, the president approved NSC 162/2, which served as the foundation for the "New Look." NSC 162/2 notably outlined a defensive policy that considered the economic viability of the nation and looked to limit defensive costs. It clearly stated, "The United States must maintain a sound economy based upon free enterprise as a basis for both high-defense productivity and for maintenance of its living standards ... [and] avoid seriously weakening the U.S. economy or undermining our fundamental values and institutions."[146] However, in order to provide sufficient security while limiting the economic repercussions, the policy statement argued for an offensive capability with "sufficient atomic weapons and effective means of delivery [that] are indispensable to U.S. security. Moreover, in the face of Soviet atomic power ... [our] atomic capability is also a major contribution to the security of our allies, as well as this country."¹⁴⁷ Furthermore, America needed "a strong military posture, with emphasis on the capability of inflicting massive retaliatory damage by offensive striking power."¹⁴⁸

Outlining the deterrent effect of atomic weapons, NSC 162/2 speculated that "the risk of Soviet aggression will be minimized by maintaining a strong security posture, with emphasis on adequate offensive retaliatory strength and defensive strength. This must be based on massive atomic capability...."¹⁴⁹ In closing the document stated,

> In the face of the developing Soviet threat, the broad aim of the U.S. security policy must be to create, prior to the achievement of mutual atomic plenty, conditions under which the United States and the free world coalition are prepared to meet the Soviet-Communist threat with resolution ... [and that] the foregoing conclusions are valid only so long as the United States maintains a retaliatory capability that cannot be neutralized by a surprise Soviet attack.¹⁵⁰

In essence, the new policy put the bulk of American defense policy into the nuclear arena. Furthermore, by establishing deterrence and retaliation as cornerstones of national defense, NSC 162/2 relied largely upon SAC and its ability to deliver atomic weapons of mass destruction.

Despite the early budget cuts in 1953, guidance outlined in NSC 162/2 returned the Air Force quickly to a planned growth of 137 wings. For the next three fiscal years, DoD again discarded the equal-share method of defense spending and allocated the majority of the budget, 47 percent, to the Air Force.¹⁵¹ With plurality of the funds going to the Air Force, SAC in turn was the priority, much to the chagrin of the other commands like TAC and ADC. The other commands in the Air Force lamented about being "SACum-sized" when it came to budgeting. While the other branches of the armed forces obviously disliked NSC 162/2 and the budget implications it held for the Army and the Navy, the JCS eventually approved the policy in December 1953.¹⁵² Admiral Radford stated that NSC 162/2 was designed for the "long pull, not a year of crisis" and that the United States "must be ready for tremendous, vast, retaliatory, and counteroffensive blows in the event of global war."¹⁵³ DoD Secretary Wilson stated the "New Look" was "a natural evolution from the crash program that was adopted following the beginning of hostilities in Korea."¹⁵⁴ The basic underlying principle of the new policy was that overwhelming nuclear firepower would in turn lessen manpower requirements that would equate to lower overall costs.¹⁵⁵

Based upon the "New Look," air power, in the form of strategic bombing, became a powerful and important extension of national policy to a level never before imagined. A single arm of one military branch now served as the standard bearer not only for military applications, but also as the centerpiece diplomatic and political tool to influence allies and foes alike. While

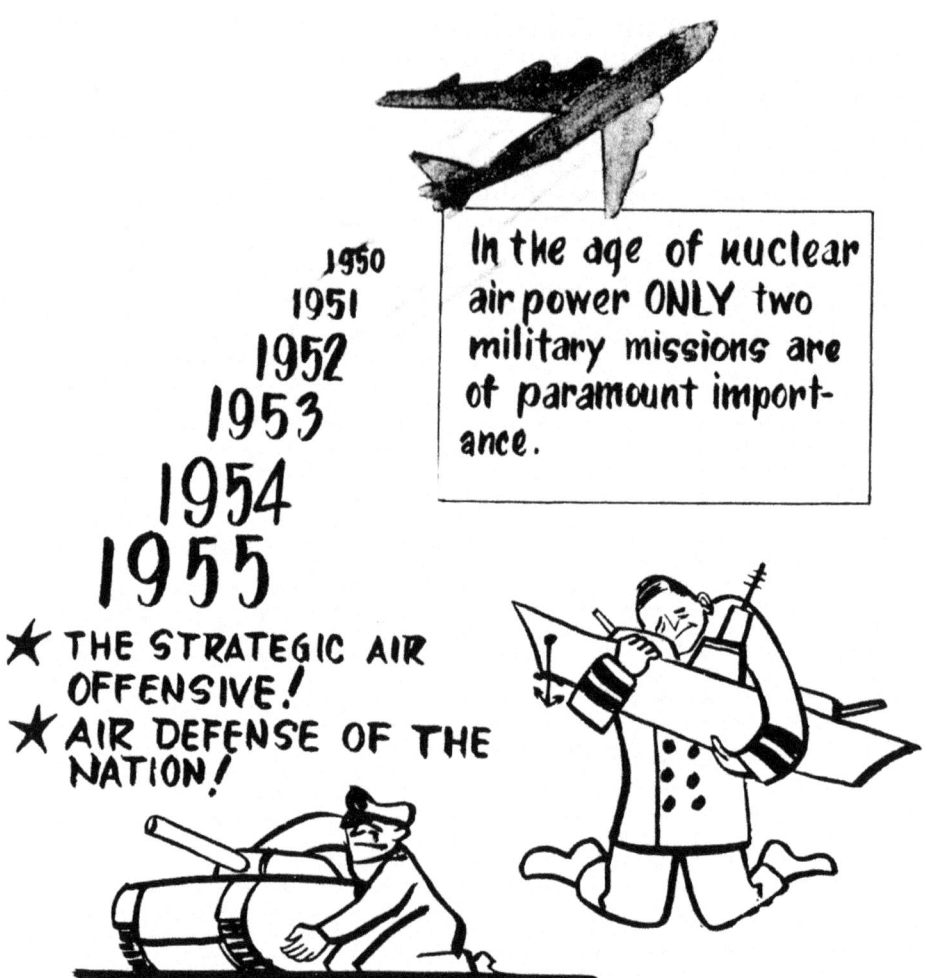

The Air Force version of national security missions in the mid–1950s ("A Decade of Security Thru Airpower," USAF Pamphlet, Box 96, LeMay Papers, Library of Congress).

no longer only a tool of precision for use in war, as originally envisioned at ACTS, strategic bombing was now an instrument for widespread destruction. In fact, the mere threat of its use was a powerful political and psychological weapon. The "New Look" and the promise of "massive retaliation" not only made SAC, with associated nuclear weapons, the preeminent element of national military power, but elevated the mere threat of strategic bombing as a means of diplomatic discourse in the international arena.

* * *

Conclusion: Turning the Corner

SAC had come a long way from its humble beginnings under Kenney's command and during LeMay's early years. By the time LeMay left the command in 1957, the influx of money, men, and machines that began to flow freely under NSC-68 funding had already made a huge difference. Additionally the AEC ramped up production of fissionable materials, and with the advent of fusion technology, thermonuclear weapons came to the fore. Throughout the 1950s the number of weapons grew exponentially, while the physical size of the bomb also shrank, giving it wider application. Additionally, the AEC's grip on the control of the weapons was also forced, with SAC gaining custody of the weapons in as early as April 1951. As a result of these changes, and under the capable leadership of LeMay, SAC matured. Standards increased, equipment was more capable, and professionalism became the standard. By the 1960s, a single integrated war plan was developed that took the totality of the American war machine into consideration and laid the foundation for joint military actions in atomic targeting and delivery. But this took years to develop. During those early years of the American atomic offensive, the Air Force found itself inheriting an entirely new application in warfare but with little capability to employ it and no doctrine to underpin it. For its first five years, America's atomic abilities remained largely stagnant and poorly resourced. General David Burchinal, one of LeMay's trusted subordinates, summed it up best:

> We weren't looking ahead; we were looking back and seeing what happened and teaching from what happened—the basic lesson, that sort of thing. I don't think we fully realized what nuclear supremacy meant that early. It was probably well into the 1950s before the full drawing of what supremacy in the nuclear field really meant to us and how much of a ticket we could write based on that supremacy.[156]

Chapter Notes

Introduction

1. U.S. Army Air Force Leaflet, Miscellaneous Historical Documents File, no. 258, Truman Presidential Library, Independence, MO.
2. Charles Sweeney, *War's End: An Eyewitness Account of America's Last Atomic Mission* (New York: Avon Publishing, 1997), 194.
3. Paul Tibbets, *Return of the Enola Gay* (New Hope, PA: Enola Gay Remembered Inc., 1998), 247; Charles Sweeney, *War's End* (New York: Avon Books, 1977), 204.
4. Tibbets, *Return*, 247.
5. *Ibid.*, 249; Sweeney, *War's End*, 208.
6. Tibbets, *Return*, 249; Sweeney, *War's End*, 211.
7. Sweeney, *War's End*, 213.
8. *Ibid.*, 213–216.
9. James Yamazaki, *Children of the Atomic Bomb* (Durham, NC: Duke University Press, 1995), 1.
10. Tibbets, *Return*, 249; Sweeney, *War's End*, 217.
11. Sweeney, *War's End*, 217.
12. *Ibid.*
13. *Ibid.*; Robert Trumball, *Nine Who Survived Hiroshima and Nagasaki* (New York: E.P. Dutton and Co., 1957), 87; Tibbets, *Return*, 250.
14. Trumball, *Nine Who Survived*, 87.
15. United States Strategic Bombing Surveys (USSBS), *The Effects of Atomic Bombs on Hiroshima and Nagasaki* (Washington, DC: U.S. Government Printing Office, 1946), 3.
16. *Ibid.*, 13.
17. *Ibid.*, 25; Trumball, *Nine Who Survived*, 82.
18. Sweeney, *War's End*, 220, 224–226.
19. Tibbets, *Return*, 250.
20. *Ibid.*
21. Yamazaki, *Children*, 6.
22. Trumball, *Nine Who Survived*, 56.
23. *Ibid.*, 31.
24. *Ibid.*, 61.
25. *Ibid.*, 17.
26. *Ibid.*, 15.
27. USSBS, *Effects of Atomic Bombs*, 15 and 18.
28. *Ibid.*, 18; Yamazaki, *Children*, 65.
29. USSBS, *Effects of Atomic Bombs*, 18.
30. *Ibid.*, 9.
31. *Ibid.*, 20.
32. *Ibid.*, 20.
33. *Ibid.*
34. *Ibid.*
35. George Gallup, *The Gallup Poll Volume 1, 1935–1948* (New York: Random House, 1972), 521–522.
36. *Ibid.*, 527.
37. John Dower, *War Without Mercy* (New York: Pantheon, 1986), 54.
38. Misc., Box 197, Official File, White House Central Files, Truman Library.
39. *Ibid.*
40. Leslie Groves, *Now It Can Be Told* (New York: DaCapo Press, 1962), 324.
41. *Ibid.*
42. *Ibid.*; Gerald DeGroot, *The Bomb: A Life* (Cambridge, MA: Harvard University Press, 2004), 91.
43. Correspondence between Truman and Cavert, August 11, 1945, Official File, Truman Library, in *Off The Record: The Private Papers of Harry S. Truman*, ed. Robert Ferrell (Colombia: University of Missouri Press, 1997) 71. DeGroot, *The Bomb*, 104.
44. Memorandum for Dean Acheson from the President, General Folder, Atomic Testing, Box 175, National Security Council—Atomic File, Subject File 1940–1953, PSF, Truman Library.
45. DeGroot, *The Bomb*, 111; E-mail between author and Erica Flanagan, Student Archivist, Truman Archive, dated 11 December, 2007. Ms. Flanagan could locate only documentation regarding Oppenheimer's quote and

could not find direct evidence of Truman's answer about the handkerchief and telling Oppenhiemer to "wipe your hands." Ms. Flanagan could locate only secondary sources regarding Truman's quote in Martin Sherwin, *American Prometheus* (New York: A.A. Knopf, 2005), 332. In an e-mail from Mr. Sherwin on 12 December 2007 to the author, he agrees that Truman's statement may be exaggerated and that the president may have embellished the story.

46. Fred Kaplan, *The Wizards of Armageddon* (New York: Simon and Schuster, 1983), 43; and Winston Churchill, address at MIT Mid-Century Convocation, March 31, 1949, available at http://libraries.mit.edu/archives/exhibits/midcentury/mid-cent-churchill.html, accessed 19 Feb 2008.

47. As the United States Army Air Forces (USAAF) became the United States Air Force (USAF) in 1947, both the terms and acronyms will be used based upon the context of a given event and when it took place.

48. Kaplan, *Wizards*, 43.

49. "National Security and the Future of the Air Forces," ppeech by Stuart Symington, Folder IV (3), Speech Material, Box 44, LeMay Papers, Manuscripts Division, Library of Congress (LOC), Washington D.C.

50. Lawrence Wittner, *Cold War America* (New York: Praeger Publishers, 1974), 7.

51. Steven Reardon, *The Formative Years: History of the Secretary of Defense Volume 1* (Washington, DC: Historical Office of the Secretary of Defense, 1984), 12; General I. Eaker, "The Army Air Forces, Its Status, Plans and Policies," speech at the National War College, June 5, 1947, Folder IV (3), Box 44, LeMay Papers, LOC, and John Sparrow, *History of Personnel Demobilization in the United States Army* (Washington, DC: Center for Military History, Facsimile Edition 1994), 21–22.

52. "Stimson Refuses Earlier Releases," *New York Times*, August 3, 1945.

53. *Ibid.*

54. Wittner, *Cold War America*, 15.

55. *Ibid.*

56. *Ibid.*; Walter S. Moody, *Building a Strategic Air Force* (Washington, DC: U.S. Air Force History and Museums Program, 1996), 50.

57. Sparrow, Appendix III, Chart II, Strength of the Army, 31 August 1945–30 April 1947, 267.

58. Moody, 50.

59. Richard H. Kohn and Joseph P. Harahan, *Strategic Air Warfare: An Interview with Generals Curtis LeMay, Leon Johnson, David Burchinal, and Jack Catton* (Washington, DC: Office of Air Force History, 1988), 74.

60. Report of the Chief of Staff USAF to the Secretary of the Air Forces, 30 Jun, 1948, pg. 7 as referenced in Sparrow, 270; Harry Borowski, *A Hollow Threat: Strategic Air Power and Containment Before Korea* (Westport, CT: Greenwood Press, 1982), 48.

61. Sparrow, 270. Figures include air force personnel.

62. Lt. Col. Frank Pancake, "The Strategic Striking Forces," *Air University Quarterly Review* No. 2 (Fall 1948), 48–56.

63. *Ibid.*

64. Michael A. Admunson and Scott Zeman, eds., *Atomic Culture: How I Learned to Stop Worrying and Love the Bomb* (Boulder: University of Colorado Press, 2006), 3.

65. Gallup, 534–535.

66. *Ibid.*, 610.

67. Reardon, *The Formative Years, 424*; Richard Rhodes, *Dark Sun* (New York: Simon and Schuster, 1995), 313.

68. "Remarks to a Group of New Democratic Senators and Representatives," April 6, 1949, *Public Papers of the Presidents of the United States—Harry S. Truman, 1949* (Washington, DC: U.S. Government Printing Office, 1964), 200.

69. Borowski, *Hollow Threat*.

70. James Abrahamson and Paul Carew, *Vanguard of American Atomic Deterrence: The Sandia Pioneers 1946–1949* (Westport, CT: Praeger Press, 2002), 120.

71. Samuel Williamson and Steven Reardon, *The Origins of U.S. Nuclear Strategy, 1945–1953* (New York: 1993), 32.

72. Spaatz Board Report, Atomic Bomb Projects File, Policy File Series, Box 20, Norstad Papers, Dwight Eisenhower Presidential Library, Abilene, KS.

73. *Ibid.*

74. Alexander de Seversky, "A Lecture on Air Power," *Air University Quarterly Review*, Vol. 1 No. 2 (Fall 1947): 38.

75. *Ibid.*

76. Spaatz Board Report.

77. *Ibid.*

78. Robert Frank Futrell, *Ideas, Concepts, Doctrine: Basic Thinking in the United States Air Force 1907–1960* (Maxwell AFB, AL: Air University Press, 1989), 237–238.

79. C. Spaatz, "Air Power in the Atomic Age," *Collier's*, 8 December 1945, Speeches and Article File, Box 268, Spaatz Papers, LOC.

80. *Ibid.*

81. *Ibid.*

82. *Ibid.*

83. Steven Ross, *American War Plans 1945–1950* (London: Frank Cass, 1996), 154.

84. *New York Times*, "Super Atom Blitz by U.S. Envisioned," October 3, 1948.

85. Moody, *Building a Strategic Air Force*, 283.

86. Col. Dale O. Smith, "Operational Con-

cepts in Modern War," *Air University Quarterly Review* Vol. II, Number 2 (Fall 1948): 14.

87. Rosenberg and W.B. Moore, "A Smoking Radiated Ruin at the End of Two Hours," Documents of American Plans for Nuclear War with the Soviet Union, 1954–1955, *International Security* Vol. 6, No. 3 (Winter 1981/82), Document One, "Memorandum Op-36C/jm, Subj: Briefing given to the representatives of all services at SAC headquarters, Offutt Air Force Base Nebraska," 18 March 1954, 27.

88. Futrell, *Ideas, Concepts, Doctrine,* 243.

89. Ross, *American War Plans 1945–1950,* 3.

90. Rosenberg and W.B. Moore, 11.

91. Alexus Grynkewich, "Advisable in the National Interest? The Relief of General George Kenney" (MA Thesis, University of Georgia, 1994), 5.

92. *Ibid.*

93. H. Richard Yarger, "Toward a Theory of Strategy: Art Lykke and the Army War College Strategy Model," available at: http://www.au.af.mil/au/awc/awcgate/army-usawc/stratpap.html, accessed 14 October 2014.

Chapter 1

1. John Lewis Gaddis, *The Cold War: A New History* (New York: Penguin Press, 2005), 29.

2. George Kennan, *Memoirs* (New York: Pantheon Books, 1967), 547–559.

3. *Ibid.*

4. George Kennan, "Sources of Soviet Conduct," *Foreign Affairs* 25, No. 4 (July 1947): 582.

5. Gaddis, *The Cold War,* 11.

6. *Ibid.*, 12.

7. *Ibid.*

8. Wittner, *Cold War America,* 9.

9. Gallup, *Gallup Poll Public Opinion 1935–1971, Volume 1* (New York: Random House, 1972), 591.

10. *Ibid.*, 665.

11. "U.S. Objectives with Respect to the USSR to Counter Soviet Threats to U.S. Security," NSC 20/4, *Foreign Relations of the United States, Vol. 1* (Washington, DC: U.S. Government Printing Office, Department of State, 1948), 663–669.

12. *Ibid.*

13. *Ibid.*

14. *Ibid.*

15. Wittner, *Cold War America* 18.

16. Williamson and Reardon, *Origins,* 26.

17. Reardon, *The Formative Years,* 310.

18. *Ibid.*

19. Williamson and Reardon, *Origins,* 52.

20. U.S. Government, *The Public Papers of the Presidents of the United States—Harry S. Truman, 1946* (Washington, DC: U.S. Government Printing Office, 1962), 74.

21. Reardon, *The Formative Years,* 310; Stephan Budiansky, *Air Power* (New York: Penguin, 2004), 346.

22. "Annual Message to the Congress on the State of the Union," January 6, 1947, U.S. Government, *The Public Papers of the Presidents of the United States-Harry S. Truman, 1947* (Washington, DC: U.S. Government Printing Office, 1962), 12.

23. Elaine Tyler May, *Homeward Bound* (New York: Basic Books, 1999), 147; Williamson and Reardon, *Origins,* 52.

24. Matt Phillips, "The Long Story of U.S. Debt, from 1790 to 2011, in 1 Little Chart," theatlantic.com, November 13, 2012, http://www.theatlantic.com/business/archive/2012/11/the-long-story-of-us-debt-from-1790-to-2011-in-1-little-chart/265185/, accessed September 9, 2014.

25. U.S. Army Center of Military History, *American Military History* (Washington, DC: U.S. Government Printing Office, 1969), 530–531; Richard F. Haynes, *The Awesome Power: Harry S. Truman as Commander in Chief* (Baton Rouge, LA: Louisiana State University Press, 1973), 120.

26. *Ibid.*

27. *Ibid.*

28. Williamson and Reardon, *Origins,* 54.

29. Reardon, *The Formative Years,* 310.

30. *Ibid.*

31. Williamson and Reardon, *Origins,* 53.

32. *Ibid.*, 312.

33. *Ibid.*

34. *Ibid.*

35. *Ibid.*, 313.

36. Williamson and Reardon, *Origins,* 78.

37. Futrell, *Ideas, Concepts, Doctrine,* 239.

38. Memorandum from Stuart Symington to Louis Johnson, September 8, 1949, B File, President's Secretary's File, Truman Presidential Library.

39. *Ibid.*

40. President's Letter of Instruction, 18 July 1948, in "*Survival in the Air Age,*" a Report by the President's Air Policy Commission (Finletter Report) (Washington, DC: U.S. Government Printing Office, 1948), v. Hereafter referred to as the Finletter Report.

41. *Ibid.*, vi.

42. Finletter Report, 160–166; Reardon, *The Formative Years,* 314.

43. Futrell, *Ideas, Concepts, Doctrine,* 227.

44. *Ibid.*

45. Finletter Report, 6–7.

46. William Borden, *There Will Be No Time* (New York: Macmillan, 1946), 212–213.

47. *Ibid.*

48. *Ibid.*, 212 and 218–225.

49. Memorandum from Stuart Symington to Louis Johnson, September 8, 1949, B File, President's Secretary's File, Truman Presidential Library.
50. Finletter Report, 11.
51. *Ibid.*, 20.
52. *Ibid.*, 24–25 and 31.
53. Reardon, *The Formative Years*, 315–316.
54. *Ibid.*
55. Finletter Report, 33.
56. Williamson and Reardon, *Origins*, 95.
57. Moody, *Building a Strategic Air Force*, 219 and 248–249.
58. Kenneth Condit, *The Joint Chiefs of Staff and National Policy Vol. II 1947–1949* (Washington, DC: Office of Joint History, 1996), 113.
59. *Ibid.*
60. Reardon, *The Formative Years*, 338.
61. *Ibid.*
62. Ross, *American War Plans 1945–1950*, 90.
63. Reardon, *The Formative Years*, 338.
64. *Ibid.*
65. Condit, *Joint Chiefs of Staff*, 121.
66. "United States Policy on Atomic Weapons, National Security Policy 30," September 10, 1948, in Thomas H. Etzold and John L. Gaddis, *Containment: Documents on American Policy and Strategy 1945–1950* (New York: Columbia University Press, 1978), 203–211.
67. Reardon, *The Formative Years*, 341. The budget allocation was actually $14.475 billion, while $525 million was designated for the stockpiling of strategic materials.
68. Reardon, *The Formative Years*, 342; Condit, *Joint Chiefs of Staff*, 124.
69. Reardon, *The Formative Years*, 343; Condit, *Joint Chiefs of Staff*, 124.
70. Reardon, *The Formative Years*, 344; Condit, *Joint Chiefs of Staff*, 128.
71. Reardon, *The Formative Years*, 345; Condit, *Joint Chiefs of Staff*, 129.
72. Reardon, *The Formative Years*, 345.
73. *Ibid.*
74. Condit, *Joint Chiefs of Staff*, 131.
75. *Ibid.*
76. Condit, *Joint Chiefs of Staff*, 134.
77. Reardon, *The Formative Years*, 347.
78. Condit, *Joint Chiefs of Staff*, 134.
79. *Ibid.*, 348.
80. *Ibid.*, 350.
81. NSC 20/4, available at https://www.mtholyoke.edu/acad/intrel/coldwar/nsc20-4.html, accessed September 15, 2014.
82. *Ibid.*, 350–351.
83. Gregg Herken, *The Winning Weapon: The Atomic Bomb in the Cold War 1945–1950* (Princeton, NJ: Princeton University Press, 1981), 278.
84. Condit, *Joint Chiefs of Staff*, 135.
85. Reardon, *The Formative Years 1947–1950*, 353.
86. Jeffry G. Barlow, *Revolt of the Admirals—The Fight for Naval Aviation 1945–1950* (Washington, DC: Naval Historical Center, 1993), 174.
87. Reardon, *The Formative Years*, 397.

Chapter 2

1. Abrahamson and Carew, *Vanguard*, 16.
2. Jack Holl, *Argonne National Laboratory 1946–1996* (Urbana: University of Illinois Press, 1996), 43.
3. Harry Truman, *Memoirs of Harry S. Truman, Volume 2: Years of Trial and Hope* (Garden City, NY: Doubleday, 1956), 7.
4. Atomic Energy Act of 1946 (Public Law 585, 79th Congress), Excerpt from Legislative History of the Atomic Energy Commission, Volume 1 (Washington, DC: U.S. Atomic Energy Commission, 1965) available at www.science.gov/~/media/bes/pdf/Atomic_Energy_Act_of_1946.pdf, accessed 12 August, 2014.
5. *Ibid.*
6. *Ibid.*
7. *Ibid.*
8. Francis Duncan and Richard G. Hewlett, *Atomic Shield: A History of the Atomic Energy Commission Volume II 1947–1952* (Berkeley: University of California Press, 1990), 1–2.
9. *Ibid.*, 2.
10. David Lilienthal, *The Journals of David E. Lilienthal, The Atomic Energy Years 1945–1950, Volume 2* (New York: Harper and Row, 1964), 132.
11. Duncan and Hewlett, *Atomic Shield*, 2.
12. Stephan Michael Schumacher, *Against the Steamroller: David Lilienthal, the Atomic Energy Commission, and the Conflict Over Militarization During Early Cold War* (Master's Thesis, California Polytechnic University, 2004), 4.
13. David E. Lilienthal, *The Atomic Energy Years*, 263.
14. *Ibid.*, 276.
15. Duncan and Hewlett, *Atomic Shield*, 1–2, 9.
16. Duncan and Hewlett, *Atomic Shield*, 1–2.
17. Duncan and Hewlett, *Atomic Shield*, 10.
18. Office of the Assistant Secretary of Defense, *History or Custody and Deployment of Nuclear Weapons July 1945 Throgh September 1977* (Washington, DC: February 1978), 6.
19. Defense Threat Reduction Agency, *Defense Nuclear Agency 1947–1997* (Washington, DC: U.S. Government Printing Office, 2002), 49.

20. *Ibid.*, 50.
21. Defense Threat Reduction Agency, *Defense Nuclear Agency 1947–1997*, 50; Abrahamson and Carew, *Vanguard*, 75.
22. Abrahamson and Carew, *Vanguard*, 76.
23. *Ibid.*, 121.
24. *Ibid.*
25. Rebecca Ullrich, *Tech Area II: A History* (Albuquerque, NM: Sandia National Laboratories, 1998), 13.
26. *Ibid.*, 14.
27. *Ibid.*, 14.
28. Abrahamson and Carew, *Vanguard*, 96.
29. *Ibid.*, 18.
30. Defense Threat Reduction Agency, *Defense Nuclear Agency 1947–1997*, 20.
31. Abrahamson and Carew, *Vanguard*, 18.
32. *Ibid.*, 20.
33. *Ibid.*, 20.
34. *Ibid.*, 37.
35. Joint Chiefs of Staff Report, "The Production of Fissionable Material: Report by the Joint Strategic Survey Committee (JCS 1745/5)" and Chief of Staff U.S. Air Force, Memo on Atomic Bomb Assembly Teams, dated 27 July 1948, in *America's Plans for War Against the Soviet Union, 1945–1950*, eds. Steven Ross and David Alan Rosenberg (New York: Garland Publishing, 1989), 28.
36. Chief of Staff U.S. Air Force Memo on Atomic Bomb Assembly Teams, dated 27 July 1948; in Ross and Rosenberg, 53.
37. Armed Forces Special Weapons Project Note, dated 2 December 1948. in Ross and Rosenberg, 62.
38. Office of the Assistant Secretary of Defense, *History of the Custody and Deployment of Nuclear Weapons July 1945 through September 1977*, 7; Reardon, *The Formative Years 1947–1950*, 427.
39. Office of the Assistant Secretary of Defense, *History or Custody and Deployment of Nuclear Weapons July 1945 through September 1977*, 7.
40. Abrahamson and Carew, *Vanguard*, 20.
41. Defense Threat Reduction Agency, *Defense Nuclear Agency 1947–1997*, 12.
42. Chuck Hansen, *U.S. Nuclear Weapons: A Secret History* (Aerofax Publishing, 1988), 124; Williamson and Reardon, *Origins*, 63.
43. *Ibid.*
44. Rhodes, *Dark Sun*, 212.
45. Reardon, *The Formative Years*, 427.
46. *Ibid.*
47. Herken, *The Winning Weapon*, 242.
48. Office of the Assistant Secretary of Defense, *History of the Custody and Deployment of Nuclear Weapons July 1945 through September 1977*, 7.
49. Defense Threat Reduction Agency, *Defense Nuclear Agency 1947–1997*, 55.

50. *Ibid.*
51. Memorandum for the Secretary of Defense, March 13, 1948, Subject: Custody of Atomic Weapons, President's Secretary's Files, Harry S. Truman Presidential Library, Independence, MO.
52. Defense Threat Reduction Agency, *Defense Nuclear Agency 1947–1997*, 55.; K. D. Nichols, *The Road to Trinity* (New York: Morrow and Company, 1987), 259.
53. *Ibid.*
54. *Ibid.*
55. Nichols, *The Road to Trinity*, 260.
56. *Ibid.*
57. Defense Threat Reduction Agency, *Defense Nuclear Agency 1947–1998*, 56.
58. General Groves retired in February 1948 and was replaced by Nichols. Defense Threat Reduction Agency, *Defense Nuclear Agency 1947–1998*, 8.
59. Abrahamson and Carew, *Vanguard*, 122.
60. Reardon, *The Formative Years*, 428.
61. Defense Threat Reduction Agency, *Defense Nuclear Agency 1947–1997*, 56; Abrahamson and Carew, *Vanguard*, 122.
62. Office of the Assistant Secretary of Defense, *History or Custody and Deployment of Nuclear Weapons*, 10.
63. Reardon, *The Formative Years*, 430.
64. Defense Threat Reduction Agency, *Defense Nuclear Agency 1947–1997*, 57.
65. *Ibid.*
66. Lilienthal, *The Journals of David E. Lilienthal, Vol. II: The Atomic Energy Years, 1945–1950*, 388.
67. *Ibid.*, 389.
68. *Ibid.*, 391.
69. *Ibid.*
70. *Ibid.*
71. Correspondence from Harry Truman to James Forrestal, dated 6 Aug 1948, President's Secretary's File, Truman Library; Reardon, *The Formative Years*, 430; Office of the Assistant Secretary of Defense, *History or Custody and Deployment of Nuclear Weapons*, 11.
72. Defense Threat Reduction Agency, *Defense Nuclear Agency 1947–1997*, 58.
73. *Ibid.*, 60.
74. *Ibid.*, 65.
75. Office of the Assistant Secretary of Defense, *History or Custody and Deployment of Nuclear Weapons*, 12.
76. Abrahamson and Carew, *Vanguard*, 150.
77. *Ibid.*, 151.
78. Reardon, *The Formative Years 1947–1950*, 431.
79. Nichols, *The Road to Trinity*, 268.
80. Defense Threat Reduction Agency, *Defense Nuclear Agency 1947–1997*, 67.
81. *Ibid.*
82. *Ibid.*, 71.

83. *Ibid.*
84. Lynn Eden, *Whole World on Fire: Organizations, Knowledge and Nuclear Weapons Devastation* (Ithaca, NY: Cornell University Press, 2004), 112.
85. Defense Threat Reduction Agency, *Defense Nuclear Agency 1947–1997*, 6.
86. Stanley Blumberg and Gwinn Owens, *Energy and Conflict: The Life and Times of Edward Teller* (New York: Putnam and Sons, 1976), 202.
87. L. Douglas Kenney, *15 Minutes: General Curtis LeMay and the Countdown to Nuclear Annihilation* (New York: St. Martin's Press, 2011), 39.
88. Herken, *The Winning Weapon*, 239.
89. *Ibid.*
90. Moody, *Building a Strategic Air Force*, 48; David Allen Rosenberg, "U.S. Nuclear Stockpile 1945 to 1950," *The Bulletin of the Atomic Scientist* Vol. 38 (May 1982), 26.
91. Rosenberg, "U.S. Nuclear Stockpile," 27.
92. Duncan and Hewlett, *Atomic Shield*, 47.
93. *Ibid.*, 48.
94. Rosenberg, "U.S. Nuclear Stockpile," 26.
95. Ross, *American War Plans 1945–1950*, 61.
96. Joint Chiefs of Staff 1745/1, "Proposed Study on the Production of Fissionable Material," dated 25 Feb 1947, in *America's Plans for War Against the Soviet Union, 1945–1950* Vol. 9, eds. Steven Ross and David Alan Rosenberg (New York: Garland Publishing, 1989), 2–3.
97. *Ibid.*, 3.
98. *Ibid.*, 5.
99. Duncan and Hewlett, *Atomic Shield*, 28.
100. *Ibid.*, 132.
101. *Ibid.*
102. *Ibid.*
103. *Ibid.*, 134.
104. Defense Threat Reduction Agency, *Defense Nuclear Agency 1947–1997*, 14.
105. Rebecca Ullrich, *Tech Area II: A History*, 15.
106. *Ibid.*
107. Degroot, *The Bomb: A Life*, 159.
108. Abrahamson and Carew, *Vanguard*, 40.
109. *Ibid.*, 41.
110. *Ibid.*
111. *Ibid.*, 42.
112. *Ibid.*, 41.
113. Letter to Commodore Vardman from Edward Hidalgo, 2 April 1946, President's Secretary's File, Harry Truman Presidential Library.
114. Moody, *Building a Strategic Air Force*, 143.
115. The Evaluation of the Atomic Bomb as a Military Weapon: The Final Report of the Joint Chiefs of Staff Evaluation Board for Operation Crossroads, 30 June 1947, 10–11. B File, President's Secretary's File, Truman Library.
116. *Ibid.*
117. David Allen Rosenberg, "American Atomic Strategy and Hydrogen Bomb Decision," *The Journal of American History* Vol. 66, No. 1 (June 1979), 66.
118. Rosenberg, "U.S. Nuclear Stockpile," 27.
119. Rosenberg, "American Atomic Strategy and Hydrogen Bomb Decision," 66.
120. Duncan and Hewlett, *Atomic Shield*, 133.
121. *Ibid.*, 138–139.
122. *Ibid.*
123. Chuck Hansen, *U.S. Nuclear Weapons: The Secret History* (Arlington, TX: AeroFax, 1988), 125.
124. Duncan and Hewlett, *Atomic Shield*, 134–135; Hansen, *U.S. Nuclear Weapons*, 125; Defense Nuclear Agency, *Defense Nuclear Agency 1947–1997*, 6.
125. Herken, *The Winning Weapon*, 225.
126. http://www.hanford.gov/page.cfm/BReactor, accessed 30 September 2014.
127. Duncan and Hewlett, *Atomic Shield*, 141.
128. David Allen Rosenberg, "U.S. Nuclear Stockpile 1945 to 1950," 27.
129. *Ibid.*, 27.
130. *Ibid.*, 26.
131. Hansen, *U.S. Nuclear Weapons*, 33.
132. http://www.hanford.gov/page.cfm/REDOX, accessed 30 Sept, 2014.
133. Duncan and Hewlett, *Atomic Shield*, 146.
134. *Ibid.*, 174.
135. Hansen, *U.S. Nuclear Weapons*, 32.
136. *Ibid.*, 125.
137. *Ibid.*, 126.
138. JCS 1823/1 Military Considerations on Delivery of More Powerful Atomic Weapons, 5 Jan 1948, Steven Ross and David Alan Rosenberg, eds., *America's Plans for War Against the Soviet Union, 1945–1950 Volume 9 The Atomic Bomb War Planning* (New York: Garland Publishing, 1989), 6.
139. *Ibid.*
140. Defense Threat Reduction Agency, *Defense Nuclear Agency 1947–1997*, 60.
141. *Ibid.*, 127.
142. Rosenberg, "U.S. Nuclear Stockpile 1945–1950," 28.
143. *Ibid.*
144. David Alan Rosenberg, "American Atomic Strategy and the Hydrogen Bomb Decision," 67.
145. *Ibid.*, 68.
146. Reardon, *The Formative Years*, 441.

147. *Ibid.*, 442.
148. Herken, *The Winning Weapon*, 289.
149. Reardon, *The Formative Years 1947–1950*, 443.
150. Report to the President by the Special Committee of the National Security Council on the Proposed Acceleration of the Atomic Weapons Program, PSF File 1940–1953, NSC-Atomic File, Atomic Energy: Advisory Committee to Atomic Energy Plans, Box 174, Truman Library.
151. *Ibid.*
152. *Ibid.*
153. Reardon, *The Formative Years*, 445.
154. *Ibid.*
155. Correspondence to Harry Truman from Brien McMahon, November 21, 1949, Atomic Energy Folder, Box 10, Naval Aide to the President Files 1945–1953, Staff Member and Office Files, Truman Library.
156. Rhodes, *Dark Sun*, 407.
157. Degroot, *The Bomb: A Life*, 161.
158. Herken, *The Winning Weapon*, 288–289.

Chapter 3

1. Executive Order 9877—Functions of the Armed Forces, July 26, 1947. Available at http://www.presidency.ucsb.edu/ws/?pid=12717, accessed 8 October 2014.
2. Reardon, *The Formative Years*, 388.
3. Draft of "Airpower in the Atomic Age" for *Collier's*, 8 December 1945, Speeches, Articles File, Box 268, Spaatz Papers, LOC.
4. General Curtis LeMay speech, Folder IV 3 (B), Box 44, General LeMay Speeches, LeMay Papers, LOC.
5. Barlow, *Revolt of the Admirals: The Fight for Naval Aviation 1945–1950*, 46.
6. Reardon, *The Formative Years*, 390.
7. Jeffrey Barlow, "Moral Courage: Vital to Navy Leadership," *Naval Aviation News* (NAN) September-October 1998, 31.
8. Barlow, *Revolt of the Admirals: The Fight for Naval Aviation 1945–1950*, 54.
9. *Ibid.*, 121.
10. Condit, *Joint Chiefs of Staff*, 92; Reardon, *The Formative Years*, 394.
11. Condit, *Joint Chiefs of Staff*, 94.
12. *Ibid.*
13. Condit, *Joint Chiefs of Staff*, 94; Reardon, *The Formative Years*, 395.
14. Barlow, *Revolt of the Admirals: The Fight for Naval Aviation 1945–1950*, 123.; Reardon, *The Formative Years*, 398.
15. Condit, *Joint Chiefs of Staff*, 94; Reardon, *The Formative Years*, 394.
16. Condit, *Joint Chiefs of Staff*, 97.
17. Reardon, *The Formative Years*, 401.
18. *Ibid.*, 400.

19. Steve Call, *Selling Air Power* (College Station, TX: Texas A&M Press, 2009), 18.
20. Barlow, *Revolt of the Admirals: The Fight for Naval Aviation 1945–1950*, 46.
21. *Ibid.*, 59.
22. Speech notes by Stuart Symington, 27 July 1948, Navy Department, Correspondence File, Box 9, Symington Papers, Truman Presidential Library.
23. *Ibid.*, 63.
24. Barlow, *Revolt of the Admirals: The Fight for Naval Aviation 1945–1950*, 137.
25. Reardon, *The Formative Years*, 411.
26. Barlow, *Revolt of the Admirals: The Fight for Naval Aviation 1945–1950*,184–186; Reardon, *The Formative Years*, 412. Apparently suffering from nervous and physical exhaustion, Forrestal died on May 22, 1949, after jumping out of his bedroom window on the 16th floor at the Bethesda Naval Hospital.
27. However, Sullivan was planning on stepping down before the cancellation. This event merely accelerated the process.
28. Barlow, *Revolt of the Admirals: The Fight for Naval Aviation 1945–1950*, 188.
29. *Ibid.*
30. Executive Office of the President, Bureau of the Budget, Memorandum for the President, April 5, 1949, Development of Atomic Weapons Program, File #11A Box 1 of 2, B File, Truman Library.
31. *Ibid.*
32. *Ibid.*
33. Williamson and Reardon, *The Origins of U.S. Nuclear Strategy*, 103.
34. *Ibid.*
35. Barlow, *Revolt of the Admirals: The Fight for Naval Aviation 1945–1950*, 207–209.
36. Barlow, "Moral Courage," 32.
37. "House's B-36 Inquiry Ends With Clearing of Officials," *New York Times*, August 26, 1949.
38. "Revolt of the Admirals," *Time* magazine, October 17, 1949; Herman Wolk, "The Battle of the B-36," *Air Force* Magazine, July 1996, Vol. 79, No. 7.
39. Revolt of the Admirals," *Time* magazine, October 17, 1949.
40. *Ibid.*
41. *Ibid.*
42. Reardon, *The Formative Years*, 416.
43. "House's B-36 Inquiry Ends with Clearing of Officials," *New York Times*. August 26, 1949.
44. "Text of Admiral Ofstie's Statement Assailing Strategic Bombing," *New York Times*, October 12, 1949.
45. *Ibid.*
46. *Ibid.*
47. "Facts and Fears," *Time* magazine, October 24, 1949.

48. *Ibid.*
49. Reardon, *The Formative Years*, 417.
50. *Ibid.*, 420.
51. Borowski, *Hollow Threat*, 30.

Chapter 4

1. John Lewis Gaddis, *The Cold War: A New History* (New York: Penguin Press, 2005), 27.
2. Arnold Offner, *Another Such Victory* (Stanford, CA: Stanford University Press, 2002), 17.
3. *Ibid.*, 16 and 31.
4. *Ibid.*, 17 and 30.
5. "Special Message to Congress on Greece and Turkey: The Truman Doctrine," *The Public Papers of the Presidents of the United States-Harry S. Truman 1947* (Washington, DC: U.S. Government Printing Office, 1962), 178.
6. May, xvii and xx.
7. "World Role for U.S.," *New York Times*, March 2, 1947.
8. Offner, *Another Such Victory*, 202–203.
9. Offner, *Another Such Victory*, 202–203; Wittner, *Cold War America*, 37.
10. Offner, *Another Such Victory*, 202–203.
11. Wittner, *Cold War America*, 46; Offner, *Another Such Victory*, 221.
12. Wittner, *Cold War America*, 44; Offner, *Another Such Victory*, 213.
13. Offner, *Another Such Victory*, 266.
14. *Ibid.*
15. Borowski, *Hollow Threat*, 19–21.
16. U.S. Strategic Bombing Survey (USSBS), Summary Report (European War), September 30, 1945, II.
17. *Ibid.*
18. Air Corps Tactical School (ACTS), A study of Proposed Air Corps Doctrine, based on a memorandum dated December 21, 1934, furnished by the War Plans Division, General Staff, January 31, 1935, quoted in Futrell, *Ideas, Concepts, and Doctrine*, 77.
19. ACTS Lecture, "The National Economic Structure," April 5, 1939, file 248.2020A-25, Albert F Simpson Historical Research Center, Maxwell AFB, AL.
20. U.S. Strategic Bombing Survey (USSBS), Summary Report (European War) September 30, 1945, 5.
21. Gerald Astor, *The Mighty Eighth* (New York: Penguin Press, 1997), 76.
22. U.S. Strategic Bombing Survey (USSBS), Summary Report (European War) September 30, 1945, 5.
23. *Ibid.*, 1.
24. *Ibid.*
25. USSBS, The Effects of Strategic Bombing on the German War Economy, Overall Economic Effects Division, October 31, 1945, 8.
26. *Ibid.*, 152.
27. *Ibid.*
28. *Ibid.*, 150.
29. *Ibid.*, 179, 178, 181, 182–183.
30. USSBS, Summary Report (European War), 16.
31. *Ibid.*, 17.
32. *Ibid.*, 10.
33. *Ibid.*
34. *Ibid.*, 16.
35. Bernard Brodie, *Strategy in the Missile Age* (Princeton, NJ: Princeton University Press, 1965), 130.
36. USSBS, *Summary Report (Pacific War) Reprint* (Maxwell AFB, AL: Air University Press, 1987), 81.
37. *Ibid.*, 82.
38. *Ibid.*
39. *Ibid.*, 50.
40. USSBS, *Summary Report (European War)*, 17.
41. U.S. Strategic Bombing Survey (USSBS), Summary Report (European War) September 30, 1945, 17.
42. Bernard Brodie, "Some Notes on the Evolution of Air Doctrine," *World Politics*, Volume 7, No. 3 (April 1955): 349–370; Kaplan, *Wizards*, 35–37.
43. Bernard Brodie, *The Ultimate Weapon* (New York: Harcourt, Brace, and Company 1946), 76.
44. *Ibid.*, 71.
45. Minority Report to Secretary of War—Military Analysis Division (Anderson Report), 11 July 1946, Garland Series, USSBS, Vol. VII (New York: Garland Publishing, 1976), 2.
46. *Ibid.*, 7.
47. Col. Dale Smith, "Operational Concepts for Modern War," *Air University Quarterly Review* Volume II, Number 2 (Fall 1948): 7.
48. *Ibid.* The underline was added by the general himself and was not done by the author.
49. *Ibid.*, 8.
50. Speech by W. Stuart Symington, "National Security and the Future of the Air Forces," given before the Economic Club of Detroit, June 17, 1946. Speech Material, Folder IV, Box 44, LeMay Papers, LOC.

Chapter 5

1. Futrell, *Ideas, Concepts, Doctrine,* 236.
2. L. Wainstein, ed., *Study S-467: The Evolution of U.S. Strategic Command and Control and Warning 1945–1971* (Arlington, VA: Institute for Defense Analyses, 1975), 10.
3. *Ibid.*
4. Reardon, *The Formative Years,* 436.
5. Williamson and Reardon, *The Origins of U.S. Nuclear Strategy 1945–1953*, 91.

6. Robert Ferrell, "Truman at Potsdam," *American Heritage*, June-July 1980, as referenced by Rhodes, *Dark Sun*, 691.
7. "United States Policy on Atomic Weapons, National Security Policy 30," September 10, 1948, in Etzold and Gaddis, *Containment: Documents on American Policy and Strategy 1945–1950*, 343.
8. *Ibid.*
9. David Alan Rosenberg, "Origins of Overkill: Nuclear Weapons and American Strategy 1945–1960," in *International Security* Vol. 7, No. 4 (Spring 1983): 13.
10. Memorandum, Vandenberg to Secretary of the Air Force, 8 November 1947, OPD 381 (5 November 1947), Record Group 341, Papers of the Chief of Staff of the U.S. Air Force, Modern Military Branch, National Archives, as referenced in Rosenberg, "Origins of Overkill," 13.
11. W.W. Butterworth, Department of State Memorandum dated September 15, 1948, in *Foreign Relations of the United States: 1948 I (Part 2)* as referenced in Etzold and Gaddis, *Containment*, 340.
12. "World Role for U.S.," *New York Times*, March 2, 1947.
13. *Ibid.*
14. Air Force Association Luncheon Speech by Gen. George Keeney, 16 September 1947, Folder IV (3) Speech Material, Box 44, LeMay Papers, LOC.
15. Memorandum for Symington from Carl Spaatz, Commanding General, Army Air Forces, Spaatz File, Box 12, Stuart Symington Papers, Truman Library.
16. Robert Frank Futrell, "The Influence of the Air Power Concept on Air Force Planning, 1945–1962," in *Military Planning in the 20th Century*, edited by Harry Borowski, 258, as referenced in Budiansky, *Air Power*, 349; DeGroot, *The Bomb: A Life*, 152–153; Kaplan, *Wizards*, 41.
17. *Ibid.*
18. Borowski, *A Hollow Threat*, 114; Moody, *Building a Strategic Air Force*, 39; Harry Borowski, "A Narrow Victory: The Berlin Blockade and the American Military Response," *Air University Review* July-August 1981, http://www.airpower.maxwell.af.mil/airchronicles./aureview/1981/jul-aug/borowski.html, accessed September 10, 2014.
19. Kohn and Harahan, *Strategic Air Warfare*, 90.
20. *Ibid.*
21. Maj. Gen. Orvil Anderson, "Air Warfare and Morality," *Air University Quarterly Review* Vol. III, Number 3 (Winter 1949): 9.
22. *Ibid.*, 13.
23. *Ibid.*
24. "U.S. Objectives 2ith Respect to the USSR to Counter Soviet Threats to U.S. Security," NSC 20/4, November 23, 1948, in Etzold and Gaddis, *Containment*, 210–211.
25. *Ibid.*
26. "U.S. Objectives with Respect to the USSR to Counter Soviet Threats to U.S. Security," NSC 20/4, November 23, 1948, in Etzold and Gaddis, *Containment*, 210–211.
27. Wittner, *Cold War America*, 46; Offner, *Another Such Victory*, 221.
28. Wittner, *Cold War America*, 44; Offner, *Another Such Victory*, 213.
29. "U.S. Objectives with Respect to the USSR to Counter Soviet Threats to U.S. Security," NSC 20/4, November 23, 1948, in Etzold and Gaddis, *Containment*, 210–211.
30. *Ibid.*
31. Rosenberg, "Origins of Overkill," 14.

Chapter 6

1. Richard Davis, *Bombing the European Axis Power* (Maxwell AFB, AL: Air University Press, 2006), 568.
2. Robert Ehlers, *Targeting the Reich: Air Intelligence and the Allied Bombing Campaigns* (Lawrence: University of Kansas Press, 2009), 165–166.
3. *Ibid.*, 177.
4. *Ibid.*, 178.
5. John Farquhar, *A Need to Know: The Role of Air Force Reconnaissance in War Planning, 1945–1953* (Maxwell AFB, AL: 2004), 53.
6. William Borgiasz, *The Strategic Air Command* (Westport, CT: Praeger Publishing, 1996), 109.
7. *Ibid.*, 112.
8. Proceedings Strategic Air Command (SAC) Commanders Conference, Ramey Air Force Base 25–26–27 April 1950. National Archives and Records Administration (NARA), Record Group 341, RG 341, Headquarters U.S. Air Force, Office of the Chief of Staff, Vice Chief of Staff Executive Service Division, General Files 1950–1953, Box 1, George Washington University, National Security Archive, Available at: http://www.alternatewars.com/WW3/WW3_Documents/AIRFORCE/SAC_Commanders_Conference_Apr_50.htm (Accessed 2 December, 2014), 14.
9. Farquhar, *A Need to Know*, 37.
10. *Ibid.*; Borgiasz, *The Strategic Air Command*, 116.
11. Heinz Hohne and Herman Zolling, *The General Was a Spy: The Truth About General Gehlen and His Spy Ring* (New York: Coward, McCann, and Geoghegan,1971), 82.
12. Farquhar, *A Need to Know*, 54.
13. *Ibid.*, 37–38.
14. *Ibid.*, 54.
15. *Ibid.*, 41.

16. *Ibid.*, 54.
17. Eden, *Whole World on Fire*, 107.
18. *Ibid.*; Geographical Imaginations: War, Space, and Security, https://www.cia.gov/library/center-for-the-study-of-intelligence/kent-csi/vol3no2/html/v03i2a10p_0001.htm, accessed 10 February 2014.
19. Eden, 107.
20. *Ibid.*
21. *Ibid.*
22. Farquhar, *A Need to Know*, 68.
23. Ross, *American War Plans*, 25.
24. Jeffry Barlow, *From Hot War to Cold: The U.S. Navy and National Security Affairs 1945–1955* (Stanford, CA: Stanford University Press, 2009), 111.
25. Ross, *American War Plans*, 26.
26. *Ibid.*, 28.
27. JPS 789 Concept of Operations for Pincher, 2 March 1946, in *Design for Global War: The Pincher Plans*, eds. Steven Ross and David Alan Rosenberg (New York: Garland Publishing, 1989), 15–16, Enclosure B.
28. "Caldron" War Plan, 2 Nov 1946, in *Pincher Campaign Plans Part 1*, eds. Steven Ross and David Alan Rosenberg (New York: Garland Publishing, 1989), 112.
29. JPS 789 Concept of Operations for Pincher, 2 March 1946, 23, Annex A to Enclosure B.
30. *Ibid.*, 25, Annex A to Enclosure B.
31. Farquhar, *A Need to Know*, 33; John E. Greenwood, "The Emergence of the Post War Strategic Air Force 1945–1953" in Air Power and Warfare: Proceedings of the Eighth Military History Symposium Air Force Academy, 1978 (Washington, DC: Office of Air Force History, 1979), 228.
32. Rosenberg, "The Origins of Overkill," 15.
33. *Ibid.*
34. Rosenberg, "American Atomic Strategy and the Hydrogen Bomb Decision," 64.
35. Ross, *American War Plans*, 55.
36. JWPC 432/7 "Tentative Overall Strategic Concept and Estimate of Initial Operations Short Title "Pincher," 18 June 1946, in *Design for Global War, The Pincher Plans*, eds. Steven Ross and David Alan Rosenberg (New York: Garland Publishing, 1989), 17, Annex A to Enclosure B.
37. Farquhar, *A Need to Know*, 35.
38. "Staff Studies of Certain Military Problems Deriving from Concept of Operations for Pincher," 13 April 1946, in *Design for Global War, The Pincher Plans*, eds. Steven Ross and David Alan Rosenberg (New York: Garland Publishing, 1989), 19.
39. Borowski, *A Hollow Threat*, 101.
40. Moody, *Building a Strategic Air Force*, 143.
41. *Ibid.*

42. Greenwood, "Emergence," 228; Moody, *Building a Strategic Air Force*, 142.
43. Ross, *American War Plans*, 28.
44. Moody, *Building a Strategic Air Force*, 148.
45. Michio Kaku and Daniel Axelrod, *To Win a Nuclear War: The Pentagon's Secret War Plans* (Boston: South End Press, 1987), 34.
46. Borowski, *A Hollow Threat*, 101.
47. Report by the Joint Strategic Survey Committee on the Final Report of the JCS Evaluation Board for Operation Crossroads, 15 June 1948, in *America's Plan for War Against the Soviet Union, 1945–1950 Vol. 9: The Atomic Bomb and War Planning Concepts and Capabilities*, eds. Steven Ross and David Alan Rosenberg (New York: Garland Publishing, 1990), 53.
48. *Ibid.*, 57.
49. Moody, *Building a Strategic Air Force*, 139.
50. *Ibid.*
51. Ross, *American War Plans*, 63.
52. *Ibid.*, 62–63.
53. JSPG 496/4, Broiler, 11 February 1948, 2, in *America's Plan for War Against the Soviet Union, 1945–1950*, eds. Steven Ross and David Alan Rosenberg (New York: Garland Publishing, 1990), Annex A, 14.
54. JSPG 496/4, Broiler, 11 February 1948, Annex C, 178.
55. Farquhar, *A Need to Know*, 52.
56. Futrell, *Ideas, Concepts, Doctrine*, 238.
57. *Ibid.*, 238.
58. *Ibid.*
59. *Ibid.*
60. Ross, *American War Plans*, 57, 69.
61. Rosenberg, "Origins of Overkill," 18; Williamson and Reardon, *The Origins of U.S. Nuclear Strategy 1945–1953*, 167.
62. Ross, *American War Plans*, 61.
63. Ross, *American War Plans*, 61. Kenneth Condit, *The Joint Chiefs of Staff and National Policy Vol. II*, 153.
64. Ross, *American War Plans*, 227.
65. Rosenberg, "Origins of Overkill," 15–16.
66. Ross, *American War Plans*, 56.
67. *Ibid.*, 56.
68. *Ibid.*
69. The gun-type components were missing the fissionable U-235. Rosenberg, "U.S. Nuclear Stockpile 1945–1950," 26.
70. Ross, *American War Plans*, 61.
71. Moody, *Building a Strategic Air Force*, 169.
72. *Ibid.*
73. Col. Dale Smith, "One Way Combat," *Air University Quarterly Review* I Vol. 1, No. 2 (Fall 47): 8.
74. Moody, *Building a Strategic Air Force*, 109.

75. *Ibid.*
76. *Ibid.*, 168.
77. *Ibid.*
78. JSPG 496/10, Crankshaft, 11 May 1948, Annex A to app. 27, in *America's Plan for War Against the Soviet Union, 1945–1950* Vol. 7, eds. Steven Ross and David Alan Rosenberg (New York: Garland Publishing, 1990), 27.
79. *Ibid.*
80. *Ibid.*
81. Center for Military History (CMA), *History of Strategic Air and Ballistic Missile Defense Volume 1 1945–1955* (Washington, DC: Center for Military History, 2009), 249.
82. *Ibid.*, 28.
83. Farquhar, *A Need to Know*, 74.
84. JSPG 496/10, *America's Plan for War Against the Soviet Union, 1945–1950* Vol. 7, 27.
85. CMA, Figure 19, 251.
86. JCS 1952/2, Weapon System Evaluation Group Report No. 1, Chapter IV, in *America's Plan for War Against the Soviet Union, 1945–1950 Vol. 13 Evaluating the Air Offensive: The WSEG 1 Study*, eds. Steven Ross and David Alan Rosenberg (New York: Garland Publishing, 1990), 167–168.
87. *Ibid.*, 168.
88. *Ibid.*
89. Reardon, *The Formative Years*, 465.
90. Ross, *American War Plans*, 90.
91. Joint Strategic Plans Committee 877/3 "Directives for the Implementation of "HALFMOON," 3 May 1948, in *America's Plan for War Against the Soviet Union, 1945–1950 Vol. 7 From Crankshaft to Halfmoon*, eds. Steven Ross and David Alan Rosenberg (New York: Garland Publishing, 1990), 12.
92. Ross, *American War Plans*, 92.
93. Joint Strategic Plans Committee 877/3, 18.
94. JCS 1952/1 "Evaluation of Current Strategic Air Offensive Plans," 21 December 1948, in *America's Plans for War Against the Soviet Union 1945–1950, The Atomic Bomb and War Planning, Concepts and Capabilities*, Vol. 9, eds. Steven Ross and David Alan Rosenberg (New York: Garland Publishing 1989), 7.
95. *Ibid.*, 8.
96. *Ibid.*, 9.
97. *Ibid.*
98. Moody, *Building a Strategic Air Force*, 199.
99. Ross, *American War Plans*, 90.
100. Reardon, *The Formative Years*, 294.
101. *Ibid.*
102. Moody, *Building a Strategic Air Force*, 211; Reardon, *The Formative Years*, 294.
103. Reardon, *The Formative Years*, 294.
104. *Ibid.*, 297.
105. Joint Strategic Plans Committee 877/3, 18.
106. Abrahamson and Carew, *Vanguard*, 61.
107. *Ibid.*, 62.
108. *Ibid.*, 151.
109. Nichols, *The Road to Trinity*, 268.
110. Moody, *Building a Strategic Air Force*, 214.
111. Kohn and Harahan, *Strategic Air Warfare*, 92–92.
112. Joint Logistics Plans Committee (JLPC) 416/12, The Logistic Feasibility of Operation Planned "HALFMOON," 15 June 1948, in *America's Plan for War Against the Soviet Union, 1945–1950 Vol. 7 From Crankshaft to Halfmoon*, eds. Steven Ross and David Alan Rosenberg (New York: Garland Publishing, 1990), 1, 9.
113. *Ibid.*, 9.
114. Moody, *Building a Strategic Air Force*, 287.
115. JLPC 416/12, Annex B to Appendix C to Enclosure B, 24.
116. Tibbets, *Return*, 216.
117. Sweeney, *War's End*, 207.
118. Proceedings Strategic Air Command (SAC) Commanders Conference, Ramey Air Force Base, 25–26–27 April 1950. National Archives and Records Administration (NARA), Record Group 341, RG 341, Headquarters U.S. Air Force, Office of the Chief of Staff, Vice Chief of Staff Executive Service Division, General Files 1950–1953, Box 1 George Washington University, National Security Archive, available at: http://www.alternatewars.com/WW3/WW3_Documents/AIR FORCE/SAC_Commanders_Conference_Apr_50.htm, accessed 2 December 2014, 216. Hereafter referred to as SAC Cmdrs Conf 25–26–27 April, 1950.
119. Ross, *American War Plans*, 95.
120. Ross, *American War Plans*, 95–96.
121. JCS 1952/11 "Evaluation of Current Strategic Air Offensive Plans," 21 December 1948, in *America's Plans for War Against the Soviet Union 1945–1950, The Atomic Bomb and War Planning, Concepts and Capabilities*, Vol. 9, eds. Steven Ross and David Alan Rosenberg (New York: Garland Publishing 1989), 4.
122. *Ibid.*, 4–5.
123. *Ibid.*, 7, 22, 11–12, 20, 24.
124. *Ibid.*, "Memorandum for the Secretary of Defense," 5a.
125. Condit, *The Joint Chiefs of Staff and National Policy Vol. II 1947–1949*, 158; JCS 1952/11Weapon System Evaluation Group, Evaluation of Effectiveness of Strategic Air Operations, 10 February 1950, in *America's Plans for War Against the Soviet Union 1945–1950, Evaluating the Air Offensive, WSEG 1*

Study, Vol. 13, eds. Steven Ross and David Alan Rosenberg (New York: Garland Publishing 1989), 163.; SAC Cmdrs Conf 25–26–27 April 1950, 208.
  126. *Ibid.*
  127. David Alan Rosenberg, "U.S. Nuclear Stockpile 1945 to 1950," 26.
  128. *Ibid.*
  129. Condit, *The Joint Chiefs of Staff*, 160; Reardon, *The Formative Years*, 365.
  130. Condit, *The Joint Chiefs of Staff*, 160.
  131. *Ibid.*
  132. Ross, *American War Plans*, 112.
  133. Ross, *American War Plans*, 112–113.
  134. Condit, *The Joint Chiefs of Staff*, 161.
  135. Draft of "Airpower in the Atomic Age" for *Collier's*, 8 December 1945, Speeches, Articles File, Box 268, Spaatz Papers, LOC.
  136. Ross, *American War Plans*, 115.
  137. Moody, *Building a Strategic Air Force*, 309.
  138. *Ibid.*, 310.
  139. *Ibid.*
  140. Condit, *The Joint Chiefs of Staff*, 161.
  141. JCS 1952/11 Weapon System Evaluation Group, Evaluation of Effectiveness of Strategic Air Operations, 10 February 1950, 163.
  142. *Ibid.*, 182.
  143. *Ibid.*
  144. JCS 1952/11 11Weapon System Evaluation Group, Evaluation of Effectiveness of Strategic Air Operations, 10 February 1950 Enclosure K, K-3.
  145. JCS 1952/11Weapon System Evaluation Group, Evaluation of Effectiveness of Strategic Air Operations, 10 February 1950, 164.
  146. *Ibid.*
  147. *Ibid.*
  148. Cmdrs Conf 25–26–27 April 1950, 211.
  149. JCS 1952/1 "Evaluation of the Current Strategic Air Offensive Plans," in *Containment, Documents on American Policy and Strategy 1945–1950*, eds. Thomas H. Etzold and John L. Gaddis (New York: Columbia University Press, 1978), 357–360.
  150. *Ibid.*
  151. WSEG Charter as referenced in John Ponturo, Analytical Support for the Joint Chiefs of Staff: The WSEG Experience 1948–1976 (Arlington, VA: Institute for Defense Analysis, 1979), xii.
  152. *Ibid.*, 2.
  153. JCS 1952/11, Enclosure K, K-3.
  154. *Ibid.*, K-4.
  155. Briefing Strategic Air Command (SAC) Commanders Conference, Ramey Air Force Base, 25–26–27 April 1950. National Archives and Records Administration (NARA), Record Group 341, RG 341, Headquarters U.S. Air Force, Office of the Chief of Staff, Vice Chief of Staff Executive Service Division, General Files 1950–1953, Box 1, George Washington University, National Security Archive, available at: http://www.alternatewars.com/WW3/WW3_Documents/AIR FORCE/SAC_Commanders_Conference_Apr _50.htm (Accessed 2 December, 2014), 15.
  156. JCS 1952/11, K-3.
  157. Briefing SAC Cmdrs Conf April 25–26–27, 1950, 21.
  158. JCS 1952/11, K-3-K-4.
  159. *Ibid.*, K-4.
  160. Briefing SAC Cmdrs Conf April 25–26–27, 1950, 13.
  161. JCS 1952/11, K-4.
  162. Briefing SAC Cmdrs Conf April 25–26–27, 1950, 5.
  163. *Ibid.*,14; Cmdrs Conf 25–26–27 April 1950, 211.
  164. Cmdrs Conf 25–26–27 April 1950, 223.
  165. Briefing SAC Cmdrs Conf April 25–26–27 1950, 16.
  166. Cmdrs Conf 25–26–27 April 1950, 221.
  167. *Ibid.*, 219.
  168. *Ibid.*
  169. JCS 1952/11, K-5.
  170. *Ibid.*
  171. *Ibid.*, K-6.
  172. Briefing SAC Cmdrs Conf, April 25–26–27 1950, 9.
  173. Cmdrs Conf 25–26–27 April 1950, 203.
  174. JCS 1844/47, enclosure 436 as quoted in Farquhar, *A Need to Know*, 111.

Chapter 7

  1. Etzold and Gaddis, "Evaluation of Effect on Soviet War Effort Resulting from the Strategic Air Offensive (Harmon Report)" in *Containment, Documents on American Policy and Strategy*, 362.
  2. *Ibid.*
  3. *Ibid.*
  4. *Ibid.*
  5. *Ibid.*
  6. *Ibid.*, 363.
  7. *Ibid.*, 364.
  8. *Ibid.*, 363.
  9. U.S. Strategic Bombing Survey (USSBS), Summary Report (European War) September 30, 1945, 16.
  10. Ehlers, *Targeting the Reich*, 3.
  11. *Ibid.*
  12. Farquhar, *A Need to Know*, 52.
  13. Eden, *Whole World on Fire*, 98.
  14. *Ibid.*, 99.
  15. *Ibid.*, 103.

16. *Ibid.*,111–112.
17. *Ibid.*, 107.
18. *Ibid.*, 110.
19. *Ibid.*, 112.
20. *Ibid.*, 161.
21. U.S. Strategic Bombing Survey (USSBS), Summary Report (European War) September 30, 1945, 17.
22. Don Pyeatt and Dennis Jenkins, *Cold War Peacemaker: The Story of Cowtown and the Convair* B-36 (Manchester, UK: Crecy Publishing, 2010), 85.
23. Briefing SAC Cmdrs Conf, April 25–26–27 1950, 14.
24. JCS 1952/11, 165.
25. Briefing SAC Cmdrs Conf, April 25–26–27 1950, 8.
26. Historical Evaluation and Research Organization, *The Development of Soviet Air Defense Doctrine and Practice: A Report Prepared for Sandia National Laboratories* (Dunn Loring, VA: DuPuy Associates, 1981), 59.
27. James Quinlivan, *Soviet Strategic Air Defense: A Long Past and an Uncertain Future* (Santa Monica, CA: RAND Corporation, 1989), 6.
28. *Ibid.*
29. *Ibid.*, 7.
30. Historical Evaluation and Research Organization, *The Development of Soviet Air Defense*, Figure 3–6, 64.
31. *Ibid.*
32. *Ibid.*
33. *Ibid.*, 65.
34. Alexander Boyd, *The Soviet Air Force Since 1918* (New York: Stein and Day Publishers, 1977), 213.
35. *Ibid.*
36. Quinlivan, *Soviet Strategic Air Defense*, 8.
37. *Ibid.*, 7–8.
38. JCS 1952/11, 175.
39. *Ibid.* Chart modified for brevity.
40. *Ibid.*, 180.
41. *Ibid.*
42. *Ibid.*
43. *Ibid.*
44. *Ibid.*
45. Futrell, *Ideas, Concepts, Doctrine*, 289.
46. U.S. Strategic Bombing Survey (USSBS), Summary Report (European War) September 30, 1945, 16.
47. *Ibid.*

Chapter 8

1. J. C. Hopkins, *The Development of Strategic Air Command 1946–1981 (A Chronological History)* (Offutt AFB, NE: Office of the Historian, Headquarters Strategic Air Command, 1982), 11.
2. *Ibid.*, 61.
3. Kohn and Harahan, *Strategic Air Warfare*, 79.
4. Hopkins, *The Development of Strategic Air Command*, 9.
5. Kohn and Harahan, *Strategic Air Warfare*, 79.
6. *Ibid.*
7. Borowski, *A Hollow Threat*, 167.
8. Curtis LeMay and Mackinlay Kantor, *Mission with LeMay* (Garden City, NY: Doubleday & Co, 1965), 433.
9. Kohn and Harahan, *Strategic Air Warfare*, 79.
10. Moody, *Building a Strategic Air Force*, 233.
11. Office of the Commanding Officer, 2d Bombardment Wing, Final Mission Report (Simulated Bombing Attack on Dayton Bomb Plot on 5, 7, 11, and 13 January 1949), Strategic Air Command History, Jan–Jun 1950, Call Number 416.01 V.1, IRIS Number 198556, Air Force Historical Research Agency, Maxwell Air Force Base, Alabama.
12. *Ibid.*
13. *Ibid.*
14. *Ibid.*, 233.
15. Strategic Air Command History, Jan-Jun 1950.
16. *Ibid.*
17. LeMay and Kantor, *Mission with LeMay*, 433.
18. *Ibid.*
19. Steven Reardon, "U.S. Strategic Bombing Doctrine Since 1945," in *Case Studies in Strategic Bombardment*, ed. R. Cargill Hall (Washington, DC: U.S. Air Force History and Museums Program, 1998), 389.
20. Moody, *Building a Strategic Air Force*, 50.
21. Remarks by General Eaker representing General Spaatz, "The Army Air Forces, Its Status, Plans, and Policies," June 5, 1947, Speech Material, Folder IV(3), Box 44, LeMay Papers, LOC.
22. Kohn and Harahan, *Strategic Air Warfare*, 82.
23. Borowski, *A Hollow Threat*, 30.
24. Herman Wolk, *Planning and Organizing the Postwar Air Force 1943–1947* (Washington, DC: Office of Air Force History, 1984), 46, 73, 75; Borowski, *A Hollow Threat*, 30.
25. Address by Major General F. L. Anderson, 3 June 1947 "Air Power and the Polar Concept, Speech Material, Folder IV(3), Box 44, LeMay Papers, LOC.
26. Undated Speech by General LeMay; Speech by Stuart Symington, September 15, 1947 at the First Annual Convention of the Air Force Association, Folder IV(3), Box 44, LeMay Papers, LOC.

27. Borgiasz, *The Strategic Air Command*, 12.
28. Wolk, *Planning and Organizing the Postwar Air Force*, 75.
29. *Ibid.*, 114.
30. Hopkins, *The Development of Strategic Air Command*, 2.
31. *Ibid.*
32. George Kenney, *General Kenney Reports* (Washington, DC: Office of Air Force History (Reprint), 1987), vii.
33. *Ibid.*
34. Grynkewich, "Advisable in the National Interest? The Relief of General George Kenney," 7, 67.
35. Wolk, *Planning and Organizing the Postwar Air Force*, 215; Moody, *Building a Strategic Air Force*, 76.
36. Wolk, 215.
37. *Ibid.*, 216.
38. *Ibid.*
39. *Ibid.*
40. Borowski, *A Hollow Threat*, 43.
41. *Ibid.*
42. *Ibid.*
43. John M Collins, "World War II NCOs," *Army Magazine* Feb. 2005, Vol. 55, No 2. Association of the United States Army Magazine, 62.
44. *Ibid.*
45. Borowski, *A Hollow Threat*, 44.
46. Moody, *Building a Strategic Air Force*, 81.
47. Borowski, *A Hollow Threat,*44.
48. *Ibid.*, 45.
49. *Ibid.*
50. Kohn and Harahan, *Strategic Air Warfare*, 78.
51. Grynkewich, "Advisable in the National Interest? The Relief of General George Kenney," 68.
52. *Ibid.*, 72.
53. *Ibid.*, 70.
54. *Ibid.*, 73.
55. *Ibid.*
56. Letter, Whitehead to Kenney, 4 July 1946, AFHRC #168.6008–3. Whitehead papers, as discussed in Grynkewich, "Advisable…?" 74.; Borowski, *A Hollow Threat*, 41.
57. After Action Report, labeled Mr. Patterson's Lunch, 30 January, 1947, AFHRC # 7103-27, Kenney papers, as discussed in Grynkewich, "Advisable…?" 75.
58. *Ibid.*
59. Borowski, *A Hollow Threat,*58; Moody, *Building a Strategic Air Force*, 86.
60. Borgiasz, *The Strategic Air Command*, 64; Moody, *Building a Strategic Air Force*, 86–87; Borowski, *A Hollow Threat*, 58–59.
61. Moody, *Building a Strategic Air Force*, 87.
62. *Ibid.*
63. Moody, *Building a Strategic Air Force*, 87.
64. Borowski, *A Hollow Threat*, 58.
65. Kohn and Harahan, *Strategic Air Warfare*, 76.
66. Grynkewich, "Advisable in the National Interest? The Relief of General George Kenney," 5.
67. Borgiasz, *The Strategic Air Command*, 64.
68. Borowski, *A Hollow Threat*, 60.
69. Kohn and Harahan, *Strategic Air Warfare*, 77.
70. Phillip S. Meilinger, *Bomber: The Early Development of Strategic Air Command* (Maxwell AFB, AL: Air University Press, 2012), 118.
71. Memorandum by the Chief of Staff, U.S. Air Force, on Requirements for the Stockpile of Atomic Weapons, JCS 1832/11, 28 December 1948, in *The Atomic Bomb and War Planning, Concepts and Capabilities,* Vol. 9, eds. Steven Ross and David Alan Rosenberg (New York: Garland Publishing, 1989), 58.
72. Harry Borowski, "Air Force Atomic Capability from V-J Day to the Berlin Blockade-Potential or Real," *Military Affairs,* Vol. 44 No. 3, 109.
73. Moody, *Building a Strategic Air Force*, 89.
74. *Ibid.*, 224.
75. *Ibid.*
76. SAC Cmdrs Conf 25–26–27 April 1950, 10.
77. USSBS, "The Effects of the Atomic Bombs on Hiroshima and Nagasaki, Extent of Fire and Limits of Blast Damage Map."
78. JCS 1952/11 Weapon System Evaluation Group, Evaluation of Effectiveness of Strategic Air Operations, 10 February 1950, 182.
79. Alwyn Lloyd, *A Cold War Legacy: Strategic Air Command 1946–1992* (Missoula, MT: Pictorial History Publishing Company, 1999), 120.
80. *Ibid.*
81. Meilinger, *Bomber: The Early Development of Strategic Air Command*, 139.
82. SAC Cmdrs Conf April 25–26–27 1950, 214; Meilinger, *Bomber*, 139.
83. SAC Cmdrs Briefing 25–25–27 April 1950, 11.
84. Borowski, *A Hollow Threat,* 59.
85. Kohn and Harahan, *Strategic Air Warfare*, 80.
86. Borowski, *A Hollow Threat,* 60: Moody, *Building a Strategic Air Force*, 88.
87. Borowski, *A Hollow Threat*, 57.
88. Moody, *Building a Strategic Air Force*, 88.
89. Borowski, *A Hollow Threat,*57.

90. Meilinger, *Bomber: The Early Development of Strategic Air Command*, 116.
91. Letter, Spaatz to Kenney, 6 May 1947, Series III, Box 5, Folder 4, Borowski Papers as discussed in Grynkewich, "Advisable…?" 82.
92. Moody, *Building a Strategic Air Force*, 87; Borowski, *A Hollow Threat*, 65.
93. Lloyd, *A Cold War Legacy*, 110.
94. *Ibid.*, 61.
95. http://usafflagranks.com/Major_General_Clements_McMullen.htm (accessed 1 November, 2014); Grynkewich, "Advisable…?" 4; Moody, *Building a Strategic Air Force*, 85; Meilinger, *Bomber: The Early Development of Strategic Air Command*, 116.
96. Los Angeles Times, "General Keeney on the State of Air Forces," 10 April 1947.
97. LeMay and Kantor, *Mission with LeMay*, 439.
98. Moody, *Building a Strategic Air Force*, 225.
99. Lindberg Report to General Vandenberg, September 14, 1948, Folder 170, Box 96, Charles Lindberg Papers (MS 325), Manuscripts and Archives, Yale University Library, New Haven, CT.
100. *Ibid.*
101. *Ibid.*
102. *Ibid.*, 2.
103. Meilinger, *Bomber: The Early Development of Strategic Air Command*, 135.
104. Lindberg Report to General Vandenberg, September 14, 1948, 2.
105. *Ibid.*
106. *Ibid.*, 3.
107. *Ibid.*
108. Grynkewich, "Advisable in the National Interest? The Relief of General George Kenney," 2.
109. Moody, *Building a Strategic Air Force*, 229.
110. *Ibid.*
111. Kohn and Harahan, *Strategic Air Warfare*, 82.
112. Lloyd, *A Cold War Legacy*, 118.
113. LeMay and Kantor, *Mission with LeMay*, 439.
114. Kohn and Harahan, *Strategic Air Warfare*, 82.
115. *Ibid.*, 430.
116. *Ibid.*, 436.
117. *Ibid.*, 432.
118. *Ibid.*, 440.
119. Phillip Meilinger, "How LeMay Transformed Strategic Air Command," *Air and Space Power Journal*, March-April 2014, 81.
120. Kohn and Harahan, *Strategic Air Warfare*, 84.
121. *Ibid.*, 97.
122. Borgiasz, *The Strategic Air Command*, 13.
123. Thomas Coffey, *Iron Eagle: The Turbulent Life of General Curtis LeMay* (New York: Avalon Books, 1986), 329–330.
124. Cmdrs Conf 25–26–27 April 1950, 228.
125. *Ibid.*

Chapter 9

1. Curtis LeMay and Bill Yenne, *Superfortress* (New York: Berkeley, 1989), xiii.
2. Alvin Croox, "Strategic Bombing in the Pacific 1942–1945" in *Case Studies in Strategic Bombardment*, 217.
3. Briefing SAC Cmdrs Conf April 25–26–27, 1950, 2.
4. USSBS, *The Strategic Air Operation of Very Heavy Bombardment in the War Against Japan (Twentieth Air Force) Final Report* (Washington, DC: U.S. Government Printing Office, 1946), 6.
5. Errol Morris, *Fog of War: Eleven Lessons from the Life of Robert S. McNamara* (Culver City, CA: Sony Pictures, 2003), video.
6. Christopher Chant, *World War II Aircraft* (London: Orbis, 1975), 112.
7. *Ibid.*
8. Carl Berger, *B-29 Superfortress* (New York: Ballentine, 1970), 32–33.
9. Headquarters Army Air Force, *Aircraft Commanders Manual for the B-29* (Reprint) (Dayton, OH: Otterbein Press, 1945), 12.
10. *Ibid.*, 5.
11. *Ibid.*, 28.
12. LeMay and Yenne, *Superfortress*, xiv.
13. Wilbur Morrison, *Point of No Return* (New York: Times Books, 1979), 25.
14. LeMay and Yenne, *Superfortress*, xiv.
15. LeMay and Kantor, *Mission with LeMay*, 323.
16. *Ibid.*
17. *Ibid.*, 321.
18. *Ibid.*, 322.
19. Morrison, *Point of No Return*, 58.
20. Graham White, *Allied Aircraft Piston Engines of World War II* (Warrendale, PA: Society of Automotive Engineers, 1995), 370.
21. LeMay speech to Ohio Society of New York, 19 November 1945. Box 41, LeMay papers, LOC.
22. LeMay and Yenne, *Superfortress*, 79.
23. Richard Campbell, *The Silverplate Bombers: A History and Registry of the Enola Gay and Other B-29s Configured to Carry Atomic Bombs* (Jefferson, NC: McFarland Publishing, 2005), 10.
24. Campbell, *The Silverplate Bombers,* 14.
25. *Ibid.*
26. Tibbets, *Return of the Enola Gay*, 230.
27. Groves, *Now It Can Be Told*, 286. Tibbets estimates that they were nine miles away

from the site of the blast when the shockwave hit.
28. Campbell, *The Silverplate Bombers*, 15.
29. *Ibid.*, 22.
30. *Ibid.*
31. *Ibid.*, 23.
32. Moody, *Building a Strategic Air Force*, 246.
33. Campbell, *The Silverplate Bombers*, 24.
34. Briefing SAC Cmdrs Conf April 25–26–27, 1950, 17.
35. Lloyd, *A Cold War Legacy*, 144.
36. Don Pyeatt and Dennis Jenkins, *Cold War Peacemaker: The Story of Cowtown and the Convair B-36* (Manchester, UK: Crecy Publishing, 2010), 49.
37. *Ibid.*, 55.
38. *Ibid.*, 124.
39. Pyeatt and Jenkins, *Cold War Peacemaker*, 70.
40. *Ibid.*
41. Enclosure K, Logistics and Base Defense, JCS 1952/11 Weapon System Evaluation Group, Evaluation of Effectiveness of Strategic Air Operations, 10 February 1950, K-12.
42. *Ibid.*
43. Briefing SAC Cmdrs Conf April 25–26–27, 1950, 17.
44. Meilinger, *Bomber: Early Development of SAC*, 87.
45. *Ibid.*
46. Pyeatt and Jenkins, *Cold War Peacemaker*, 70.
47. JCS 1952/11Weapon System Evaluation Group, Evaluation of Effectiveness of Strategic Air Operations, 10 February 1950, 164.
48. Briefing SAC Cmdrs Conf April 25–26–27, 1950, 7–8.
49. Lloyd, *A Cold War Legacy*, 99.
50. Briefing SAC Cmdrs Conf April 25–26–27, 1950, 17.
51. Lloyd, *A Cold War Legacy*, 136.
52. Borgiasz, *The Strategic Air Command*, 81.
53. Enclosure F, Bomber Operational Capabilities, JCS 1952/11 Weapon System Evaluation Group, Evaluation of Effectiveness of Strategic Air Operations, 10 February 1950, F-10.
54. Borgiasz, *The Strategic Air Command*, 81.
55. Enclosure K, Logistics and Base Defense, JCS 1952/11 Weapon System Evaluation Group, Evaluation of Effectiveness of Strategic Air Operations, 10 February 1950, K-3.
56. Lloyd, *A Cold War Legacy*, 102.
57. Borgiasz, *The Strategic Air Command*, 80–81.
58. Enclosure K, Logistics and Base Defense, JCS 1952/11 Weapon System Evaluation Group, Evaluation of Effectiveness of Strategic Air Operations, 10 February 1950, K-13.
59. Briefing SAC Cmdrs Conf April 25–26–27, 1950, 3.
60. SAC Cmdrs Conf 25–26–27 April 1950, 222.
61. Rudolf Ventresca, *Organizational Structure for Air National Guard Tactical Aircraft Maintenance* (Maxwell AFB, AL: Air University Press, 1991), 6.
62. *Ibid.*
63. Borgiasz, *The Strategic Air Command*, 82.
64. *Ibid.*, 83.
65. *Ibid.*
66. "Man in the First Plane," *Time* magazine, September 4, 1950.
67. JCS 1952/11 Weapon System Evaluation Group, Evaluation of Effectiveness of Strategic Air Operations, 10 February 1950, 188.
68. JCS 1952/11 Weapon System Evaluation Group, Evaluation of Effectiveness of Strategic Air Operations, 10 February 1950, Enclosure D, 29.
69. JCS 1952/11 Weapon System Evaluation Group, Evaluation of Effectiveness of Strategic Air Operations, 10 February 1950, 188.
70. *Ibid.*, Enclosure F, F-25.
71. JCS 1952/11 Weapon System Evaluation Group, Evaluation of Effectiveness of Strategic Air Operations, 10 February 1950, Enclosure D, D-44.
72. *Ibid.*
73. *Ibid.*
74. *Ibid.*, D-47.
75. *Ibid.*
76. Briefing SAC Cmdrs Conf April 25–26–27, 1950, 16.
77. *Ibid.*, D-44.
78. *Ibid.*, Enclosure D, D-45.
79. Briefing SAC Cmdrs Conf April 25–26–27, 1950, 16.
80. Historical Division, Office of Information, *Development of Airborne Armament 1910–1961* (Air Force Systems Command, 1961); JCS 1952/11 Weapon System Evaluation Group, Evaluation of Effectiveness of Strategic Air Operations, 10 February 1950, 187.
81. Dennis Jenkins, *Magnesium Overcast: The Story of the Convair B-36* (North Branch, MN: Specialty Press, 2002), 151.
82. Air Force Historical Publication Series, *Development of Airborne Armament 1910–1961 Volume 1 Bombing Systems,* http://www.alternatewars.com/SAC/AirborneArmament/Volume_I.html (accessed December 23, 2014).
83. *Ibid.*
84. Pyeatt and Jenkins, *Cold War Peacemaker*, 70; Lloyd, *A Cold War Legacy*, 145.
85. Historical Division, Office of Information, *Development of Airborne Armament 1910–1961*.
86. History of B-36 Procurement: Presented

to the House Armed Services Committee, F.H. Smith, B-36 Subject File, Box 119, Nathan Twining Papers, LOC.
87. *Ibid.*
88. Futrell, *Ideas, Concepts, Doctrine,* 231.
89. *Ibid.*
90. Richard Tregaskis, "Without Fighters Our Bombers Are Sitting Ducks," *Collier's,* October 8, 1949, 16.
91. *Ibid.,* 60.
92. Pyeatt and Jenkins, *Cold War Peacemaker,* 103.
93. *Time* magazine, September 4, 1950. Online access available at http://www.time.com/covers/0,16641,19500904,00.html (accessed March 20, 2007).
94. Briefing SAC Cmdrs Conf April 25–26–27, 1950, 14.
95. *Ibid.*
96. Marcelle Size Knaack, *Encyclopedia of U.S. Air Force Aircraft and Missile Systems* (Washington, DC: Office of Air Force History, 1978), 32.
97. *Ibid.*
98. *Ibid.,* 34.
99. *Ibid.*
100. SAC Cmdrs Conf 25–26–27 April 1950, 219–220.
101. *Ibid.,* 220.
102. Futrell, 254.
103. *Ibid.*
104. *Ibid.*

Conclusion

1. "Report to the President by the Special Committee of the National Security Council on the Proposed Acceleration of the Atomic Energy Program," October 10, 1949, B File, #11A Box 1 of 2, President's Secretary's File, Truman Library.
2. *Ibid.*
3. George H. Gallup, *The Gallup Poll, Public Opinion 1935–1971, Volume 2 1949–1953* (New York: Random House, 1972), 791–792.
4. *Ibid.*
5. *Ibid.,* 839.
6. *Ibid.*
7. *Ibid.,* 929.
8. "Annual Message to the Congress of the State of the Union," January 4, 1950, U.S. Government, *The Public Papers of the Presidents of the United States—Harry S. Truman,* 1950 (Washington D.C.: U.S. Government Printing Office, 1962), 10.
9. *Ibid.,* 7.
10. *Ibid.,* 5.
11. David Kunsman and Douglas Lawson, *A Primer in U.S. Strategic Nuclear Policy* (Albuquerque, NM: Sandia National Laboratories, 2001), 28; Condit, *The Joint Chiefs of Staff,* 560.
12. Allen R. Millet and Peter Maslowski, *For the Common Defense—A Military History of the United States of America* (New York: The Free Press, Macmillan, 1994), 513.
13. Williamson and Reardon, *The Origins of U.S. Nuclear Strategy 1945–1953,* 133.
14. *Ibid.*
15. *Ibid.*
16. "United States Objectives and Programs for National Security," NSC 68, April 14, 1950 in Etzold and Gaddis, *Containment, Documents on American Policy and Strategy,* 387.
17. *Ibid.,* 426–438.
18. *Ibid.,* 438.
19. *Ibid.,* 400, 416–417.
20. *Ibid.,* 442.
21. Williamson and Reardon, *The Origins of U.S. Nuclear Strategy,* 136–137; Offner, *Another Such Victory,* 366.
22. Offner, *Another Such Victory,* 366, 383.
23. Dean Acheson, *Present at the Creation* (New York: Norton, 1969), 374.
24. Williamson and Reardon, *The Origins of U.S. Nuclear Strategy,* 137.
25. Wittner, *Cold War America,* 79.
26. Office of the Historian, Headquarters Strategic Air Command, *The Development of Strategic Air Command 1946–1981 (A Chronological History),* 28.
27. *Ibid.,* 46.
28. "Memorandum Op-36C/jm," 18 March 1954, addendum to Rosenberg and Moore, "Smoking Radiating Ruin at the End of Two Hours."
29. *Ibid.,* 349.
30. "Memorandum Op-36C/jm," 18 March, 1954, addendum to Rosenberg and Moore, "Smoking Radiating Ruin at the End of Two Hours."
31. Gallup, *The Gallup Poll, Public Opinion 1935–1971, Vol. 2,* 897. The respondents to this poll had been screened in a previous question asking, "Will you tell me what the term 'cold war' means?" 58 percent answered correctly.
32. *Ibid.,* 906. The remaining six percent had no opinion.
33. *Ibid.,* 648.
34. Paul Boyer, *By Bomb's Early Light: American Thought and Culture at the Dawn of the Atomic Age* (Chapel Hill: University of North Carolina Press, 1985), 334.
35. *Ibid.,* 336.
36. Degroot, *The Bomb,* 245, 248.
37. "Special Message to Congress Reporting in the Situation in Korea," July 19, 1950. *Public Papers of the Presidents of the United States—Harry Truman,* 532.
38. *Ibid.*

39. *Ibid.*, 747.
40. *Ibid.*, 71.
41. Condit, *The Joint Chiefs of Staff*, 531; "Report to the President by the Special Committee of the National Security Council on the Proposed Acceleration of the Atomic Energy Program," October 10, 1949, Expansion of Atomic Energy File, Advisory Committee Atomic Energy, Box 174, NSC-Atomic File, Subject File 1940–1953, Personal Secretary File, Truman Library.
42. Enclosure to Correspondence from Brien McMahon to Harry S. Truman, May 30, 1952, entitled "The Scale and Scope of Atomic Production: A Chronology of Leading Events," 13, Thermonuclear Folder, Atomic Weapons, Box 176, NSC-Atomic File, Subject File 1940–1953, Personal Secretary File, Truman Library.
43. *Ibid.*
44. *Ibid.*
45. *Ibid.*
46. Condit, *The Joint Chiefs of Staff*, 533–534; "Report to the President by the Special Committee of the National Security Council on the Proposed Acceleration of the Atomic Energy Program, 2.
47. Condit, *The Joint Chiefs of Staff*, 553; "Report to the President by the Special Committee of the National Security Council on the Proposed Acceleration of the Atomic Energy Program, 2.
48. Special Committee Report, 8.
49. *Ibid.*, 9.
50. Rosenberg, "American Atomic Strategy and Hydrogen Bomb Decision," 78; Enclosure to Correspondence from Brian McMahon to Harry S. Truman, May 30, 1952, entitled "The Scale and Scope of Atomic Production: A Chronology of Leading Events," 14, Box 176, NSC-Atomic File 1940–1953, Personal Secretary File, Truman Library.
51. Williamson and Reardon, *The Origins of U.S. Nuclear Strategy*, 152–153; Rosenberg, "The Origins of Overkill," 23.
52. Memorandum for the Executive Secretary, National Security Council, May 14, 1952, President's Secretary's File, Truman Library.
53. Rhodes, *Dark Sun*, 252–253.
54. Condit, *The Joint Chiefs of Staff*, 546.
55. *Ibid.*
56. Rhodes, *Dark Sun*, 248.
57. Condit, *The Joint Chiefs of Staff*, 542.
58. *Ibid.*, 252.
59. Rhodes, *Dark Sun*, 381.
60. Condit, *The Joint Chiefs of Staff*, 543; Rosenberg, "American Atomic Strategy and Hydrogen Bomb Decision," 79.
61. Enclosure to Correspondence from Brien McMahon to Harry S. Truman, May 30, 1952, entitled "The Scale and Scope of Atomic Production: A Chronology of Leading Events," 14.
62. Condit, *The Joint Chiefs of Staff*, 546.
63. *Ibid.*, 543.
64. Condit, 543; Kunsman and Lawson, 26.
65. Condit, *The Joint Chiefs of Staff*, 543.
66. Rosenberg, "American Atomic Strategy and Hydrogen Bomb Decision," 80; and Enclosure to Correspondence from Brien McMahon to Harry S. Truman, May 30, 1952, entitled "The Scale and Scope of Atomic Production: A Chronology of Leading Events," 15; Condit, *The Joint Chiefs of Staff*, 544; Kunsman and Lawson, *A Primer in U.S. Strategic Nuclear Policy*, 27.
67. Rosenberg, "American Atomic Strategy," 80.
68. Condit, *The Joint Chiefs of Staff*, 544.
69. *Ibid.*, 545; Enclosure to Correspondence from Brien McMahon to Harry S. Truman, May 30, 1952, entitled "The Scale and Scope of Atomic Production: A Chronology of Leading Events," 15; Kunsman and Lawson, *A Primer in U.S. Strategic Nuclear Policy*, 27.
70. Enclosure to Correspondence from Brien McMahon to Harry S. Truman, May 30, 1952, entitled "The Scale and Scope of Atomic Production: A Chronology of Leading Events," 15.
71. Correspondence to Harry S. Truman from Brien McMahon, November 21, 1949, Atomic Energy Folder, Box 10, Naval Aide to the President Files 1945–1953, Staff Member and Office Files, Truman Library.
72. *Ibid.*
73. *Ibid.*
74. *Ibid.*
75. Condit, *The Joint Chiefs of Staff*, 548.
76. Memo, JCS to SecDef, "The United States Military Position with Respect to Development of the Thermonuclear Weapon," 23 November 1949, as referenced in Condit, *The Joint Chiefs of Staff*, 548–549.
77. *Ibid.*
78. Memo, JCS to Sec Def, "Request for Comments on Military Views of Members of General Advisory Committee," 13 Jan 1950 (derived from JCS 2096, CCS 471.6 (12–14–49) sec 1, as referenced in Condit, *The Joint Chiefs of Staff*, 555; Rhodes, *Dark Sun*, 406.
79. Omar Bradley to Secretary of Defense, January 13, Bradley Folder, General File, President's Secretary's File, Truman Library, as referenced in Rosenberg, "American Atomic Strategy and Hydrogen Bomb Decision," 83.
80. Condit, *The Joint Chiefs of Staff*, 550.
81. *Ibid.*, 557.
82. *Ibid.*
83. Correspondence from Harry Truman to David Lilienthal, January 31, 1950, Thermonuclear Folder, Box 176, Subject File, 1940–1953 NSC-Atomic File, Presidents Secretary File, Truman Library.

84. Rhodes, *Dark Sun*, 407.
85. Statement by the President on the Hydrogen Bomb, January 31, 1950, *Public Papers of Harry S. Truman, January 1 to December 31, 1950* (Washington, DC: U.S. Government Printing Office, 1965), 138.
86. Gallup, *The Gallup Poll, Public Opinion 1935–1971, Vol. 2 1949–1953*, 888.
87. *Ibid.*, 895.
88. *Ibid.*
89. Memorandum For: Mr. Robert LeBaron, Chairman Military Liaison Committee to the AEC, Subject: A Basis for Estimating Maximum Soviet Capabilities for Atomic Warfare, 16 February 1950, Atomic Energy Folder-Russia, Box 175, President's Secretary's File, Truman Library.
90. *Ibid.*
91. *Ibid.*; Rosenberg, "American Atomic Strategy and Hydrogen Bomb Decision," 84.
92. *Ibid.*
93. *Ibid.*, 85.
94. Norman Moss, *Men Who Play God: The Story of the H-Bomb and How the World Came to Live with It* (New York: Harper and Row, 1968), 51.
95. Stanley Blumberg and Gwinn Owens, *Energy and Conflict: The Life and Times of Edward Teller* (New York: Putnam and Sons, 1976), 213.
96. "A Terrible Weapon and a Courageous Decision," *Fort Worth Star Telegram*, February 2, 1950, in Folder 1, Correspondence File C-General, Box 2 Symington Papers, Truman Library.
97. *Ibid.*
98. Correspondence, Stuart Symington to Louis Johnson, 8 November, 1949, Atomic Energy File, Box 175, NSC Atomic File, Subject File 1940–1953, President's Secretary's File, Truman Library.
99. *Ibid.*
100. *Ibid.*
101. *Ibid.*
102. *Ibid.*
103. Futrell, *Ideas, Concepts, Doctrine*, 317.
104. *Ibid.*; Moody, *Building a Strategic Air Force*, 394. The air force also changed its organizational nomenclature, counting "wings" instead of "groups."
105. Futrell, *Ideas, Concepts, Doctrine*, 320 and 322.
106. Williamson and Reardon, *Origins of U.S. Nuclear Strategy*, 144.
107. Moody, *Building a Strategic Air Force*, 446.
108. *Ibid.*
109. Futrell, *Ideas, Concepts, Doctrine*, 323.
110. *Ibid.*, 324.
111. *Ibid.*
112. *Ibid.*; Rosenberg, "The Origins of Overkill," 22.
113. Futrell, *Ideas, Concepts, Doctrine*, 324.
114. *Ibid.*, 325, 419–420.
115. *Ibid.*, 421.
116. Budiansky, *Air Power*, 366; Rosenberg, "The Origins of Overkill," 22.
117. Moody, *Building a Strategic Air Force*, 403.
118. *Ibid.*
119. *Ibid.*
120. Rosenberg and Moore, Document One, "Memorandum Op-36C/jm, Subj: Briefing given to the representatives of all services at SAC headquarters, Offutt Air Force Base Nebraska," 18 March 1954, 23.
121. *Ibid.*
122. J.C. Hopkins, *The Development of Strategic Air Command 1946–1981* (Offutt AFB, NE: Office of the Historian, Headquarters Strategic Air Command, 1982), 20 and 40.
123. Mark Lorell, *Bomber Research and Development Since 1945* (Santa Monica, CA: RAND Corporation, 1995), 16–17.
124. Memorandum for the President, James Lay Jr., September 10, 1952, NSC Atomic File, President's Secretary's File, Truman Library.
125. Rosenberg, "The Origins of Overkill," 18.
126. Steven L. Reardon, "U.S. Strategic Bombardment Doctrine Since 1945," in R. Cargill Hall, *Case Studies*, 409.
127. *Ibid.*, 408–409.
128. General Nathan F. Twining, Chamber of Commerce Banquet Speech, Galveston Texas, February 9, 1954, 1954 Folder, Speeches and Writing File, Box 153, General Nathan F. Twining Papers, LOC, as referenced in Hall, *Case Studies*, 408.
129. Kaplan, *Wizards*, 79.
130. Karl Clausewitz, *On War*, ed. Michael Howard and Peter Paret (Princeton: Princeton University Press, 1976), 69; Kaplan, *Wizards*, 79.
131. Kaplan, *Wizards*, 79–81.
132. Colonel Willis G. Carter, "Strategic Bombardment and National Objectives," *Air University Quarterly Review*, Volume IV, Spring 1951, No. 3, 10.
133. *Ibid.*, 11.
134. Gallup, *The Gallup Poll, Public Opinion 1935–1971, Vol. 2, 1949–1953*, 965.
135. *Ibid.*
136. Herman S. Wolk "The New Look," *Air Force Magazine*, August 2003, Vol. 86, No. 8, 81.
137. Rosenberg, "Origins of Overkill," 28.
138. Samuel Wells, "The Origins of Massive Retaliation," *Political Science Quarterly* Vol. 96, No. 1 (Spring 1981): 31; Kunsman and Lawson, *A Primer in U.S. Strategic Nuclear Policy*, 33.

139. "Text of Eisenhower's 'Feast or Famine' Defense Policy," *New York Times*, September 26, 1952.
140. Gallup, *The Gallup Poll, Public Opinion 1935–1971, Vol. 2 1949–1953*, 1073.
141. Futrell, *Ideas, Concepts, Doctrine*, 421.
142. *Ibid.*, 421–422; Glen H. Snyder, *Strategy, Politics, and Defense Budgets* (New York: Columbia University Press, 1962), 429.
143. Legislative Leadership Meeting, Supplemental Notes, May 12, 1953, Staff Notes, Jan-Dec 43 Folder, Box 4, DDE Diary Series, Ann Whitman File, Papers as President, Eisenhower Library.
144. Rosenberg, "The Origins of Overkill," 28; Wells, "Origins," 44.
145. Snyder, *Strategy, Politics*, 407.
146. NSC 162/2, A Report to the National Security Council by The Executive Secretary on Basic National Security Policy, Oct 30, 1953, Folder NSC 162/2(2), Box 11, Disaster File, National Security Council Staff: Papers, 1948–1961, National Security Council, White House Office Papers, Eisenhower Library.
147. *Ibid.*, 7–8.
148. *Ibid.*, 5.
149. *Ibid.*, 19.
150. *Ibid.*, 25.
151. Alfred Goldberg, ed., *A History of the United States Air Force, 1907–1957* (Princeton, NJ: D. Van Nostrand, 1957), 117; Rosenberg, "Origins of Overkill," 29.
152. Wells, "Origins," 46.
153. Wolk, *Planning and Organizing the Postwar Air Force*, 82.
154. Futrell, *Ideas, Concepts, Doctrine*, 425.
155. Snyder, *Strategy, Politics*, 437.
156. Kohn, *Strategic Air Warfare*, 82.

Bibliography

Published References

Abrahamson, James, and Paul Carew. *Vanguard of American Atomic Deterrence: The Sandia Pioneers 1946–1949*. Westport, CT: Praeger Press, 2002.
Acheson, Dean. *Present at the Creation*. New York: Norton, 1969.
Admunson, Michael, and Scott Zeman, eds. *Atomic Culture: How I Learned to Stop Worrying and Love the Bomb*. Boulder: University of Colorado Press, 2004.
Air Policy Commission. "Survival in the Air Age" (Finletter Report). Washington, D.C.: US Government Printing Office, 1948.
Astor, Gerald. *The Mighty Eighth*. New York: Penguin Press, 1997.
Barlow, Jeffrey. *From Hot War to Cold: The US Navy and National Security Affairs 1945–1955*. Stanford, CA: Stanford University Press, 2009.
_____. *Revolt of the Admirals: The Fight for Naval Aviation 1945–1950*. Washington, D.C.: Naval Historical Center, 1993.
Berger, Carl. *B-29: The Superfortress*. New York: Ballantine, 1970.
Blumberg, Stanley, and Gwinn Owens. *Energy and Conflict: The Life and Times of Edward Teller*. New York: Putnam and Sons, 1976.
Borden, William. *There Will Be No Time*. New York: Macmillan, 1946.
Borgiasz, William. *The Strategic Air Command*. Westport, CT: Praeger Publishing, 1996.
Borowski, Harry. *Hollow Threat*. Westport, CT: Greenwood Press, 1982.
Boyd, Alexander. *The Soviet Air Force Since 1918*. New York: Stein and Day Publishers, 1977.
Boyer, Paul. *By Bomb's Early Light: American Thought and Culture at the Dawn of the Atomic Age*. Chapel Hill: University of North Carolina Press, 1985.
Brodie, Bernard. *Strategy in the Missile Age*. Princeton, NJ: Princeton University Press, 1965.
_____. *The Ultimate Weapon*. New York: Harcourt, Brace, and Company, 1946.
Call, Steve. *Selling Air Power*. College Station: Texas A&M Press, 2009.
Campbell, Richard. *The Silverplate Bombers: A History and Registry of the Enola Gay and Other B-29s Configured to Carry Atomic Bombs*. Jefferson, NC: McFarland, 2005.
Center for Military History. *History of Strategic Air and Ballistic Missile Defense Volume 1, 1945–1955*. Washington, D.C.: Center for Military History, 2009.
Chant, Christopher. *World War II Aircraft*. London: Orbis, 1975.
Clausewitz, Karl. *On War*. Edited by Michael Howard and Peter Paret. Princeton, NJ: Princeton University Press, 1976.
Coffey, Thomas. *Iron Eagle: The Turbulent Life of General Curtis LeMay*. New York: Avalon Books, 1986.
Condit, Kenneth. *The Joint Chiefs of Staff and National Policy Vol. II, 1947–1949*. Washington, D.C.: Office of Joint History, 1996.
Davis, Richard. *Bombing the European Axis Power*. Maxwell AFB, AL: Air University Press, 2006.

Defense Threat Reduction Agency. *Defense Nuclear Agency 1947–1997.* Washington, D.C.: US Government Printing Office, 2002.
DeGroot, Gerald. *The Bomb: A Life.* Cambridge, MA: Harvard University Press, 2004.
Dower, John. *War Without Mercy.* New York: Pantheon, 1986.
Duncan, Francis, and Richard Hewlett. *Atomic Shield: A History of the Atomic Energy Commission Volume II, 1947–1952.* Berkeley, CA: University of California Press, 1990.
Eden, Lynn. *Whole World on Fire: Organizations, Knowledge and Nuclear Weapons Devastation.* Ithaca, NY: Cornell University Press, 2004.
Ehlers, Robert. *Targeting the Reich: Air Intelligence and the Allied Bombing Campaigns.* Lawrence, KS: University of Kansas Press, 2009.
Etzold, Thomas, and John L. Gaddis. *Containment: Documents on American Policy and Strategy 1945–1950.* New York: Columbia University Press, 1978.
Farquhar, John. *A Need to Know: The Role of Air Force Reconnaissance in War Planning, 1945–1953.* Maxwell AFB, AL: Air University Press, 2004.
Ferrell, Robert, ed. *Off the Record: The Private Papers of Harry S. Truman.* Columbia, MO: University of Missouri Press, 1997.
Futrell, Robert Frank. *Ideas, Concepts, Doctrine: Basic Thinking in the United States Air Force, 1907–1960.* Maxwell AFB, AL: Air University Press, 1989.
Gaddis, John L. *The Cold War: A New History.* New York: Penguin Press, 2005.
Gallup, George. *The Gallup Poll, Public Opinion 1935–1971, Volume 1, 1935–1948.* New York: Random House, 1972.
_____. *The Gallup Poll, Public Opinion 1935–1971, Volume 2, 1949–1971.* New York: Random House, 1972.
Goldberg, Alfred, ed. *A History of the United States Air Force, 1907–1957.* Princeton, NJ: D. Van Nostrand, 1957.
Groves, Leslie. *Now It Can Be Told.* New York: Da Capo Press, 1962.
Hall, R. Cargill, ed. *Case Studies in Strategic Bombardment.* Washington, D.C.: US Air Force History and Museums Program, 1998.
Hansen, Chuck. *US Nuclear Weapons: The Secret History.* Arlington, TX: Aerofax Publishing, 1988.
Haynes, Richard F. *The Awesome Power: Harry S. Truman as Commander in Chief.* Baton Rouge: Louisiana State University Press, 1973.
Headquarters Army Air Force. *Aircraft Commanders Manual for the B-29* (Reprint). Dayton, OH: Otterbein Press, 1945.
Herken, Gregg. *The Winning Weapon: The Atomic Bomb in the Cold War 1945–1950.* Princeton, NJ: Princeton University Press, 1981.
Historical Evaluation and Research Organization. *The Development of Soviet Air Defense Doctrine and Practice: A Report Prepared for Sandia National Laboratories.* Dunn Loring, VA: DuPuy Associates, 1981.
Hohne, Heinz, and Herman Zolling. *The General Was a Spy: The Truth About General Gehlen and His Spy Ring.* New York: Coward, McCann, and Geoghegan, 1971.
Holl, Jack. *Argonne National Laboratory 1946–1996.* Urbana: University of Illinois Press, 1996.
Hopkins, J.C. *The Development of Strategic Air Command 1946–1981 (A Chronological History).* Offutt AFB, NE: Office of the Historian, Headquarters Strategic Air Command, 1982.
Jenkins, Dennis. *Magnesium Overcast: The Story of the Convair B-36.* North Branch, MN: Specialty Press, 2002.
Kaku, Michio, and Daniel Axelrod. *To Win a Nuclear War: The Pentagon's Secret War Plans.* Black Rose Books Ltd., 1987.
Kaplan, Fred. *The Wizards of Armageddon.* Stanford, CA: Stanford University Press, 1983.
Keeney, Douglas. *15 Minutes: General Curtis LeMay and the Countdown to Nuclear Annihilation.* New York: St. Martin's Press, 2011.
Kennan, George. *Memoirs.* New York: Pantheon Books, 1967.
Kenney, George. *General Kenney Reports.* Washington, D.C.: Office of Air Force History (Reprint), 1987.

Knaack, Marcelle. *Encyclopedia of US Air Force Aircraft and Missile Systems*. Washington, D.C.: Office of Air Force History, 1978.
Kohn, Richard H., and Joseph P. Harahan. *Strategic Air Warfare: An Interview with Generals Curtis LeMay, Leon Johnson, David Burchinal, and Jack Catton*. Washington, D.C.: Office of Air Force History, 1988.
Kunsman, David, and Douglas Lawson. *A Primer in US Strategic Nuclear Policy*. Albuquerque, NM: Sandia National Laboratories, 2001.
LeMay, Curtis, and MacKinlay Kantor. *Mission with LeMay*. Garden City, NY: Doubleday, 1965.
LeMay, Curtis, and Bill Yenne. *Superfortress*. New York: Berkeley, 1989.
Lilienthal, David. *The Journals of David E. Lilienthal, The Atomic Energy Years 1945–1950, Volume 2*. New York: Harper and Row, 1964.
Lloyd, Alwyn. *A Cold War Legacy: Strategic Air Command 1946–1992*. Missoula, MT: Pictorial History Publishing Company, 1999.
Lorell, Mark. *Bomber Research and Development Since 1945*. Santa Monica, CA: RAND Corporation, 1995.
May, Elaine Tyler. *Homeward Bound: American Families in the Cold War Era*. New York: Basic Books, 1999.
Meilinger, Philip S. *Bomber: The Early Development of Strategic Air Command*. Maxwell AFB, AL: Air University Press, 2012.
Millet, Allen, and Peter Maslowski. *For the Common Defense: A Military History of the United States of America*. New York: The Free Press, Macmillan, 1994.
Moody, Walter S. *Building a Strategic Air Force*. Washington, D.C.: US Air Force History and Museums Program, 1996.
Morrison, Wilbur. *Point of No Return*. New York: Times Books, 1979.
Moss, Norman. *Men Who Play God: The Story of the H-Bomb and How the World Came to Live with It*. New York: Harper and Row, 1968.
Nichols, K.D. *The Road to Trinity*. New York: Morrow and Company, 1987.
Office of the Assistant Secretary of Defense. *History or Custody and Deployment of Nuclear Weapons July 1945 through September 1977*. Washington, D.C.: U.S. Government Printing Office, February 1978.
Office of the Federal Register, National Archives and Records Service, General Services Administration. *The Public Papers of the Presidents of the United States—Harry S. Truman, 1946*. Washington, D.C.: US Government Printing Office, 1962.
_____. *The Public Papers of the Presidents of the United States—Harry S. Truman 1947*. Washington, D.C.: U.S. Government Printing Office, 1962.
_____. *The Public Papers of the Presidents of the United States—Harry S. Truman 1950*. Washington, D.C.: U.S. Government Printing Office, 1962.
Offner, Arnold. *Another Such Victory*. Stanford, CA: Stanford University Press, 2002.
Pyeatt, Don, and Dennis Jenkins. *Cold War Peacemaker: The Story of Cowtown and the Convair B-36*. Manchester, UK: Crecy Publishing, 2010.
Quinlivan, James. *Soviet Strategic Air Defense: A Long Past and an Uncertain Future*. Santa Monica, CA: RAND Corporation, 1989.
Reardon, Steven. *The Formative Years: History of the Secretary of Defense Volume 1*. Washington, D.C.: Historical Office of the Secretary of Defense, 1984.
Rhodes, Richard. *Dark Sun*. New York: Simon & Schuster, 1995.
Ross, Steven. *American War Plans 1945–1950*. London: Frank Cass, 1996.
Ross, Steven, and David Alan Rosenberg, eds. *America's Plans for War Against the Soviet Union, 1945–1950, Volume 2 Design for Global War*. New York: Garland Publishing, 1989.
_____ and _____. *America's Plans for War Against the Soviet Union 1945–1950, Volume 3 Pincher Campaign Plans*. New York: Garland Publishing, 1989.
_____ and _____. *America's Plan for War Against the Soviet Union, 1945–1950 Volume 7 From Crankshaft to Halfmoon*. New York: Garland Publishing, 1990.
_____ and _____. *America's Plans for War Against the Soviet Union, 1945–1950 Volume 9 The Atomic Bomb War Planning, Concepts, and Capabilities*. New York: Garland Publishing, 1989.

Bibliography

_____and _____. *America's Plan for War Against the Soviet Union, 1945–1950 Volume 13 Evaluating the Air Offensive: The WSEG 1 Study.* New York: Garland Publishing, 1990.

Sherwin, Martin. *American Prometheus.* New York: A.A. Knopf, 2005.

Snyder, Glen. *Strategy, Politics, and Defense Budgets.* New York: Columbia University Press, 1962.

Sparrow, John. *History of Personnel Demobilization in the United States Army.* Washington, D.C.: Center for Military History, Facsimile Edition, 1994.

Sweeney, Charles. *War's End: An Eyewitness of America's Last Atomic Mission.* New York: Avon Publishing, 1997.

Tibbets, Paul. *Return of the Enola Gay.* New Hope, PA: Enola Gay Remembered, 1998.

Truman, Harry. *Memoirs of Harry S. Truman, Volume 2, Years of Trial and Hope.* Garden City, NY: Doubleday, 1956.

Trumball, Robert. *Nine Who Survived Hiroshima and Nagasaki.* New York: E.P. Dutton, 1957.

Ullrich, Rebecca. *Tech Area II: A History.* Albuquerque, NM: Sandia National Laboratories, 1998.

United States Army Center of Military History. *American Military History.* Washington, D.C.: US Government Printing Office, 1969.

United States Department of State. "US Objectives with Respect to the USSR to Counter Soviet Threats to US Security," NSC 20/4, *Foreign Relations of the United States, Vol. 1.* Washington, D.C.: US Government Printing Office, Department of State, 1948.

United States Strategic Bombing Surveys (USSBS). *The Effects of Atomic Bombs on Hiroshima and Nagasaki.* Washington, D.C.: US Government Printing Office, 1946.

_____. *The Effects of Strategic Bombing on the German War Economy, Overall Economic Effects Division, October 31, 1945.* Washington, D.C.: US Government Printing Office, 1945.

_____. *Minority Report to Secretary of War-Military Analysis Division (Anderson Report), 11 July 1946.* Garland Series, USSBS, Volume VII, New York: Garland Publishing, 1976.

_____. *The Strategic Air Operation of Very Heavy Bombardment in the War Against Japan (Twentieth Air Force) Final Report.* Washington, D.C.: US Government Printing Office, 1946.

_____. *Summary Report (European War) September 30, 1945.* Washington, D.C.: US Government Printing Office, 1945.

_____. *Summary Report (Pacific War) Reprint.* Maxwell AFB, AL: Air University Press, 1987.

Ventresca, Rudolf. *Organizational Structure for Air National Guard Tactical Aircraft Maintenance.* Maxwell AFB, AL: Air University Press, 1991.

Wainstein, L., ed. *Study S-467: The Evolution of US Strategic Command and Control and Warning 1945–1971.* Arlington, VA: Institute for Defense Analyses, 1975.

White, Graham. *Allied Aircraft Piston Engines of World War II.* Warrendale, PA: Society of Automotive Engineers, 1995.

Williamson, Samuel, and Steven Reardon. *The Origins of US Nuclear Strategy, 1945–1953.* New York: Palgrave, 1993.

Wittner, Lawrence. *Cold War America.* New York: Praeger Publishers, 1974.

Wolk, Herman. *Planning and Organizing the Postwar Air Force 1943–1947.* Washington, D.C.: Office of Air Force History, 1984.

Yamazaki, James. *Children of the Atomic Bomb.* Durham, NC: Duke University Press, 1995.

Unpublished Sources

Alfred Simpson Historical Research Center, Maxwell AFB, AL.
    Air Corps Tactical School (ACTS) Lectures, File 248.2020A-25
    Strategic Air Command History, Call Number 416.01 V.1, IRIS Number 198556

Dwight David Eisenhower Presidential Library, Abilene, KS.
    Dwight David Eisenhower Diary Series, Ann Whitman File

National Security Council Papers, 1948–1961, White House Office Papers
  Papers of Lauris Norstad
George Washington University National Security Archive (Online).
  National Archives and Records Administration (NARA), Record Group 341, RG 341
Harry S. Truman Presidential Library, Independence, MO.
  B File
  Miscellaneous Historical Documents File
  Papers of Stuart S. Symington
  Personal Secretary Files
  President's Secretary's File
  Staff Members and Office Files
  White House Central Files
Manuscripts Division, Library of Congress, Washington, D.C.
  Papers of General Curtis E. LeMay
  Papers of Carl A. Spaatz
  Papers of Nathan Twining
Yale University Library, Manuscripts and Archives, New Haven CT
  Papers of Charles Lindbergh

Periodical and Journal Articles

Anderson, Orvil. "Air Warfare and Morality." *Air University Quarterly Review* Vol. III, Number 3 (Winter 1949).
Barlow, Jeffery. "Moral Courage: Vital to Navy Leadership." *Naval Aviation News*, September-October 1998.
Borowski, Harry. "Air Force Atomic Capability from V-J Day to the Berlin Blockade—Potential or Real." *Military Affairs*, Vol. 44, No. 3.
_____. "A Narrow Victory: The Berlin Blockade and the American Military Response." *Air University Review*, July-August 1981.
Brodie, Bernard. "Some Notes on the Evolution of Air Doctrine." *World Politics*, Vol. 7, No. 3 (April 1955).
Collins, John. "Word War II NCOs." *Army Magazine*, Vol. 55, No. 2 (February 2005). Association of the United States Army Magazine.
de Seversky, Alexander. "A Lecture on Air Power." *Air University Quarterly Review*, Vol. 1 No. 2 (Fall 1947).
"Facts and Fears." *Time* (October 24, 1949). http://www.time.com/time/magazine/article/0,9171,805110,00.html (accessed 20 June 2008).
"General Keeney on the State of Air Forces." *Los Angeles Times*, 10 April 1947.
"House's B-36 Inquiry Ends with Clearing of Officials." *New York Times*, August 26, 1949.
Kennan, George. "Sources of Soviet Conduct." *Foreign Affairs*, 25, No. 4 (July 1947).
"Man in the First Plane." *Time* (September 4, 1950). http://www.time.com/timemagazine/article/0,9171,856658,00.html (accessed June 21, 2008).
Meilinger, Phillip. "How LeMay Transformed Strategic Air Command." *Air and Space Power Journal*, March-April 2014.
Pancake, Frank. "The Strategic Striking Forces." *Air University Quarterly Review*, No. 2 (Fall 1948).
"Revolt of the Admirals." *Time* (October 17, 1949). http://www.time.com/time/magazine/article/0,9171,853921,00.html (accessed 21 June 2008).
Rosenberg, David Alan. "American Atomic Strategy and Hydrogen Bomb Decision." *The Journal of American History*, 66, No. 1 (June 1979).
_____. "US Nuclear Stockpile 1945 to 1950." *The Bulletin of the Atomic Scientist* Vol. 38 (May 1982).
Rosenberg, David Alan, and W.B. Moore. "A Smoking Radiated Ruin at the End of Two Hours." Documents of American Plans for Nuclear War with the Soviet Union, 1954–1955. *International Security*, Vol. 6, No. 3 (Winter 1981/82).

Smith, Dale. "One Way Combat." *Air University Quarterly Review,* Vol. 1, No. 2 (Fall 1947).
———. "Operational Concepts in Modern War." *Air University Quarterly Review* Vol. II, Number 2 (Fall 1948).
"Super Atom Blitz by U.S. Envisioned." *New York Times*, October 3, 1948.
"A Terrible Weapon and a Courageous Decision." *Fort Worth Star Telegram*, February 2, 1950.
"Text of Admiral Ofstie's Statement Assailing Strategic Bombing." *New York Times,* October 12, 1949.
Tregaskis, Richard. "Without Fighters Our Bombers Are Sitting Ducks." *Collier's*, October 8, 1949.
Wells, Samuel. "The Origins of Massive Retaliation." *Political Science Quarterly* Vol. 96, No. 1 (Spring 1981).
Wolk, Herman. "The Battle of the B-36." *Air Force Magazine*, July 1996, Vol. 79, No. 7.
———. "The New Look." *Air Force Magazine,* August 2003, Vol. 86, No 8.
"World Role for US." *New York Times,* March 2, 1947.

Manuscripts

Greenwood, John E. "The Emergence of the Post War Strategic Air Force 1945–1953." *Air Power and Warfare: Proceedings of the Eighth Military History Symposium Air Force Academy, 1978.* Washington, D.C.: Office of Air Force History, 1979.
Grynkewich, Alexus, "Advisable in the National Interest? The Relief of General George Kenney." Master's thesis, University of Georgia, 1994.
Schumacher, Stephan, Michael. "Against the Steamroller: David Lilienthal, the Atomic Energy Commission, and the Conflict Over Militarization During Early Cold War." Master's thesis, California Polytechnic University, 2004.

Electronic Sources

Air Force Historical Publication Series. "Development of Airborne Armament 1910–1961 Volume 1 Bombing Systems." Available at http://www.alternatewars.com/SAC/AirborneArmament/Volume_I.html (accessed December 23, 2014).
Atomic Energy Act of 1946. "(Public Law 585, 79th Congress), Excerpt from Legislative History of the Atomic Energy Commission, Volume 1 (Washington, D.C.; U.S. Atomic Energy Commission, 1965)." Available at: ww.science.gov/~/media/bes/pdf/Atomic_Energy_Act_of_1946.pdf (accessed August 12, 2014).
Geographical Imaginations: War, Space, and Security. Bombing Encyclopedia of the World. Available at https://www.cia.gov/library/center-for-the-study-of-intelligence/kent-csi/vol3no2/html/v03i2a10p_0001.htm (accessed February 10, 2014).
MIT Institute Library. "Winston Churchill Address at MIT." Mid-Century Convocation, March 31, 1949, available at http://libraries.mit.edu/archives/exhibits/midcentury/mid-cent-churchill.html (accessed February 19, 2008).
National Security Council. "NSC 20/4 U.S. Objectives with Respect to the USSR to Counter Soviet Threats to U.S. Security." Available at https://www.mtholyoke.edu/acad/intrel/coldwar/nsc20-4.html (accessed September 15, 2014).
Phillips, Matt. "The Long History of US Debt in One Little Chart." Available at http://www.theatlantic.com/business/archive/2012/11/the-long-story-of-us-debt-from-1790-to-2011-in-1-little-chart/265185/ (accessed November 10, 2014).
U.S. Department of Energy. "Reduction Oxidation Plant." Available at http://www.hanford.gov/page.cfm/REDOX (accessed September 30, 2014).
University of California, The American Presidents Project. "Executive Order 9877—Functions of the Armed Forces, July 26, 1947." Available at http://www.presidency.ucsb.edu/ws/?pid=12717 (accessed October 8, 2014).
Yarger, Richard. "Toward a Theory of Strategy: Art Lykke and the Army War College Strat-

egy Model." Available at: http://www.au.af.mil/au/awc/awcgate/army-usawc/stratpap. html (accessed October 14, 2014).

Video

Morris, Erol. *Fog of War: Eleven Lessons from the Life of Robert S. McNamara.* Culver City, CA: Sony Pictures, 2003.

Index

Able Test (Nuclear) 55
Abwehr 98
Acheson Dean 11, 40, 176, 178
Air Corps Tactical School (ACTS) 81, 92, 189, 192
Air Defense Command (ADC) 139, 191
Air Force Armament Laboratory 168
Air Force Chief of Staff 12, 16, 44, 66, 91, 120, 150, 188
Air Force, Secretary of 12, 27, 28, 70, 87
Air Force, U.S. (USAF) 2–5, 13, 16, 17, 18, 19, 20, 22, 26, 27, 28, 29, 30, 31, 32, 33, 35, 36, 44, 47, 49, 50, 51, 65, 66, 67, 68, 69, 70, 71, 72, 73, 74, 80, 82, 87, 92, 96, 97, 98, 99, 100, 101, 102, 104, 106, 112, 115, 116, 118, 120, 122, 124, 130, 133, 134, 137, 138, 140, 141, 142, 145, 146, 149, 150, 151, 155, 156, 158, 163, 164, 167, 170, 172, 175, 179, 180, 185, 186, 187, 188, 189, 191, 193
Air Policy Commission 27
Air Training Command (ATC) 148
Air University Quarterly Review (AUQR) 13, 17, 19, 86, 93, 108, 188
Air War Planning Documents (AWPD) 156
AJ-1 Savage 69
Army Air Force, U.S. (USAAF) 10, 13, 18, 79–86, 96, 98, 103, 110, 126, 130, 133, 137–141, 148–149, 155–156, 160, 163
Army, U.S. 12–13, 15, 16, 19, 26–27, 29, 31, 32, 33, 35–37, 41, 43, 51, 65, 68, 77, 115, 118, 141, 175, 186, 191
AJAX, Operation 42, 44, 113
Allied Central Interpretation Unit (ACIU) 96, 97, 129
American Legion 138
Anderson, Frank 138
Anderson, Orville 86–87, 93, 188
Andrews Field, Maryland 139, 151
Anti Aircraft Artillery (AAA) 110, 130, 131, 132
Archangel, Russia 77
Armed Forces Special Weapons Project (AFSWP) 42–43, 45–48, 50–51, 56, 69, 88, 102, 108, 112–114
Army Analysis Division 86
Army Chief of Staff 10, 140
Army General Classification Test (AGCT) 141–142, 164
Arnold, H. H. "Hap" 10, 11, 16, 138, 140, 156
Astrakhan, USSR 89
Atomic Energy Act, 1946 (McMahon Act) 15, 46, 52
Atomic Energy Commission (AEC) 2–4, 15–16, 21, 27, 32, 38–39, 40–52, 53, 56–57, 59, 61–64, 75, 88–89, 102–103, 112, 114, 128, 175, 179, 180–185, 187, 193
Austin, Warren 39

B Reactor 57–60
B-17 Flying Fortress 27, 155
B-24 Liberator 122, 155
B-29 Superfortress 7–9, 45–46, 48, 88–89, 101, 107–109, 112–113, 115, 119, 120–122, 129, 130–132, 135–136, 141, 147, 149–150, 154–155, 156, 157, 158–159, 160–165, 168–170, 187; KB-29 119–120; RB-29 129; Silverplate 45–48, 69, 88, 158–159; WB-29 63
B-36 Peacemaker 27, 66–67, 71–74, 108, 119–121, 123, 131, 135–136, 154–155, 159–165, 168–169, 170, 172, 175, 178, 185, 187; RB-36 129, 178
B-50 69, 107–108, 115, 120–121, 131–132, 135, 146, 154–155, 159–161, 163–165, 168–169, 178, 187
B-58 Hustler 130, 187
Bacher, Robert 40
Baker Test (Nuclear) 55
Baku, USSR 98, 101
Baldwin, Hanson 78, 91
BANJO, Operation 50
Baruch Plan 37, 39, 56, 90, 103, 143
Beahan, Raymond, Kermit 8
Berlin Blockade (Airlift) 33, 47, 48–50, 69, 75, 88, 110–113, 116, 120, 135, 166

223

Index

Bock's Car (B-29) 115
Bolling Field, Washington, D.C. 139
Bolshevik 95
Bombardiers 8, 102, 136, 144, 148
Bombing Encyclopedia of the World 99, 128
Borden, William (*There Will be No Time*) 28–29
Borgiasz, William (*Strategic Air Command*) 2
Borowski, Harry (*Hollow Threat*) 2
Bradbury, Norris 47, 55
Bradley, Omar 74, 183, 186
Brereton, Louis 42, 44, 48
Brodie, Bernard (*The Ultimate Weapon*) 86, 188
Budgetary Advisory Committee (BAC) 32, 33, 34
Bulgaria 78, 94
Burchinal, David 193
Burke, Arleigh 73
Butterworth, W.W. 91

C-54 Skymaster 112–113, 121
C-97 Stratofreighter 113
Cairo-Suez Region 101, 107, 111, 113, 114, 000
Capone, Al 78
Carpenter, Donald 48–50, 69
Carswell Air Force Base 136, 161
Castle Bravo (Nuclear Test) 185
Catton, Jack 93, 114, 145
Cavert, Sam 11
Central Intelligence Agency (CIA) 97
Chiang, Kai-shek 118
Chickenpox, Aircraft 113
Chief of Naval Operations (CNO) 32, 33, 67–70, 74, 103, 116, 120
Chief of Staff, Air Force 10, 12, 16, 44, 66, 68, 74, 90–91, 120, 139, 144, 150, 153, 180, 188
China 35, 84, 111, 118, 154, 156, 175
Churchill, Winston 11
Circular Error Probable (CEP) 145, 146, 147, 165, 166
Clausewitz, Carl 188
Clifford, Clark 48
CMR Division 57
Cold War 1, 3, 23, 34, 75, 77, 86, 89, 96, 179
Collier's Magazine 18, 118, 170
Combined Bomber Offensive (CBO) 15, 80, 82–86, 92, 95–96, 100–101, 106, 122, 125–126, 128, 130, 132–133, 163, 168, 170–171
Connally, Thomas 39
Continental Air Force (CAF) 138–139
Convair Fort Worth 160, 185, 187
COWBOY, Operation 50
CROSSROADS, Operation 54–57, 60–61, 73, 92, 103
Culter, Robert 190
Czecholsovakia 33, 78, 88, 94, 110

D Reactor 57, 59–60
Davis Monthan Air Force Base 136
Dayton, Ohio 135, 137, 146, 178, 187
Defense, Secretary of 13, 31, 34–35, 50, 65, 71, 176, 179, 186
DeGroot, Gerard 179
Democratic Party 14, 78, 189
Denfeld, Louis 32–33, 68–69, 70, 74, 116, 120
Denver 138
de Seversky, Alexander 17
Dewey, Thomas 34, 79
Director of the Bureau of the Budget 71
Directorate of Artillery 130
Directorate of Intelligence, USAF 92
Donbass, USSR 101
Dorland, Gil 43
DR Reactor 59
Dualism Conference 152

East Indies 85
EASTWIND, Operation 50
Economic Club of Detroit 12
Eielson Air Force Base 63, 119
8th Air Force 81–82, 122, 130, 133, 146, 152, 171
Eisenhower, Dwight 47, 65, 117, 140, 153, 185, 187, 189, 190
Electronic Countermeasures (ECM) 120, 122, 129, 166, 167
Electronic Intelligence (ELINT) 98
Enola Gay 115
Espanola, New Mexico 54
Ethiopia 84, 125
Europe 12, 14–16, 24, 30, 34, 48, 78–82, 88, 93, 94, 96, 98–100, 103–104, 108, 110–113, 117–118, 121, 125, 133, 135, 137, 169, 170
Executive Order 9835 78
Executive Order 9877 65, 67–68

F Reactor 57
F-84 Thunderstreak 122, 129, 171–172, 178
F-89 Scorpion 27
Federal Council of the Churches of Christ in American 11
Fermi, Enrico 38, 182
Ferret, Mission 98
15th Air Force 137, 141, 143
5th Air Force 139
Finletter, Thomas K. 28, 186
Finletter Comission Report (Survival in the Air Age) 28–30, 35, 141, 177, 186
Fiscal Year 23, 26, 29–33, 34–36, 70, 93–94, 112, 117, 140, 159, 190–191
Fission 42, 45, 53, 56–62, 64, 75, 114, 175, 179–180, 182–183, 193
509th Bombardment Group 88, 102, 146, 152, 158
Flieger Abwehr Kannone (FLAK) 82
Foreign Affairs (Journal) 23
Forrestal, James 13, 28, 71

228　Index

Webb, James 49
Webster, William 62
Wendover Field 42–43, 159
WHIPPOORWILL, Operation 50
Whitehead, Ennis 142–143
Wilson, Carroll 57, 59
Wolfe, K. B. 143
Wonderful Project 137
World War I 77, 84, 138
World War II 15, 17, 20, 25, 37, 70, 73, 77, 81, 85–87, 126, 138, 155
Worth, Cedric 72–73
Wright-Patterson Air Force Base 119
Wringer Project 97, 127

X Division 56
XF-85 Goblin Fighter 172
X-Ray Shot (Nuclear Test) 61
XXI Bomber Command 9, 101, 155

Y-12 Seperation Plant 53
Yakoshima Island, Japan 7
Yarmouth, United Kingdom 84
Yeager, Chuck 170
Yoke Shot (Nuclear Test) 61

Z Division 42–43, 55, 57, 60, 113
Zacharias, Jerrod 43
Zebra Shot (Nuclear Test) 61

Index

Romania 78, 94
Rosenberg, Allen 3
Rosenberg, Julius, and Ethel 178
Ross, Stephen 3
Royal Air Force 32, 80, 84, 88, 168
Royal Navy Fleet Air Arm 32
Royall, Kenneth 46–47, 49
Russell, Richard 10, 39

Saddletee Modification 72, 159, 161
Sandia Base, Albuquerque 42–44, 46–47, 50, 55–56, 107, 113, 159
Sandstone Test (Nuclear) 47, 56, 60–62, 180
Schweinfurt, Germany 82
Secretary of State 11, 34, 40, 190
Senate Special Committee on Atomic Energy 38
7th Bombardment Group 136, 152
Sherman, Forrest P 74
Sing Sing Prison 178
Smith, Bedell 190
Smith, Cyril 38
SOLARIUM Operation 190
Soviet Air Force 100
Soviet Union 1–4, 11–12, 19–21, 23–24, 27, 30, 37, 63, 72, 77–80, 88, 89, 91, 93–94, 96–100, 103–107, 109–115, 119–120, 125, 127–128, 131, 133, 161, 166, 172, 189, 121–123, 129–132, 134–155, 159–160, 163–167, 170–171, 173, 177–178, 182, 187–188, 191–193
Spaatz, Carl 16, 18, 66, 68–69, 91–92, 102–103, 106, 118, 137, 139, 140, 142–145, 148, 150
Spaatz Board 16–17, 49, 97
Spain 84
Special Weapons Unit 50, 114
Stalingrad, USSR 107
Standing Operating Procedure (SOP) 137
Stimson, Robert 80, 89–90
Strategic Air Command (SAC) 1–4, 11–12, 19–21, 30, 72, 91, 93, 96–97, 104–121, 122–123, 127–132, 134–155, 159–162, 163–173, 177–178, 182, 182, 187–188, 191–193
Strategic Vulnerabilities Branch (SVB) 128
Strauss, Lewis 40, 181–182, 185
Streett, St. Clair 142–143
Suez Canal 100–101, 107, 111, 113–115
Sullivan, John 70–71
Surface to Air Missile (SAM) 110
Sweeney, Charles 7–9, 115
Symington, Stuart 12, 27, 29, 47, 70, 72, 74, 87, 91, 140–142, 180, 185, 186

Tactical Air Command (TAC) 139
Taifun Rocket 110
Target Folders 99, 122
Teller, Edward 52, 181, 185
Tennessee Valley Authority (TVA) 40
13th Air Force 143

38th Engineering Bn. 42
301st Bombardment Group 88
307th Bombardment Group 88
311 Air Division 127
Tibbets, Paul 9, 115, 150–152
Time magazine 165
Tinian Island 7, 9
Tip Toe Project 173
Tregaskis, Richard 170
Truman, Harry 2, 4, 10–11, 13–15, 20, 23, 25–31, 33–39, 47–49, 52–53, 56–57, 63–68, 70–71, 75, 77–79, 88, 89–90, 92, 94, 112, 117, 120, 138, 140, 153, 175–182, 184–187, 189–190
Truman Doctrine 34, 78–79, 94
20th Air Force 8
20th Bombardment Squadron 136
27th Bombardment Group 88
28th Bombardment Group 88
2761 Engineering Bn. 42
Twinning, Nathan 188

ULTRA Intercepts 126
United Air Lines 164
United Nations 37, 39, 90, 142
USS *United States* 70–71, 74, 170
Unlimited, Operation 50, 114
Urakami Valley, Japan 8, 9
Ural Region, USSR 96, 101
Uranium 52, 54–55, 57–59
U.S. Air Forces in Europe (USAFE) 88, 135
U.S. Strategic Bombing Survey (USSBS) 9, 51, 77, 80–86, 93, 97, 103, 125–129, 133, 146, 176

Vandenberg, Hoyt 16, 74, 90–91, 112–113, 120, 124, 150–151, 153, 172, 180, 186, 188
VanZant, James 72
Very Heavy Bombardment (VHB) 138, 156
Very Long Range Bomber (VLR) 156
VIII Fighter Command 82
V-J Day 77
Vladivostok, USSR 77
Volga Region, USSR 101
Vultee Corporation 72

Walker Air Force Base, NM 147
War, Secretary of 13, 28, 80, 86, 89, 143
Warplans: Broiler 4, 20, 53, 103–105, 107–112, 116, 126; Earshot 102; Halfmoon 4, 20, 30, 32, 33–34, 69, 110–117, 120, 126–127; Makefast 101–103; Offtackle 3–4, 20, 116–123, 126–127, 131, 146, 161–164, 167, 171–172, 179; Pincher 4, 20, 100–105, 110, 126; Trojan 116–117, 120, 124, 179
Warsaw Pact 1
Waymack, William 40
Weapons Sytem Evaluation Group (WSEG) 120–123, 125–126, 129, 131–133, 146, 161, 163, 166

226 Index

Marshall, George C. 10, 11, 33–34, 40, 186
Marshall Plan (European Recovery Plan) 34, 78–79, 94, 118
Marxism 24
Massachusetts Institute of Technology (MIT) 11, 29
Massive Retaliation 18, 192
Matthews, Francis 74
Maxwell Field 81, 151, 152
McKellar, Kenneth 40
McMahon, Brien 15–16, 38–39, 64, 179, 181–183, 185
McMullen, Clements 139, 143–151
McNarney, Joseph 140
Medal of Honor 137
Megaton (Mt) 1, 64
Meilinger, Phillip (*Bomber: The Formation and Early Years of SAC*) 3
MiG-15 109, 122, 130–132, 169
MiG-9 131
Military Air Transport Service (MATS) 112, 114, 121
Military Liaison Committee (MLC) 16, 38, 41–42, 45–50, 57, 59–62, 69, 114, 184
Military Operating Skill (MOS) 148
Millikin, Eugene 39
Mistubishi 8, 9
Mitchell, William, Billy 65
MK III Bomb "Fat Man" (Implosion Design) 8, 16, 42, 44–46, 48, 51, 53–57, 60–62, 69, 89, 114–115, 117, 120, 158
MK IV Bomb 44, 51, 56, 60–62, 120, 158
MK V Bomb 61
Montgomery, J. B. 20, 164, 171
Moody, Walter, (*Building a Strategic Air Force*) 2
Moscow, USSR 23, 101, 107, 111, 116, 100

Nagasaki, Japan 7–10, 16, 45, 51, 54, 61–62, 115, 155
National Military Establishment (NME) 3, 16, 19, 21, 25, 27, 30–35, 46–52, 62, 65, 89, 90
National Security Council (NSC) 24, 112, 134, 175, 180, 100
National Security Council Policy: 7 31; 30 21, 89, 90, 91, 103; 162/2 151, 190–192; 20/2 89; 20/4 21, 24, 31, 34, 63, 93, 94–95, 99, 103, 105, 112, 117, 118, 125, 177, 180; 68 24, 36, 51, 126, 153, 176, 177–179, 186, 189–190, 193
National War College 137
Naval War College 69
Navy, Secretary of 70, 71–72, 74
Navy, U.S. 4, 12–13, 16, 19, 26–27, 29, 31–33, 35, 49–51, 54–55, 65–74, 85, 112, 120, 169, 170, 175, 186, 191
New Look 189–192
New Mexico 42–43, 54, 147
New York 163
New York Times 78, 91

Newport Conference 69, 112
Nichols, Ken 46–48, 51, 61, 114
Nimitz, Chester 67, 103
Nitze, Paul 176–177
Norden Bombsight 81
Norstad, Lauris 16, 149, 151
NUTMEG, Operation 50

Odlum, Floyd 72
Offner, Arnold 79
Offutt Air Force Base 11, 151, 153
Ofstie, Ralph 73–74
Okinawa, Japan 9, 111, 113, 114
OP-23 Office 73
Operations Analysis Branch 145, 150
Oppenheimer, J Robert 11, 38, 54–55, 182–183
Ostfriesland 65
OVERLORD Operation 100
Oxnard Municipal Airfield 43

P2V Neptune 69
P-51 Mustang 27
P-80 Shooting Star 169
Pace, Frank 71
Parsons, William 48
Partridge, Earl 97, 109
Patterson, Robert 13, 28, 143
Pax Americana 13
Pax Atomica 14
Pax Britannica 13
Pearl Harbor 18, 29
Physical Vulnerabilities Branch (PVB) 128
Pike, Sumner 40, 182
Ploesti, Romania 101
Plutonium 45, 54–60
Poland 78, 94
Polonium-Beryllium 57–59
Powers, Tommy 109, 151
Protivo Vozdushnaya Oborona Strany (PVO Strany) 109, 122, 129–133, 162, 168–169, 172–173

R-3350 engine 155–159
R-4360 Engine 108, 159, 162
Radar: APQ-13 136, 165–168; APQ-23 136, 165–166, 168; APQ-24 147, 165–169
Radford, Arthur 73, 191
Radiation 9–10, 45, 59, 129
RB-47 129, 178
Rear Area Assembly Team (RAT) 42
Reconstruction Finance Corporation 43
Red Army 1, 2, 5, 24, 88, 89, 93, 100, 104, 109, 111, 118–119, 125, 130, 175
Reduction-Oxidation (Redox) 59
Reliable Project 169
Remainder Method 26
Republican Party 25, 40, 78, 178
Retardation Missions 118–119
"Revolt of the Admirals" 33, 93, 169, 172
Rhine River 111, 118

Fort Worth Star Telegram 185
43rd Bombardment Group 152
46th Bombardment Squadron 136
49th Bombardment Squadron 152
Forward Area Assembly Team (FAT) 42, 113
Fusion 64, 180, 181, 193

Gaddis, John Lewis 23–24
Galley, Daniel 67
Gehlen, Reinhard 98
General Advisory Committee (GAC) 38, 46, 64, 181–182, 185
Genetrix Project 98
Global Electronics Modification (GEM) 159
Great Britain 32, 111
Great Depression 25–26, 94
Greek Civil War 33
Ground Control Intercept (GCI) 109, 110, 116
Groves, Leslie 10–11, 16, 37–38, 40–43, 46, 52, 54–55, 57–59, 62
Gulf of Mexico 136

H Reactor 59
Hanford Engineering Works (HEW) 54, 57–60, 62
Harmon Report 125–126
Hart, Thomas 39
Hickenlooper, Bourke 40
Hinshaw-Brewster Report 29
Hitler, Adolf 77–78
Hobson Plan 164–165
House Subcommittee on Armed Forces Appropriations 35
House Un-American Activities Committee (HUAC) 178
Hull, John 121
Human Intelligence (HUMIT) 126
Hungary 78, 94

Ickes, Harold 13
Integrated Air Defense (IAD) 20, 67, 96, 162
Intercontinental Ballistic Missiles (ICBM) 173
Interior, Secretary 13
Ipswich, United Kingdom 84

Jackson, C.D. 190
Johnson, Edwin 13, 38–39
Johnson, Leon 137, 145, 148
Johnson, Louis 35, 63, 71–72, 74, 176, 179, 183–185
Joint Chiefs of Staff (JCS) 2, 29–31, 33–35, 53, 62–64, 69, 74, 77, 99, 102, 116–117, 120, 123–124, 126, 128, 140, 146, 177, 179, 181–184, 186–187, 191
Joint Chiefs of Staff Report 1745/1 53
Joint Chiefs of Staff Report 1952/1 120, 124
Joint Committee on Atomic Energy (JCAE) 16, 38–41, 64, 181
Joint Intelligence Committee (JIC) 99
Joint Logistics Plans Committee (JLPC) 115

Joint Strategic Plans Division (JSPD) 103
Joint Strategic Plans Group (JSPG) 53, 79
Joint Strategic Survey Committee (JSSC) 44, 62
Joint War Plans Committee (JWPC) 79, 100, 103, 106

K-25 Gaseous Diffusion Plant 54
Kazan, USSR 98
Kelly Air Force Base 151
Kennan, George 23–24, 30–31, 77, 106, 176–177
Key West Conference 68, 112
Key West, Naval Air Station 68
Kharkov, USSR 107
Kiloton (Kt) 61, 64, 105, 146, 166
Kirtland Air Force Base 47–48
Kistiakowsky, George 43
Kokura, Japan 8-Jul
Korea 4, 35–36, 51, 60, 109, 111, 122, 126, 130–131, 176–177, 179, 184, 186–187, 189, 191
Kremlin 23, 177
Kuomintang 118
Kuzbass, USSR 101
Kyoto, Japan 89–90
Kyushu, Japan 7, 8

LA-11 Fighter 131
Landry, R. B. 71
Lead, Crews 147, 187
Leahy, William 103
LeMay, Curtis 4, 9, 11–12, 19–20, 66, 88, 92–93, 101, 106–107, 119, 122–123, 133, 135–137, 142, 144, 146–148, 151–153, 155–158, 164–165, 167–168, 170–171, 173, 178, 183, 187, 192, 193
Leningrad, USSR 98, 107, 111, 116
Levitated Core 59
Lilienthal, Davide E. 40–41, 44, 46–49, 52–53, 62, 179, 181, 182–183
Lindbergh, Charles 149–152
Little Boy Bomb (Gun type) 16, 48, 54–56, 58, 61, 69, 89, 115, 117, 137, 146–147, 158, 181
London, United Kingdom 84
Long Telegram (Mr. X) 23, 176–177
Loper, Herbert 184
Los Angeles Times 149
Lovett, Robert 186
Luftwaffe 82, 84, 122, 125, 130, 167, 170

M Division 56
MacArthur, Douglas 139, 140
Manchuria 111
Manhattan Engineering District (Project) 2–3, 10, 15, 37–39, 41, 52, 54–56, 181–182, 184
Mao Tse-Tung 35, 118, 175
Marianas Island Chain 154
Marine Corps, U.S. 19, 74

www.ingramcontent.com/pod-product-compliance
Ingram Content Group UK Ltd.
Pitfield, Milton Keynes, MK11 3LW, UK
UKHW021845140426
5217IPUK00022B/1592